DISCARDED

HORSEMEN OF THE ESOPHAGUS

HORSEMEN
OF THE
ESOPHAGUS

COMPETITIVE EATING AND
THE BIG FAT AMERICAN DREAM

JASON FAGONE

Crown Publishers • New York

Wondering about the meaning of the weight on the front cover of this book?
To find out the answer, visit www.jasonfagone.com.

Photo credits:

Photo of David "Coondog" O'Karma and Takeru Kobayashi, used by permission of Steve Addicks..
Photo of Tim "Eater X" Janus at the World's Greatest Shoo-Fly Pie Bake-Off & Eating Contest,
used by permission of Rockvale Outlets.
Photo of Bill "El Wingador" Simmons, used by permission of Bill Walsh.

Text credits:

Excerpts from Eric "Badlands" Booker's *Hungry & Focused* LP used by permission of Eric Booker.
Excerpts from David "Coondog" O'Karma's writing used by permission of David O'Karma.
Excerpts of songs from the *Blueberry Musical* by Doug Guy used by permission of J. Douglas Guy III.
Excerpts from the AICE website used by permission of Arnold Chapman.

Published in the United States by Crown Publishers, an imprint of the
Crown Publishing Group, a division of Random House, Inc., New York.
www.crownpublishing.com

Crown is a trademark and the Crown colophon
is a registered trademark of Random House, Inc.

Library of Congress Cataloging-in-Publication Data
Fagone, Jason.
Horsemen of the esophagus : competitive eating and the big
fat American dream / Jason Fagone.—1st ed.

p. cm.

1. Gastronomy. 2. Food habits—United States. 3. Contests—United States. I. Title.
641'.013—dc22   2006000666

ISBN-13: 978-0-307-23738-5
ISBN-10: 0-307-23738-9

Printed in the United States of America

Design by Lenny Henderson

10 9 8 7 6 5 4 3 2 1

First Edition

To my parents, Frank and Sharyn, for everything

Contents

HORSEMEN OF THE ESOPHAGUS

Back home a momentous change was coming over the United States. There was a new President, William Howard Taft, and he took office weighing three hundred and thirty-two pounds. All over the country men began to look at themselves. They were used to drinking great quantities of beer. They customarily devoured loaves of bread and ate prodigiously of the sausage meats of poured offal that lay on the lunch counters of the saloons. The august Pierpont Morgan . . . ate breakfasts of steaks and chops, eggs, pancakes, broiled fish, rolls and butter, fresh fruit and cream. The consumption of food was a sacrament of success. A man who carried a great stomach before him was thought to be in his prime. Women went into hospitals to die of burst bladders, collapsed lungs, overtaxed hearts and meningitis of the spine. There was a heavy traffic to the spas and sulphur springs, where the purgative was valued as an inducement to the appetite. America was a great farting country. All this began to change when Taft moved into the White House. His accession to the one mythic office in the American imagination weighed everyone down. His great figure immediately expressed the apotheosis of that style of man.

—E. L. Doctorow, *Ragtime*

Wait a minute, America isn't the hot-dog champion? Well, how could you let that happen? This whole nation is stuffing its face! Can't one of us do it at record speed?

—Hank Hill

THE PASSION OF THE TOAST

S H E   H A S   P I C K E D   a fine day to grace Southern California with Her presence. The sun is shining, the sky is blue. Gulls loop above the Venice Beach boardwalk in jazzy little arcs. The February air is warm, but not warm enough to melt the grilled cheese sandwich through which She has chosen to broadcast her message of peace. Anyway, She's packed inside a plastic box, surrounded by cotton balls, and encased in a frame for protection. Ten years ago the image of the Virgin Mary appeared on a grilled cheese sandwich in the frying pan of Diana Duyser, a Florida jewelry designer. Now, She is here.

The Blessed Virgin, in recent years, has been appearing less and less in crop formations and curvy building glass. She seems to prefer, as holy vehicles, specific kinds of food. She has not seared Herself onto a piece of ahi sushi, or a crepe suzette. She has not arranged Her visage in mosaic form using the grains of a delicate risotto. Instead, She has chosen as vehicles to become flesh a popcorn kernel, a Funyun, and a Rold Gold Honey Mustard pretzel twist—and, here, now, a grilled cheese sandwich. Even deities change with the times. In 2005, Our Lady seems to be a voracious snacker. The Virgin's palate is no longer demure. She's hungry.

This afternoon, when it comes to appetite, the old girl is flat outclassed. In fifteen minutes, here at Venice Beach, the World Grilled Cheese Eating Championship will be decided. It's an eating contest. Whoever eats the most grilled cheese sandwiches in ten minutes wins $3,500. The prize pot has attracted some of the hungriest people in the world—people who eat under the banner of the International Federation of Competitive Eating, also known as the IFOCE or the Federation. They consider themselves professionals, and athletes. Guys like Eric "Badlands" Booker, a 420-pound subway conductor, rapper, and world champion in the donut, corned beef hash, and cheesecake disciplines. "Hungry" Charles Hardy, who just half an hour ago tattooed the initials "IFOCE" onto his right bicep. Ed "Cookie" Jarvis, a Long Island realtor who embroiders his numerous eating titles onto a gargantuan flowing robe with his portrait airbrushed on the front, flanked by a lightning bolt. Rich and Carlene LeFevre, the First Couple of competitive eating—a pair of sweetly manic retirees from the outskirts of Las Vegas. Carlene is a consistent top-five finisher, and Rich, nicknamed "The Locust," holds records in Spam (6 pounds in 12 minutes), chili (one and a half gallons in 10 minutes), and corny dogs (18½ in 10 minutes).

Even the Locust's accomplishments pale in comparison to America's greatest eater, now sitting in the concrete bleachers, beaming, her ponytail held in place by two star-shaped barrettes. Sonya Thomas. Five feet five, 103 pounds. She calls herself "The Black Widow" because she gleefully devours the males; she may or may not be playing on an Asian stereotype. Her eating titles are so numerous that promoters list them alphabetically: asparagus, baked beans, chicken nuggets, chicken wings, eggs, fruitcake, giant burger, hamburger, jambalaya, Maine lobster, meatballs, oysters, pulled pork, quesadilla, sweet potato casserole, tacos, toasted ravioli, Turducken...

"BROTHERS AND SISTERS!"

It's starting. The voice is miked up. It booms from the concrete expanse near the stretch of boardwalk called Muscle Beach, named after an outdoor gym where exhibitionists yank dumbbells. Beyond the gym, toward the beach, is a concrete amphitheater, with bleachers that face the stage and a stage that faces the Pacific. The stage sits directly underneath a giant concrete barbell, looming like a relic of some extinct bodybuilding race. The stage's speakers broadcast the voice, which is saying:

"There are moments in our days when we are suddenly LOST."

Conversations stop. One hundred and fifty curious heads swivel toward the man onstage in the dark blazer and the straw boater hat. This is the contest emcee: George Shea, chairman of the IFOCE, which bills itself as "the governing body of all stomach-centric sport." His hands, clasped together over his crotch, hold a microphone. He looks down and widens his stance dramatically as the opening lament of Moby's "Natural Blues" emerges from the PA system.

"We hum along doing the million things that Americans do, and then suddenly we are STRUCK—"

A woman, excited, screams.

"—and we wonder why. There is no trigger. There is no reason. And yet there it is. Sadness. Isolation. Loss. Why?"

Shea pauses, then answers his question:

"Because the PURSUITS of our lives have OBSCURED our lives, ladies and gentlemen. It is not only the hustle and bustle, the cars, and the kids, the debts and the acquisitions—it is something more."

Often, Shea refers to competitive eating as the country's "fastest-growing sport," and he likes to say, tongue two-thirds in cheek, that eating is now number five in America's heart after baseball, basketball, football, and golf, having surpassed hockey and badminton. Today's contest is just one of a hundred scheduled for 2005, up from about seventy in 2004. Prize pots surge, TV deals dangle . . .

"We cannot SEE!" Shea is saying. "We cannot HEAR! We cannot THINK! And that is why . . . she has come! Amid no fanfare whatsoever!"

"A woman!" says Shea. "Grilling a cheese sandwich!"

The music shifts to a gentle adult contemporary track. George Shea bleeds all aggression from his voice.

"Ladies and gentlemen. It is said that pearls are the precipitate of sunlight, slowed and bent by the ocean until it forms a nugget of beauty inside the lowly mollusk. And likewise, this grilled cheese sandwich is the precipitate of the divine spirit"—and here the music shifts again, to a dark minor-key vamp, and Shea's voice skews evil—"captured here on Earth in the most unlikely of places, delivered to us in the image of the Virgin Mary!"

Shea has sensitive features, an aristocratic nose, and neat black hair. Good-looking, compact. Perfect posture. His voice is melodious but powerful—precise, all syllables enunciated, with the pitch control of a cabaret singer and the gestural excess of a dinner-theater Hamlet.

"It is the bane of our species," he says, "that we are warped most when we know it the least, ladies and gentlemen. It is time to put aside the pursuits that push us through our day, because this change is here today as an athletic and religious experience. TODAY WE HOLD THE GOLDENPALACE .COM WORLD GRILLED CHEESE EATING CHAMPIONSHIP! An all-you-can-eat contest that will stand as an homage, as a recognition, a dramatic illustration of the message delivered [to] us by the Virgin Mary Grilled Cheese Sandwich!"

The music softens. Shea ushers onstage a representative of GoldenPalace .com, Steve Baker. Last November, GoldenPalace.com bought the sandwich for $28,000 on eBay, hoping to use it for promotional stunts like this one. Wearing a grubby sweatshirt, jeans, and two-day stubble, Baker raises the Virgin Mary Grilled Cheese above his head and proclaims:

"The Passion of the Toast lives."

Baker steps down into the crowd, now a sea of limbs holding digicams and angling for a keepsake shot. He parades the sandwich, which Shea calls "the culinary version of the Shroud of Turin," into the digicam throng, and then the sandwich is placed onto an easel, at the side of the stage, to make way for the gurgitators.

The eaters take their places at the long horizontal eating table one by one, accompanied by a rock song. The top eaters merit a sobriquet or a simple recitation of their feats: Carlene LeFevre becomes "the Martha Stewart of mastication"; the Spam record of husband Rich is heralded, to oohs and ahhs; "Jalapeño" Jed Donahue is announced as having swallowed 152 of his namesake peppers. Sonya Thomas is described as "a cross between Anna Kournikova, Billie Jean King, and a jackal wild on the Serengeti." Other accomplished eaters include Long Island's Don "Moses" Lerman, Zen master of raw butter, matzo balls, and baked beans; and Frank Wach, a Chicagoan and "a rookie out of the toasted ravioli circuit." Eric "Badlands" Booker styles himself a rapper, and at every contest he treats the audience to a cut from his family-friendly, 100-percent-eating-themed LP, *Hungry & Focused*. Today he drops "The Sweet Science of Competitive Eating":

> *I'll be that top gurgitator extraordinaire,*
> *one that eats to the beat in a flash and flair*
> *eat you outta house and home, no thought or care*

fridge empty, cupboards bare . . .
y'know my name, I got that fame
for cramming food down my esophageal drain . . .
Yo, when I say grill, y'all say cheese!
Grill!
Cheese!
Grill!
Cheese!

The best introductions accompany the least accomplished eaters, because the newbies are blank slates, allowing Shea to concoct mythic pasts. "Captain" Cade Hardin, the audience learns, once ate twenty-two bowls of Captain Crunch cereal in three minutes, "but it ripped up the roof of his mouth, and he was traumatized, both physically and emotionally, and he left the competitive eating circuit for seventeen years," says Shea. "Today, his first time back at the table, a round of applause for the bravery of this man." The crowd duly applauds. One fresh-faced guy, the audience is told—to the strains of "Gangsta's Paradise"—recently "consumed two rolls of unleavened bread," says Shea. "And it raised in his stomach and created an enormous amount of pressure. And he fell to the ground writhing in what appeared to be pain. But when his family came to his side and knelt over him, they realized it was *ecstasy*. I. FEEL. GOOD. FOR THE FIRST TIME IN MY LIFE. And his father . . . said, 'Go, my son, join the EYE-EFF-OH-CEE-EEE. Join the eaters.' And so he did, ladies and gentlemen. Twenty-eight years of age, Maaaaatt Simpsonnnnnnnnnn!!!"

The best introduction belongs to Allen "The Shredder" Goldstein, a muscular up-and-comer from Long Island. He has coordinated an elaborate routine with Shea using the eighties hair-rock ballad "Sister Christian." With the song's dulcet piano intro as his backdrop, Shea tells the audience that despite Shredder's Camaro-driving, iron-pumping ways, he has an "emotional side. A soft side that the WOMEN love . . . that's right." Shea times it so that when he says "right," Night Ranger kicks into their famous pre-chorus vamp—"It's trrooooo"—that rocks into the famous chorus:

"MO-TO-RIN'!"

Dun-dun-CHIK!

On the downstrokes of each electric guitar chug, Shea and Shredder, in unison, pump their fists and raise them skyward.

"WHAT'S! YOUR! PRICE! FOR FLIGHT!"

The swelling crowd—maybe 200 to 250 people now—laughs and cheers. They're primed. So are the eaters. Minutes ago they saw the GoldenPalace .com guy unload the giant tray of sandwiches from his truck. The eaters gathered around, inspecting the material.

"I hope they're greasy," Carlene LeFevre said. "They'll just slide right down."

The eaters, all fifteen, stand next to each other at a long table on the stage. Each eater has two plates of five grilled cheese sandwiches in front of him, along with at least two cups of water—one for drinking, one for dunking. All of the top eaters pre-moisten their food by dunking, which eases the food's journey down the esophagus and kick-starts digestion once it passes through the esophageal sphincter and into the stomach.

Their hands are not allowed to touch the food until Shea gives the word. He counts down from ten, and the crowd joins him: "Two . . . One . . . Go! Oh my good gracious, we have begun. But it is not simply a contest, it is a journey, my friends, a journey down the alimentary canal, a journey to self-discovery, self-realization. Eric 'Badlands' Booker, here at the center of the table. Sonya Thomas to *his* right and Ron Koch to *her* right. The big men, the two pillars of competitive eating, the two horsemen of the esophagus, 'Hungry' Charles Hardy and Edward 'Cookie' Jarvis, here at this portion of the table. . . ."

The eaters rip in, dunking the sandwiches in the water cups and cramming them mouthward with no regard for manners or decorum. Quick-staining cheeks go unwiped; grabby hands churn the food. As performers, the eaters are very Dizzy Gillespie—dimples plump, eyes laser-locked on the chow, never looking at the audience. *Violent* is a word that comes to mind. *Assault* is another. It's scary, the suddenness with which the contest has morphed from chipper carny-barker mode to an insectoid (The Locust!) creepiness, the whole of sunny, chilled-out Southern Cal smushed to the length of this table. How can they not choke? How can they not explode?

Rich "The Locust" LeFevre, who looks like somebody's geeky uncle with his big plastic glasses and gray comb-over, is particularly fearsome, splashing a several-foot-diameter area with his first thrust of bread into water, soaking his own shirt. He rotates the sandwich once it reaches his lips, twirls it like it's corn on the cob, and mashes it inward, toward his pinker parts, the force spraying bits in a scatter pattern around his swampy water cup. He never alters his food-shoveling rhythm, a gluttonous metronome. There's debris, lots of it. Little ropes of bread, cheese, and water leak and splash onto the tablecloth below. This is not normal.

After a minute or two, individual eating styles become easier to discern. Carlene LeFevre bobs her head up and down, like she's listening to a Strokes song through a wireless brain transceiver, in a move that's been dubbed "the Carlene Pop." Badlands Booker listens to his own rap CD on his iPod. Standing at the center of the table, he finishes his first plate—that's five sandwiches—at the 51-second mark. Badlands uses his copious blowfish cheeks to store the food. "Remember, ladies and gentlemen," says Shea, "competitive eating is the battleground upon which Gaaawwd and Lucifer battle for men's souls!"

And now, at the two-and-a-half-minute mark, Sonya Thomas has ten sandwiches down the hatch.

"Nostradamus, born in the early sixteenth century, actually mentioned the Grilled Cheese Championship in his poetic yet cryptic quatrains," says Shea. "He said, 'And at one point under the bright sky, they shall gather to eat, they shall gather to eat the cheese that has been pouched in bread and grilled!'"

Six minutes left, and Shea has "never seen Eric with such rhythm." But Sonya Thomas, Shea has already noted, "is moving very quickly, my friends." Sonya eats with no recognizable style. She knows that style bleeds speed. She's a machine. Efficient. Just flat *fast*. "Ladies and gentlemen," says Shea, "the universe has no edge and no center, and like Sonya Thomas's stomach, it is ever-expanding . . . Is she the best eater in the world? No. That is Kobayashi." Shea is talking about Japan's Takeru Kobayashi, who, in 2001, at the age of twenty-three, *doubled* the Nathan's hot dog record. "Is she the best eater in America?" continues Shea. "Yes. Without question. Will I phrase everything hereto forward in the form of a question? No."

Three minutes and thirty seconds left, and Sonya has a small but solid lead. The LeFevres, Badlands Booker, and "Jalapeño" Jed Donahue are still eating at full tilt, but the rest have started to fall off. "They face," says Shea, "a mission similar to that of Federal Reserve Chairman Alan Greenspan—namely to balance the forces of inflation and deflation." The outcome is certain, but there's still drama in watching Sonya's tally rise and rise. With a minute and thirty left, Shea loses it. He screams, "Oh! My! GOD! LADIES AND GENTLEMEN! HERE UNDER THE SUN, THE CLOUDS HAVE PARTED TO ALLOW US HERE TODAY TO DEMONSTRATE OUR COMMITMENT TO THE VIRGIN MARY AND TO VICTORY IN THE WORLD OF COMPETITIVE EATING! I AM ABSOLUTELY OVERWHELMED BY EMOTION! I HAVE NOT FELT THIS MUCH EMOTION SINCE THE BIRTH OF MY FIRST CHILD, A SON!"

Shea's voice cracks with emotion.

"I am feeling the spirit overcome me, ladies and gentlemen! TWENTY-THREE GRILLED CHEESE SANDWICHES, SONYA THOMAS, LADIES AND GENTLEMEN!"

Shea starts speaking in tongues.

"Ten, nine, eight . . ."

A flurry of last-minute face-stuffing, then Shea ends it. "Put down your grilled cheeses. Oh. Oh. Oh. Just shake it off, ladies and gentlemen. I don't remember a moment of it. I don't remember . . ."

An IFOCE official goes from plate to plate, tallying sandwiches. In a slight upset, Carlene LeFevre has beaten the big boys from New York to take third place with just shy of twenty-one grilled cheeses. She giggles, raises her hand in acknowledgment of the crowd, then leans over and wipes her mouth on her husband's shirt. Jed Donahue and Rich LeFevre, both on the slim side, tie for second with twenty-three sandwiches. Sonya Thomas, of course, takes first with twenty-five. "That's the fifth time I've come in second to Sonya," says Rich LeFevre. "It's getting boring."

George Shea presents Sonya with the championship belt that says WORLD GRILLED CHEESE EATING CHAMPION in gold letters. She holds it up high above her head and grins for the cameras. Then she reaches down, grabs her twenty-sixth grilled cheese, takes a ponderous bite, and laughs.

part one

COONDOG O'KARMA'S
GOT NOTHING

Takeru Kobayashi and David "Coondog" O'Karma at the filming for Fox's *Glutton Bowl.*
During Coondog's 2005 trip to Japan, he ate, drank, and slept with this photo on a lanyard
around his neck. (Steve Addicks)

1

IN GORGING, TRUTH

THE DAY AFTER George W. Bush won his second term, a friend of mine e-mailed me, "How about this as a possible theme for your book?"

americans are big, fat, infantile, stupid assholes who love to shovel shit down their throats, and so to shovel more shit down one's throat than any other is to be truly king of america.

At that point I had been covering eating contests for three months. In the thick of a nasty presidential election and a dumb bloody war fueled by certain American appetites, I had been humping around the country on Southwest Airlines, taking notes on the exploits of professional gluttons. It was hard not to make the connection. One Saturday in October, I flew to Jackson, Mississippi, for a Krystal-brand hamburger contest. When I woke up the next morning in my Red Roof Inn in an asphalt no-man's-land next to a Whataburger franchise (TRY OUR TRIPLE MEAT AND TRIPLE CHEESE), an anonymous Bush adviser informed me, via the online *New York Times,* "We're an empire now," and anyone who didn't agree was "in what we call the reality-based community." The adviser said that "when we act, we create our own reality. . . . We're history's actors . . . and you, all of you, will be left to just study what we do." Pass the gravy, suckers. I walked fifty yards to the Waffle House and ate my reality-based eggs along with fifteen or twenty other Jacksonians, all of them non-historical actors like me. Somebody had left a *Clarion-Ledger* on the counter, with headlines like N. KOREAN NUKES LIKELY POWELL TOPIC and UTAH BIOWEAPONS TEST SITE TO GROW. I walked to the fair, where the Federation's gurgitators* visited terrible indignities upon their hamburgers under a sweltering sun. In the bleachers, I talked to a man with one tooth who said he eats all day and never gets full. I met two men from Texas who'd driven eleven hours to compete here. "I think it's sort of a celebration," said one. "A celebration of our prosperity. We're able to do this, so we might as well do it, I guess." After the contest, the TV cameras descended upon Nick Blackburn, a roly-poly local who had placed third. I interviewed his loudest supporter, a youngish guy with black spiky hair, who said he was Nick's pastor. If Christ happened upon an eating contest, I asked, what would Jesus do? "God knows our heart," the pastor said. "He judges what's in our hearts, not the stupid things we do." He laughed. "If he did that, we'd *all* be in trouble."

The Federation's critics are easy to find, having left a trail of acerbic, disapproving quotes in thousands of newspaper and wire stories about competitive eating. Food historians like Barbara Haber ("It's the fall of Rome, my dear") and physicians like the Harvard Medical School's George Blackburn ("This is sick, abnormal behavior") have lined up to take a whack, as have foreign critics such as *The Guardian,* which in the same 2002 article that quoted Blackburn called competitive eating "a sport for our degraded times" and connected its rise to "an unprecedented boom in the American economy fuelled by rampant consumption." In 2003, consumer advocate Ralph Nader sounded the alarm about four "signs of societal decay": three involved corporate greed and congressional gerrymandering, and the fourth was competitive eating. The Federation's chairman, George Shea, responded to Nader by talking up his Turducken contest. A Turducken is a chicken stuffed into a duck stuffed into a turkey. Shea called his contest "the first real advancement in Thanksgiving since the Indians sat down with the Pilgrims." Shea's counterattacks tend to mix deadpan charm and gentle mockery. "There are those who object to our sport," Shea told me when I

---

* The word "gurgitator" is actually a registered trademark of the Federation, but, perhaps owing to its dull-edged awkwardness, the competitors preferred to call themselves "eaters." The fan site trencherwomen.com later made the term gendered, separating "gurgitators" (men) from "gurgitrices" (women), though the proper word probably should have been "gurgitatrices."

asked if it was wise to promote gluttony in the fattest nation on earth,* "and for the moment I'd like to refer to them as," and Shea's voice sped up and dropped a half-octave to let me in on the joke, "knee-jerk reactionaries and philistines." He continued, normal-voiced, "A lot of people have had trouble separating this superficial visual of people stuffing their faces with large quantities of food with the stereotype of the Ugly American. That is not where I am. I see beauty. I see physical poetry."

Poetry, exactly. Shea's eating contests were poetic in their blatancy, their brazen mixture of every American trait that seemed to terrify the rest of the planet: our hunger for natural resources that may melt the ice caps and flood Europe, our hunger for cheap thrills that turns Muslim swing voters into car bombers.† If anti-American zealots anywhere in the world wanted to perform a minstrel show of our culture, this is what they'd come up with. Competitive eating was a symbolic hairball coughed up by the American id. It was meaningful like a tumor was meaningful. It seemed to have a purpose, a message, and its message was this: Look upon our gurgitators, ye Mighty, and despair. Behold these new supergluttons, these ambassadors of the American appetite, these horsemen of the esophagus.

There was a time, of course—a year and fifteen pounds ago—when I didn't watch people gorge themselves in public and try to figure out what it meant, or if it meant anything at all. I was a serious journalist with a good job. I wrote for a magazine in Philadelphia. I wrote about doctors, developers, politicians, and the occasional eccentric who wanted to change the world. I had never heard of the Belt of Fat Theory. I couldn't tell the difference between "Hungry" Charles Hardy and Hungry Hungry Hippo. I couldn't rap a single verse of competitive-eating-themed hip-hop. The only thing I knew about competitive eating was what everybody else knows: that every year, some skinny Japanese guy kicks all of our American asses in hot dogs.

---

* Now that residents of several E.U. countries have been found to be more obese than Americans, and obesity panics have taken hold in Britain and France, any Europeans who mock the girth of our nation are merely throwing stones at fat houses. Luckily for them, American-style eating contests are still totally mockable.

† Not to mention the contests' wankish indifference to the 800 million global hungry and also the 12 percent of American households our own Department of Agriculture considers "food-insecure."

I was okay with all of that.

Then, one day in the summer of 2004, while using my magazine's Internet connection to distract myself from thinking about my doctors and developers and politicians and eccentrics who wanted to change the world, I came across the Federation's website, ifoce.com.

The outer rim of the donut hole.

Across the top of the page, a banner spelled out INTERNATIONAL FEDERATION OF COMPETITIVE EATING. The site's design was unremarkable except for an illustration on the page's upper left: a heraldic seal with two facing lions. Upon closer inspection, the lions were eating a hot dog from both ends while pawing tubes of mustard and ketchup that crossed, like swords, to form an X. A Latin inscription read IN VORO VERITAS.

In Gorging, Truth.

I clicked "Media Inquiries."

Within a day or two I got a call back from Rich Shea, younger brother of George Shea. In the meantime I had done some more reading. I had discovered that my hometown, Philly, hosted an annual chicken-wing contest called Wing Bowl. A couple of times since I had moved to Philly, friends and strangers had tried to tell me about Wing Bowl, but I must have blown them off. On the phone, Rich Shea explained the significance of Wing Bowl's greatest champion, a truck driver named Bill "El Wingador" Simmons. "Wingador's done a lot for competitive eating, certainly in Philly," Rich said. "So, you know, he could be the Moses Malone—did Moses Malone play for the Sixers? He could be the Doctor J"—he paused, thought of something better—"the *G. Love and Special Wing Sauce* of competitive eating." He laughed.

Rich talked quickly and thought quickly. He explained that he and his brother maintained a public relations firm in New York—Shea Communications—and their bread-and-butter clients were legitimate types like detectives and commercial real estate managers. The Federation was a separate track of the business, run from the same loft office in Chelsea. The Sheas got into the eating game in the late eighties, when both of them graduated from college, one after the other, and went to work in New York City for two old-school PR guys from the era when PR guys were called "press agents." The two old-school PR guys were the ones who invented the biggest eating contest in the world, the Nathan's Famous Hot Dog contest, back in the 1970s. The brothers eventually took over the Nathan's account and formed the Federation in 1997 with the goal of extruding that single hot dog contest into a gluttonous empire.

And they were getting close. The Federation claimed to have 300 active eater-members. Rich said that by the end of 2004, the Federation would have sanctioned about seventy-five contests that year, anywhere from three to ten per month. This was in addition to a handful of non-Federation contests that came in two flavors: indie and bootleg. The indie contests—one or two per month—were organized under the umbrella of an offshoot league called the Association of Independent Competitive Eaters, or AICE. Because AICE was newer, its contests were far smaller than the Federation's. As for the bootleg contests, they were harder to characterize: dozens, maybe hundreds, of minor spectacles at low-rent venues, at America's crummy bars, small-town carnivals, drive-time radio stations.

Eaters had options, but there was a catch. They couldn't mix and match. The Federation required its top talent to sign exclusive eighteen-month management contracts, and it had not been reluctant to shoot off cease-and-desist letters to wayward eaters it suspected of breaching the contract. Ambitious eaters—those who desired the imprimatur of a league—were therefore forced to pick either AICE or the Federation. Most eaters went with the Federation because it was bigger in every way: bigger stage, bigger money, bigger media. The Federation contests were sponsored by food companies, mostly, but also by municipal festivals and casinos on Indian reservations. The Sheas earned a per-contest fee from each sponsor, usually in the mid-four to low-five figures. The sponsors also put up the prize money, which Rich described as "a thousand dollars here, a thousand dollars there." In 2004, the total cash prize money was more than $60,000, of which the top American eater, Sonya Thomas, took home at least $17,000, plus a car—but the prizes, the number of contests, and the fan base were all growing; in 2005, sponsors would dole out more than $160,000, and Sonya would double her cash winnings. "It appeals to our competitive nature," Rich told me, adding, "You could also argue it's packaging and promotion and marketing. We've been very careful with how we've presented it." The Shea brothers had targeted "that guy demo," landing the horny eighteen-to-thirty-four set that loved *Maxim* and *FHM*. Capturing the guy demo allowed them to pitch eating specials to the Travel Channel, the Food Network, the Discovery Channel, and even such bigger fish as Fox. In 2004, ESPN scored 765,000 household viewers for its first live broadcast of the Nathan's contest.

Eventually, said Rich, he and his brother hoped to convert eating from a hobby into a professional sport, like bass fishing. "That's sort of the curve we're looking at," Rich said.

He didn't mention it, but in 2001, the B.A.S.S. league sold to ESPN for a purported $35 million.

Eating contests weren't invented by the Shea brothers or their mentors, or even by Americans. Anthropological studies and old copies of scurrilous newspapers suggest that the will to gorge is universal. Speed and volume competitions pop up in Greek myth, in the *Eddas* of Norse myth,* and even in what may be mankind's first novel, Apuleius's *Golden Ass,* written in the second century A.D.: "Last night at supper, I was challenged to an eating race by some people at my table and tried to swallow too large a mouthful of polenta cheese." (Choking ensued.) Ethnographies show that eating contests were regular events at lavish Native American potlatch feasts, and there's historical evidence of rice contests in Japan, beefsteak contests in Britain, mango contests in India. Even in France, that supposed bastion of foody sanity, *les goinfres* (pigs) compete to pound *le fromage* at seasonal festivals.

We're different because we have more of it, more types of contests in more places. We do it broader and bigger, and unlike the British, the French, and the Germans—whose health ministry explicitly condemned the German variation of eating contests, called *Wettessen,* in a letter to a researcher of mine—we make no apologies. We unabashedly marry the public-gorging impulse to our most sacred American rituals (the catching of the greased pig followed by the pie contest followed by the reading of the Declaration of Independence on the Fourth of July) and give organized gluttony an iconic role in our most iconic movies. One of the feel-good pinnacles of *Cool Hand Luke,* Paul Newman's epic prison flick, is the scene in which Luke wins over his fellow prisoners by declaring, casually, that he can eat fifty hardboiled

---

* The god Loki loses to a giant. Both eat all of their meat, but the giant eats his plate, too, proving that competitive eating really does have a strategic component.

eggs—"Yeah, well, it'll be somethin' to do," says Luke—commencing days of fevered speculation, betting, logistical preparation, training meals, and exercise leading up to the eventual eating performance itself. Luke eats the fifty eggs, winning his buddy Dragline a ton of cash and triumphing existentially over his captors by making prison seem like fun. Also uplifting, though in a different sense, is the infamous blueberry-pie-eating scene in *Stand by Me.* A young boy in a small town, cruelly nicknamed "Lardass" and taunted by classmates and adults alike, gets revenge by entering a pie contest and vomiting on one of his competitors. Lardass ignites a chain reaction: "Girlfriends barfed on boyfriends. Kids barfed on their parents. A fat lady barfed in her purse. The Donnelly twins barfed on each other. And the Women's Auxiliary barfed all over the Benevolent Order of Antelopes . . ."

I never found a newspaper clipping that described a "total barf-o-rama" like the one in *Stand by Me,* but minus the barf-o-rama, it could be any contest in any small town. Prison masculinity tests like the one in *Cool Hand Luke* also have a basis in reality, if my interview with a Baltimore gurgitator nicknamed Tony Hustle, formerly incarcerated in the state of Maryland for armed robbery, is any indication. When it comes to contest lore, fact trumps fiction. The great Damon Runyon, the bard of 1920s Broadway, staged a fictional eating contest for his short story "A Piece of Pie," but for my money, his nonfiction account of an eating contest in the March 5, 1920, *New York American* is more pleasurable. Runyon, reporting from the Yankees training camp in Florida, describes preparations for a "gustatory grapple" between the sportswriters (especially a top eater-scribe named Irwin Cobb) and the ballplayers (primarily Babe Ruth, for obvious reasons):

> It was decided that Mr. Cobb should start from scratch with Ruth, and that they shall spot their competitors one Virginia ham each, and a double porterhouse. George Mogridge, who is managing Ruth, insisted on a rule that Mr. Cobb shall not be permitted to tell any stories during the encounter, as George says his man cannot do a menu justice if he has to stop and laugh, while Mr. Cobb's ability to laugh and eat at the same time is well known. He can emit a raucous guffaw and chamber a Dill pickle simultaneously.

Maybe because of the nature of the subject, it's impossible to find a boring account of an eating contest, even if you go all the way back to the beginning—back as far as 1793, when a newspaper in York, Pennsylvania, noted that "two young men of this County, an hour after dining, undertook to eat twenty-four ginger Cakes each, to have them gratis provided they accomplished it." In sclerotic nineteenth-century New York City, fat mayors and even fatter aldermen settled bets with their jaws while corrupt Tammany Hall racketeers treated their armies of tenement dwellers to pie-eating contests at lavish picnics. On the ambrosial frontier of pre-smog Los Angeles, a gold-rusher's daughter challenged her friends to "an eating race" of peaches, while on the mean, fallen frontier, in the mining town of Galena, Montana, the Fourth of July "was ushered in by the booming of giant powder which shook the buildings from roof to basement," followed by "the soupeating contest between Sperindo Perrcri, superintendent of the Savage mine, and Defenbaugh, watchman at the Red Cloud, for the championship of the Hills and a silver-striking hammer." The contests belched out the fierce impulses of a new country. By the turn of the century, every town from Rolla, Missouri, to Bountiful, Utah, speed-ate pies on the Fourth. Contests attracted chowhounds from the most dignified institutions (academia, the church, the military[*]) and lifted nobodies to mythic heights.[†] An eating contest was a natural icebreaker for picnics, summer camps, and county fairs because it swallowed people's differences in its broad, low humor—though there was a certain breed of contest that did the exact opposite, that heightened differences, and cruelly so. From the late nineteenth century through the Great Depression, whites recruited blacks—often little kids—to eat watermelons. The supposed voracity of the black appetite had its roots in the minstrel-show tradition. NO MINSTREL SHOW, IF YOU PLEASE, protested one conservative[‡] black newspaper in 1922: "The comic supplement Negro, the water melon eating Negro, is the one which our enemies would have us resemble."

---

[*] U.S. troops have battled with food on navy battleships and inside Trident nuclear submarines; they have staged eating contests while stationed in Paris in 1918 (pie), Italy in 1945 (pie), Vietnam in 1968 (eggs), and Beirut in 1984 (dog biscuits).

[†] The eating prowess of "Honest Red" Dugan, a poor Lower Manhattan cabdriver who died in 1911, scored him a *Times* obituary longer than that of most congressmen.

[‡] So conservative, in fact, that it had refused to criticize the governor of Missouri when he vetoed an anti-lynching bill.

As America grew more body-conscious, the stigma of public gluttony spread to whites. In 1946, the wife of the Army's top eater, PFC Chester Salvatori, divorced him "on grounds of cruelty" because she was "humiliated by the publicity that came from her husband's feats in eating," according to a wire story. Once the occasion for manly pride, eating contests now faded into the hidden recesses of personal biography, to be trotted out later for laughs should the person become famous, as in the case of Colonel Parker (whose biographer notes that he promoted a contest, once, before he met Elvis), and the segregationist George Wallace (who is shown at a pie contest in an old college snapshot, gazing "pensively at the floor," according to a biographer), and even Al Gore Jr., whose eventual political profilers couldn't resist noting that a young Al Gore, working as a cub reporter in Tennessee, once reported on a Whopper-eating contest at Burger King.*

Eating contests lost their swagger. Adults ceded the competition table to little kids and frat boys. Contests grew stunty and tame.

And then the Federation came along, and eating contests became big and dangerous and wild again. Into the delicate ecosystem of American gurgitation, the Federation introduced several new elements: first, a full-time promoter—the Shea brothers—and, second, a core group of pioneering gurgitators, the first people in history to self-identify as professional eaters. "We did all the footwork years ago," as "Hungry" Charles Hardy told me. "Traveling here, traveling there. We didn't really make no kinda money. We pretty much took it to where it was today."

I started calling eaters in September 2004, starting with the veterans like Hardy and Ed "Cookie" Jarvis and Don "Moses" Lerman. They all said they were amazed by eating's trajectory, its quick-rising legitimacy. "The life has been a lot better, eating on the circuit," Hardy said, owing to the uptick in

---

* Gore's fastidious coverage of the event ("one of the contestants regurgitated his first three Whoppers on the table and dampened the morale of his competitors") was later interpreted by one profiler as proof of Gore's resolve not to skate by on merely his "pedigree" and his "cum laude Ivy League diploma," and to get his hands dirty by taking on what the profiler called "stories like that." It was seen to be revealing of his inner character, which is probably why it was so much fun to learn, from the *Los Angeles Times* in early 2006, that the disgraced lobbyist Jack Abramoff, who elevated mere conflict of interest to a lucrative criminal art, once organized "a Quarter Pounder–eating contest at a McDonald's, with some proceeds going to the American Cancer Society"—a fundraising effort that the Wonkette weblog called "uniquely ironic."

prize pots. Ed Jarvis said, "Let's face it. We're on ESPN. If that's not professional sports, I don't know what is." Don Lerman said, "I think in three years it'll be as big as PGA golf. In five years it may be in the Olympics."* The one eater to offer me a reality check was Arnie "Chowhound" Chapman, the renegade with the league of his own. He told me he wanted eating to be chilled-out and shticky, not corporate. Arnie was the bizarro-world version of the Federation guys, believing them all delusional and the Federation morally depraved. "The elite eaters," Arnie said, "they're addicted to adulation, they're addicted to publicity."

Arnie was half right. There were definite hints of pride and obsession in those early calls, not least in Arnie's own anti-Federation spiel. Ed said he maintained a trophy room. "It's like a shrine," Ed said. "I mean, people look in and they're like, 'God.'" Don had a trophy room, too. And a weight problem. "Since I'm thirty, I've been fighting obesity," Don said. Ed was pushing four hundred and also trying to lose weight.† The day I talked to him, he was pondering an upcoming cannoli contest. Ed was the cannoli champ, but was thinking about not defending his title. "It's rough on the body," he said. "One, you're eating 11,000 calories. Two, there's no money. Three, all that said, the bottom line is 'What am I doing this for?' I'm basically putting 11,000 calories into my body with the chance I could get hurt. What for? There's gotta be a cause." Even Arnie admitted, "I'm even a little concerned about myself. I'm now 245 pounds. I've never been that heavy before."

---

* As a publicity stunt for a Spam-eating contest, George Shea once arranged an Olympic-style "torch run" using a can of Spam mounted on a chair leg. He later told the *Washington Post* it was "the first-ever meat-based torch run in the United States, if not the world." He also claimed to have lobbied unsuccessfully for eating's inclusion in the Olympics: "I strongly believe that we have overtaken curling in the overall pantheon of sports," he told the *McGill Daily* (whose interviewer, by the way, had decided to call Shea after "musing about what could be accomplished in the world if all the money spent on eating contests in the U.S. per year were to be diverted toward, say, treating preventable disease in sub-Saharan Africa," only to be wooed by Shea's deadpan savvy into publishing a full Q&A of their exchange), "and I think tennis is next."

† Caveat: pinning down an eater's poundage is more difficult than it may seem. One reason is that the eaters' weights fluctuate significantly; Don "Moses" Lerman has weighed as much as 250 pounds and as little as 142. Also, the official "weigh-in" ceremonies have been known to produce odd numbers, and the IFOCE's "bib sheets," which list eaters' weights and heights, are rarely updated. Absent any canonical source, I tend to trust what the eaters tell me. Still, all weights in this book should be considered estimates.

Slander, rivalry, hubris, recklessness: that was half of the Shakespearean palette, the exact half you'd expect to find in a group of pro gluttons. But the more eaters I called, and the more I pushed past their immediate need to impress upon me that they weren't a bunch of freaks, the more I saw that they really weren't. I got a sense of the other half of the palette, the subtler shades. With a few conspicuous exceptions, the eaters didn't seem to be life-long publicity hounds or career eccentrics. They had wives and kids. They had jobs as construction workers, social workers, bankers, engineers, lawyers. I would come to know them as genuinely sweet and generous guys, most of them. Except for their collective waist size, they were as averagely American as the Americans in campaign commercials. They had to know that competitive eating was a marketing ploy, and yet—out of some psychic contortion it was too soon for me to guess at—rarely spoke of it that way. Eating, to them, wasn't a ploy. It was fun. It was a chance to compete, to travel the country and make a little money, or at least break even. It was a chance to be on ESPN.

How many people get to be on ESPN?

And beyond the obvious rewards were the intangibles, borne of the fact that eating was a community, one with its own distinct interior culture, its own goals and sacred controversies. (The controversies, if anything, legitimize the community, as sociologist Gary Alan Fine told me: "It means ... there are some things that matter.") Charles Hardy, who in a few months would tattoo the letters "IFOCE" on his right bicep, said, "We're like one big family." Ed Jarvis said, "I'm with a group, not by myself ... It's nice to have a group." They readily talked trash and bestowed compliments, too. He's fast (said Don of Ed), he's got capacity, he's got technique, "he believes in what he does." Belief/believes/believer. The eaters kept conjugating that word. I talked to another eater, twenty-seven-year-old Tim "Eater X" Janus, who told me the story of the first time George Shea offered to pay for his hotel room at an out-of-state contest. "I was pretty flattered, actually," Tim said. "I knew it could lead to big things ... I don't know, it's just neat to see people believe in you, for anything, really."

It didn't seem that it could be so welcoming, this weird little corner of the culture, but there it was, warm and cozy, teeming with improbably hopeful activity. In *The Control of Nature,* John McPhee writes that the founders of

New Orleans built a city "where almost any camper would be loath to pitch a tent." Here on the pro gluttony circuit, atop the same cultural terrain that made me feel, in my bitterest moments, ashamed to be an American, the eaters were planting their dearest desires—for fair and honest competition, for a pat on the back, to get noticed, to prove themselves, to make their kids and spouses proud.

Life/liberty/pursuit of happiness by way of eating/shitting/vomiting/shilling.

In Gorging, Truth.

Could it work?

Could the eaters really draw blood from this stone? Could they extract, from this grotesque spectacle, meaning? And if they could, did that mean the spectacle wasn't as grotesque as it seemed to someone like me, looking in from the outside? Was there something nourishing hidden within American trash culture?

Look, to be clear: these were my own existential questions. Not the eaters'. The eaters weren't staying up nights wondering if they could extract meaning from the grotesque. Eating wasn't grotesque, it was cool, and if the eaters did stay up nights, it was to trade stomach-stretching techniques on the phone or check the latest eating gossip on beautifulbrian.com.

This is where we converged. Seriousness. The eaters took eating seriously—they trained, they spent their money and time, risked their health and their relationships—and I felt like I should take eating as seriously as they did. That didn't mean adopting a persona and joining the circuit as a gurgitator, although once, at a pastrami contest at New York's Second Avenue Deli, I did step up to the competition table myself, about which the less said the better.*

No: serious, to me, meant, on a basic level, going to a ton of contests.

---

* Okay, I'll say this: prior to the contest, I agonized about how far I should push myself—i.e., whether it was the better part of valor to stop if I felt like I was about to vomit, or to keep going, so as to more fully empathize with the discomfort my subjects often endure. As it turned out, owing to the chewiness of the meat and also my inability to resist the urge, every ten seconds or so, to pick up a napkin and wipe my face, I ended up eating one sandwich in ten minutes. One.

Starting with a Krystal hamburger qualifier in Knoxville, Tennessee, on September 19, 2004, and ending with a blueberry pie contest in Machias, Maine, on August 20, 2005, I would eventually attend twenty-seven eating contests in thirteen states and two continents, including seventeen Federation contests, five AICE contests, two local TV contests, one sports radio contest, one contest sponsored by a United Church of Christ congregation, and one contest organized by a Japanese weatherman. I would attend, for instance, four Krystal hamburger events and five Nathan's hot-dog events. I would attend the Gameworks World Tex Mex Roll-Eating Championship Presented by Great Lakes Crossing at the Great Lakes Crossing Mall in Auburn Hills, Michigan. The World's Greatest Shoo-Fly Pie-Eating Championship at the Rockvale Outlets in Lancaster, Pennsylvania. The ACME World Oyster Eating Championship in Metairie, Louisiana. The World Cheesecake-Eating Championship in Brooklyn. The Entenmann's Pies Thanksgiving Invitational in the Chelsea district of New York City. The Ball Park Fiesta Bowl National Hot Dog Eating Championship in Tempe, Arizona. The Third Annual International Chili Society's World Championship Chili Eating Contest at Mandalay Bay Hotel and Casino in Las Vegas. And after enough contests, after filling enough notebooks with columns of numbers signifying quantities of meats and sweets, I would become akin to an actual serious beat reporter covering an actual serious beat—which was my goal starting out. I wanted the coverage *itself,* not just the effort, to be serious. I wanted to cover eating as if it were important. Not mock-important.* Truly important.

It was possible, of course, that it wasn't important—that it was all just empty calories, signifying nothing. It was possible that the eaters weren't harbingers of the coming apocalypse, just an excuse for headline writers to make bad puns. Appetite for Destruction. Cool Hand Puke. Lord of the

---

* The *New York Post*'s Gersh Kuntzman, writing in the IFOCE's newsletter *The Gurgitator* ("Life on the Circuit"): "... the Land of the Rising Bun is the one remaining breeding ground for the next generation of gustatory gladiators. Whether it's in their elementary schools, where kids learn about the legendary eaters like Nakajima, Shirota, and Arai, or in the buffet academies, where potential stars are groomed for eating greatness, Japan prepares while the rest of the world errs ..."

Wings.* Wing Eaters Peck for Position. Frankly Speaking. Great Balls of Matzo. Getting Stuffed.† A Competitor With Guts. Big Eater Can Stomach the Competition. Man Bites Dogs, Over and Over. She Meats Expectations. This isn't a knock on reporters—I am one—but, for most of us, an eating piece isn't a project, it's a blessed break from *other* projects, which is why eating always gets shoehorned into a few standard and easy-to-pull-off formats: (1) the shlocky thirty-second "brite" segment at the end of a local newscast; (2) the half-playful, half-serious newspaper feature; (3) the puffy, sprawling alt-weekly profile of the alt-weekly's town's most prominent eater; or (4) the stripped-down News of the Weird brief sandwiched contextless between other, wildly unrelated briefs.‡

And they fail. They all fail to capture the mad galumphing experience of an eating contest, a really good one, when the crowd's into it, gawking, screaming, and the food's detonated on contact with a merciless line of teeth and jaws, and Shea's on his game—*we cannot SEE, we cannot HEAR, we need something MORE!*—and when, scanning the crowd's faces, I can tell that we're all feeling something, something intense, maybe revulsion, maybe joy, maybe just a deep curiosity, but it's more than can be expressed in a thirty-second brite or a fifty-word brief. Whatever's happening doesn't feel shabby or small, but instead—I swear to the Virgin Mary Grilled Cheese—broad and big and consequential, as though America has vomited up its deepest hope and deepest dread in one place and now something worthwhile having to do with this *big, fat, infantile, stupid* country can be learned, or accomplished. The whole goopy range of it, everything that makes America so undeniably great and infuriating, loved and hated, everything that makes me want to buy a ranch in Montana one day and move to Scandinavia the next: a cross-section of the promise and the threat we represent to the world and to ourselves.

---

* The title, I'm sad to say, of my own article about the Philadelphia Wing Bowl.
† There's a definite and creepy sexual subtext to some of the headlines, a gleeful, violative aggression; somebody once told a friend of mine that he hated this book's title because it seemed like someone was "getting orally raped."
‡ Page 6 news briefs, *Ottawa Sun*, November 27, 2005: (1) Toronto boy falls off a building and dies; (2) Colorado teen faces a year in prison for hitting and killing a bicyclist "while text-messaging"; (3) Sonya Thomas eats a Thanksgiving turkey in twelve minutes; (4) tribal leaders in South Africa oppose government's outlawing of virginity tests for young girls.

I wanted to capture that range. And I wanted to do it by writing about the eaters, who were living it. That meant I needed eaters of a certain type. Eaters who embodied eating's risks (meaning they competed often enough to strain their bodies) and also its rewards (meaning they were talented and high-ranked). I needed eaters with a good chance of transcending the pro circuit's intrinsic comedy, tragedy, slander, and bad food to achieve true athletic grace, maybe even redemption.

I found three of the lucky ones, and latched on.

I'm talking about Bill "El Wingador" Simmons, chicken-wing champion of the world. I'm talking about Tim "Eater X" Janus, tiramisu-eating champion of the world.

I'm talking, especially, about David "Coondog" O'Karma, tag-team bratwurst champion of Canton, Ohio.

2

THE FIFTY-DOG DAY

DAVE O'KARMA is a painting contractor. He paints houses in Cuyahoga Falls, Ohio, where he lives with his second wife, Lisa, and his stepdaughter, Juanita. Dave stands tall but not straight, a slouching six-two with a paint-ladder tan and nicely toned biceps and unfortunate brown hair. The hair is shaved to the skin except for a stripe down the middle. The edge definition of the stripe varies from true mohawk to amorphous mop. Except for the mohawk, he looks like Jesus, if Jesus could bench 250, or else he looks like Peter Pan, if Peter Pan were middle-aged, and a redneck. Dave wears a floppy fishing hat and T-shirts with the sleeves torn off and the necks ripped vertically down to the nipple. His nose is a perfect arrow pointing to a salt-and-pepper beard that terminates in a goatee. When he walks, there's a sense that his neck is leading him independent of his body. When he sits, his long limbs either fold into his chest, fetally, or kick across the furniture like a kid stuck in a dentist's waiting room. One of Dave's friends, a columnist for an Akron newspaper, describes Dave as "kind of brilliant" and "sort of a savant," an analysis that Dave agrees with. "I'm pretty sure I'm a low-level genius," Dave says. His voice is high and nasal. "Look, I'm not college-educated, you know? But I'm self-taught. I live by a fuckin' library. If I ever lost everything, I'd be one of those homeless people living in the library, carrying their clothes and reading books." He even published a book of his own, once. It was a book of poetry called *Wit and Whimsy of a White-Trash Jesus*. The white-trash Jesus was him, Dave O'Karma.

When this story began, in the first summer of the new millenium, Dave was forty-four years old. He and Lisa had been married for two years. They had a newly merged family. Dave's house was in flux. Lisa was attending nursing school. New stepdaughter Juanita was applying to colleges. Dave's son, Adam—who had just moved in with Dave's ex-wife, to Dave's chagrin—would start high school in a few months. Exciting things were happening to Dave's loved ones, but not to Dave, who had always wanted to be a writer but never had any luck with his poems or screenplays. Now he was forty-four years old. His family had left him behind, and so had the rest of America, his cultural referents (John Lennon, Kurt Vonnegut Jr.) rendered quaint by cable news and empire.

Dave figured: *Man, you ran out of time.*

One afternoon in July, Dave stopped at the grocery store on his way home from work. Standing in the checkout line, he thumbed the July 25, 2000, issue of *National Examiner.* The cover promised embarrassing stories about Michael Jordan, Johnny Carson, and Patty Hearst. On page five, he saw this:

"And the WEINER is . . ."

100-lb. hot-dog-eating champion gulps down 25 franks to win the prized Mustard Belt title

A 5-foot-6, 100-pound Japanese native gobbled down 25 all-American hot dogs in 12 minutes to earn a world record and a yellow belt in gluttony.

Kazutoyo Arai swallowed up the other 17 competitors at Nathan's Famous Fourth of July Hot Dog Eating Contest in Coney Island, N.Y., taking home the Mustard Yellow International Belt, the holy grail of timed gastronomic excess . . .

Last year's champion, 300-plus-pound Steve Keiner of New Jersey, couldn't cut the mustard for fifth place, even after having a dentist sharpen his teeth to give him an "edge."

Dave thought: Yes.

He loved the part about the dentist and the sharpened teeth; he loved the bad puns ("couldn't cut the mustard") and the article's accompanying pictures of the svelte victorious Japanese and the fat vanquished Americans with great names like "Hungry" Charles Hardy and Syd "Mongo" Goldstein. Dave vibrated, immediately, *yes* to the whole ridiculous thing.

Dave had actually done this before, eating competitively. As a nerdy eleventh-grader at Falls High, Dave competed in a pizza-eating contest on Cleveland television in 1972. His opponent, a square-jawed Italian named "Mushmouth," had once claimed that "when it comes to pizza, don't mess with a dago." Dave wore a shirt that said KING COONDOG O'KARMA in block letters. He messed with the dago, and won. "I thought I'd choke to death," he told the *Cuyahoga Falls City Press*.

He still had the old newspaper clip somewhere in his attic.

There in the supermarket, Dave closed the *National Examiner* and threw it onto the conveyor belt with the rest of his groceries. Within days he sent an e-mail to the Federation's George Shea. Lest Shea dismiss him as a wannabe, Dave listed his eating résumé from the seventies—the pizza title, yes, and also a "world record" from the time he ate 45 eggs in 8 minutes and 10 seconds on a Cleveland radio station on the Fourth of July, and another "world record" in donut eating (25 in 12 minutes)—point being, *I'm a pedigreed eater. I've done this before. I'm pretty good.*

Shea e-mailed back the next day, inviting Dave to sign up for one of a dozen qualifying contests for the 2001 Nathan's hot dog championship. The closest qualifier was in Middletown, New York, a seven-hour drive from Cuyahoga Falls. The date was ten months away.

For ten months, Dave painted houses by day and surfed eating websites by night, studying photos of the great eaters of the day. Finally, the contest in Middletown. Dave rented a big Dodge and took Lisa and Juanita and Adam on their first trip as a new family. The morning of the contest, Dave walked two miles from his hotel to the Galleria mall, the site of the contest, to try his first-ever Nathan's hot dog. (He had been training with cheap grocery-store dogs.) He took his first bite and it was almost like the dog bit back, with its taut natural casing and its Mace-like sting of garlic. It was disgusting. He figured he wouldn't eat more than five hot dogs, total, in twelve minutes.

But he ate seventeen, and won.

"It's Coondog O'Karma!" shouted the IFOCE's George Shea. "Coondog O'Karma of Ohio is the new Nathan's Middletown Hot Dog Eating champion, and will be going to Coney Island on the Fourth of July!"

As soon as Dave and his family got home, they started getting calls. ESPN radio wanted an interview. Dave stepped into the "Coondog" character he'd invented back in 1972—a funny, tough, arrogant, superaccomplished, proud son of the Midwest—and told the reporters that a sense of forgotten glory and solemn devotion had motivated him to pick up his fork, after a long retirement, and eat once again.

Dave invited Adam to the Nathan's finals in New York. Adam was excited. He'd never been to New York. So, on July 2, the two of them flew from Cleveland to La Guardia, and when they passed above the Statue of Liberty, Adam turned to Dave and said "Big Time." Dave hadn't been to the Big Time since he was four years old. He and Adam hopped in a cab and rode to their comped hotel, where Dave stood in the lobby with Adam, looking up at the big ceiling, nodding his head. He caught the eye of the bellhop and said, "Are there any other famous people staying here besides me?"

"And who might you be, sir?"

"I'm Coondog O'Karma. I'm the Middletown hot dog eating champion."

"No shit."

The next day, July 3, he was Coondog, *fully* Coondog, when he walked to City Hall for the traditional weigh-in with the mayor. Big Time. Giuliani wasn't there yet, and neither were the Japanese eaters—just the American eaters and a bunch of TV crews, including one from Germany and one from a Tokyo TV eating show called *TV Champion*, with which even the IFOCE officials were only vaguely familiar. The Tokyo crew was attached to a Japanese TV host in a black tuxedo.

Coondog spotted his idols standing in the sun, wearing white Nathan's T-shirts that said EAT ALL THAT YOU CAN EAT. They were all here in the (abundant) flesh, and Coondog introduced himself around: Steve "The Appetite" Addicks, Ed "Cookie" Jarvis, "Hungry" Charles Hardy . . .

"Oh my God, you're 'Hungry' Charles Hardy!"

Hardy, weighed down with bling, smiled and said, in what Coondog later referred to as a "whisky-coated rasp":

"Welcome to the club, Coondog."

Suddenly there was a hubbub, heads whipsawing, TV cameras swiveling. Coondog assumed it was the mayor and his entourage.

Nope. The Japanese.

They emerged from an unseen vehicle and walked toward the Americans. There were two this year, one fewer than last year. The first was Kazutoyo Arai, age thirty-four, the hero of Coondog's *National Examiner* article from one year back. He had won last year's contest with twenty-five and one-eighth hot dogs, a new world record. Arai, nicknamed "The Rabbit" because when he ate he took mincing bites and bobbed his head with a steady rhythm, was a short, gentle man with shiny jet-black hair parted down the exact middle of his forehead. He weighed 100 pounds exactly. His family owned a butcher shop in Saitama, Japan, but none of the American eaters or American journalists knew that; they just knew him as the champ, so they swarmed him. Including Coondog, who pointed at the Mustard Yellow Belt the Rabbit was holding—a cheap prop glued with rhinestones—and held out his upturned hands.

"Can I hold it?"

The Rabbit, nodding, handed over the belt in a gesture of transoceanic trust. Coondog immediately lifted it high above his head, way out of the Rabbit's reach.

"MINE!" Coondog sneered, catching the eye of the German cameraman, who asked, "Who are you?"

"I'm Coondog O'Karma, and I'm here to take back the hot dog belt!"

So while the foreign crews fawned over the Americans and the American crews fawned over the Rabbit, nobody noticed the cute little Japanese kid with the short spiky blond hair and the white T-shirt and the maroon running shorts, sitting there on a park bench. This was Takeru Kobayashi, the second Japanese eater. Twenty-three years old. A kid, really. At least one of the Americans thought Kobayashi was the Rabbit's son. His name hadn't been mentioned in the City of New York's press release; he was surrounded by zero TV cameras and zero journalists. The only thing the American eaters knew for sure was that he had beaten the Rabbit in Japan, and that his nickname was "The Prince." The Americans had heard rumors, though. Don Lerman heard he ate seventy-five hot dogs, and assumed the dogs were those little cocktail franks. Krazy Kevin heard thirty hot dogs, which was still ludicrously high.

Coondog was curious.

He walked over to the park bench, where Koby sat next to the tuxedoed Japanese TV host.

"What's his name?" said Coondog.

The host glared at Coondog. Off-camera, he was not friendly.* But Coondog saw an opening. He saw that Koby was looking at his chest, at his T-shirt. It was custom-made, depicting a hot dog and the phrase JUST EAT IT written in mustard.

"You want it?" said Coondog, and he took the shirt off his back and handed it to Koby.

"You like?"

Koby grinned.

Giuliani arrived, donned one of Shea's straw boater hats, weighed the eaters, and took questions, including one from the Japanese TV host.

"What are you going to do if Japan wins again?"

"I'll resign."

The eaters scattered. Dave and Adam hopped on the subway and rode around, aimlessly, with no particular destination. Later that night, Coondog stopped by a Nathan's party at an Irish pub in the financial district. All the eaters were there, including the Japanese. Coondog spotted a CNN reporter and tried to charm her. Then he saw Koby. He bought him a Coors Light.

"You wanna arm-wrestle?"

Coondog put his elbow on the bar. Koby understood and put his elbow up, too. They wrestled; Coondog won. He grabbed another beer and held it up.

"You want to do a contest, right?"

Koby understood this, too. Koby and Coondog chugged the beers as fast as they could. Coondog would later claim that he won. The CNN reporter watched, but her camera wasn't running. Coondog, she said, that was great—can you get him to do it again?

Coondog said he'd try, and walked over to the bartender to get two more

---

* The next morning, on the chartered bus from the Millennium hotel to Coney Island, Coondog tries to trade with the Rabbit for his TV Tokyo headband, and the Japanese host/interpreter interferes brusquely. Coondog says to the Rabbit, "How do I say, 'Your interpreter is an asshole?'"

beers. By the time he got back, Koby's handlers had spirited him away. He was gone.

The next day, the Fourth of July, it rained lightly. It was gray and soupy. Five hundred people gathered at Surf and Stillwell Avenues on Coney Island, in front of the original Nathan's Famous stand, where a stage had been erected with a long table and a tarplike backdrop decorated with blue and yellow Nathan's signage and balloons. The crowd was a patchwork of umbrellas; the dozens of cameramen, including a guy from CNN, had wrapped their equipment with trash bags. Some spectators held signs that had been passed out by IFOCE officials to give the appearance of actual eating fandom. DOG-GINATOR RULES. BEAT THE RABBIT. Nathan's CEO, Wayne Norbitz, wandered the area in a yellow polo shirt, and was cornered by the tuxedoed Japanese TV host, who told him, in Japanese, "I'm sorry, but we're going to have the Japanese win again this year." Norbitz smiled and put his hands around the host's neck. The host pretended he was choking.

The contest had come a long way in a very short time. Just eight years earlier, it was so small and obscure that Norbitz himself had to solicit contestants from the ranks of Coney Island's passersby. Since the Federation's George Shea took over the contest in the early nineties, he had made it bigger and more visually outlandish but also more regimented and predictable, laying the logistical foundation for the eventual live ESPN broadcast that would begin in 2004. The Nathan's contest of George Shea was a highly choreographed affair. There was a production script. There were run-throughs the morning of the contest. "Everything is kind of rehearsed," says Mike "The Scholar" Devito, the 1990, 1993, and 1994 Nathan's champion and the Federation's ex-commissioner. "It's a show with a contest at the end." In 2001, Devito was fulfilling his commissioner's duty to act as the "head judge," the one who relays hot dog totals from the judges, who squat in front of the tables, to the card girls, also known as "Bunnettes," who display the totals on flippable blue cards they hold high above their heads, so audience members can keep track of the leaders.

As for the Federation officials like Devito and Shea, they already knew how many hot dogs the eaters would eat. Eric Booker, Don Lerman, Charles Hardy, and Ed Jarvis would all hover around twenty dogs. Arai would do twenty-five. Maybe, if it was a really rare and special day—"a great show," says Devito—someone would eat thirty.

At noon, Shea kicked off the show by introducing the eaters one by one. Hardy pumped his fists, Jarvis draped himself with the American flag, Coondog ripped his shirt and glared at the audience with a mean grin. Then the Japanese: Koby first, giving Dave a high five as he walked onstage. He wore a white headband that said TV TOKYO and made his ears stick out. The Rabbit came out last, as the reigning champ, and foisted the Mustard Yellow Belt high above his head. Eric Booker, perhaps the largest eater on stage and certainly the blackest, stood between the Rabbit and Koby for purposes of the TV visual.

In the seconds before the countdown, Arai closed his eyes as if he were meditating. Koby arranged his five large yellow cups of water. The crowd chanted something indecipherable. The Rabbit slapped both of his cheeks, hard, as IFOCE officials brought each eater two paper plates of five hot dogs each.

"Join me please," said Shea. "Ten! Nine! Eight! Seven! Six! Five! Four! Three! Two! One! Ohhhhhh! . . . We're here to see who's going to take home this bout . . ."

The deejay cued "Disco Inferno" and, with that, kicked off the most boring eight-minute stretch of the day. In a twelve-minute contest, nothing interesting happens until the final third, when you start getting totals and a feel for the front-runners. "It's the last few minutes that's going to determine the outcome," says Mike Devito.

It was a reasonable expectation. Except, after only three minutes, the little Japanese kid with the jutting ears and cute spiky hair had almost broken the world record—*and he still had nine minutes left to go.*

One of the first to realize something was amiss was Don "Moses" Lerman, the veteran matzo-ball champ.* "All of a sudden," Don recalls, "I've got eight and the Japanese guy's got fifteen. And when you hear that, you say to yourself, in your mind, should I put my body through this trauma, you know, this workout, if I can't *catch* him?"

---

* In eating circles, a veteran is someone who has been competing since 2000.

Lerman, calling upon his years of experience, was able to focus and continue eating, but most of the other eaters weren't so cool-headed. Perhaps the next eater to notice was Steve "the Appetite" Addicks, a locomotive mechanic from Baltimore. Addicks was stationed directly to Koby's left. In photos from that day, Addicks was pictured with his mouth open, spilling half-chewed dog meat, head cranked toward Kobayashi with a look of pure confusion. Koby was eating his hot dogs with an inhuman ease. While the Rabbit kept the dog and bun together as an intact unit, dunking the whole thing and stuffing it, Koby was separating the dog from the bun. What's more, he was breaking each dog in half, then eating both halves at the same time, after which he dunked and ate the bun. Koby's judge was Gersh Kuntzman, a *New York Post* scribe and the original competitive-eating beat reporter. Gersh and other reporters would later dub Koby's eating style "the Solomon Method."

"I was in awe," says Steve Addicks. "It was amazing. I was standing next to something that—it's like, ah, I don't know—it was almost a religious experience, you know? Something that I was so close to see, that very few people will ever be able to witness, as far as the magnitude of what it meant to me as an eater. It was just like"—he makes a whooshing sound—"whoa . . . I'm sitting there watching a miracle."

It didn't take long for recognition to filter down the table in both directions, sped by the increasingly panicked statements of head judge Mike Devito, who kept looking imploringly at judge Gersh Kuntzman, who was squatting in front of the table with a pack of numbers printed on yellow sheets of paper. His numbers went to thirty. The Bunnettes' flippable cards only went to twenty-five. The yellow sheets were just in case. When he was handed the pack earlier that day, he thought it was a joke; you'd never need that many. Now, as Devito looked to Gersh for verification—was this for real?—Gersh gave him the thumbs-up, and worried that he would run out of numbers.

After three minutes and twenty-four seconds, Koby had finished his twenty-second hot dog.

"Oh my God, ladies and gentlemen," said George Shea, "twenty-two hot dogs and buns!"

Some perspective: the key benchmark of greatness in competitive eating, akin to rolling a 300 game in bowling or scoring under par in golf, is to eat 20 hot dogs in 12 minutes. This is called "doing the deuce." By the time an eater has "done the deuce," he has consumed 4.4 pounds of solid food and perhaps 2 pounds of water; he has eaten 6,180 calories, 403 grams of fat, and almost 14 grams of sodium. By the time an eater has "done the deuce," he is ready to lie down someplace air-conditioned, close to a toilet. But Koby, already at twenty-two, wasn't flagging. The Rabbit was in a distant second with fourteen hot dogs, and the rest of the eaters were in single digits.

"We need more hot dogs over here!"

"Ladies and gentlemen," said Shea, "Kobayashi, Takeru Kobayashi of Japan, has broken the American record—"

"—and the world record," interrupted someone else—

"—in under five minutes in this contest."

On the right end of the table, Coondog was well on his way to 20 hot dogs. He thought he was doing great. He thought all the cheering was for *him*. Then his counter told him, "The little Japanese kid just finished twenty-seven."

"No fuckin' way," said Coondog.

"Way," said the counter.

Coondog looked out into the audience and found Adam, his son. Adam was waving his hands wildly, gesturing for Coondog to hurry up. His eyes were wide. Coondog finally looked over at Koby, watched him for a few seconds, threw one of his hot dogs into the crowd, and put down his buns. So did Steve Addicks. "Gentleman" Joe Menchetti took off his shirt and executed what he would later call "a combination throwing in the towel and waving the white flag," exposing his ample belly. Someone yelled for him to put his shirt back on. The Japanese host screamed:

"KOOOBAYYYAAASHIIIIIII!!!!!!"

"KOOOBAYYYAAASHIIIIIII!!!!!!"

"KOOOBAYYYAAASHIIIIIII!!!!!!"

"Twenty-nine!"

"Twenty-nine hot dogs and buns!"

And on the face of George Shea—this man who could quote Virgil in the original Latin and often worked Shakespeare references into his monologues, which had become, through long practice, these great loquacious jets of ballyhoo that he could spray into audiences for twenty minutes at a time without breaking a sweat or dangling a participle—on the face of George Shea, a public man, a carny barker as cynical and wised-up as they come, you could see that the muscles had gone slack. Shea looked at Kobayashi, opened his mouth, and faintly shook his head. The man who invented the modern "sport" of competitive eating had just witnessed its remaking. George Shea, for maybe two seconds, was speechless.

He turned away from Koby and looked into the crowd. "One away," he said. One away from the magic number.

The Bunnette, having run out of flippable cards, held up a yellow sheet that said thirty.

There was a roar.

In the pit, Gersh Kuntzman ran out of numbers. He started furiously writing Koby's totals on the backs of yellow sheets with a ballpoint pen. Thirty-four. Thirty-six.

The crowd chanted, "For-ty! For-ty! For-ty!"

Gersh kept scribbling. Forty-six. Forty-seven.

"Forty-seven hot dogs and buns in twelve minutes!"

"KOOOBAYYYAAASHIIIIIII!!!!!!"

"KOOOBAYYYAAASHIIIIIII!!!!!!"

"KOOOBAYYYAAASHIIIIIII!!!!!!"

"Ladies and gentlemen, count down with me if you will! Ten! Nine! Eight! Seven! Six!"

"KOBAYAAAASHIIIIIII!!!!!"

"Five! Four! Three! Two!"

"KOBAYAHSIIIII!"

"One!"

And on the back of a yellow piece of paper, held high above the head of the victorious Takeru Kobayashi, was a Sharpie'd number representing his final total:

50

"Yo sha!" yelled Koby. ("All right!")

The deejay played an upbeat song as Shea announced the winners. In third place was "Hungry" Charles Hardy, who, as the top American, was draped with the Stars and Stripes previously worn by Ed Jarvis. Hardy bent over the table. The flag did nothing to disguise his obvious pain. In second, the Rabbit with thirty-one hot dogs—six more than his prior world record and, on any other day, an astounding total. But it was Koby who now held aloft the giant gold trophy and the Mustard Yellow Belt. He grinned and grinned. He appeared energetic, bouncy, as though he could run a marathon. His countrymen surrounded him, congratulating him in Japanese:

"You're a beast!" said the Rabbit.

"Aren't you happy?" asked the Japanese TV host.

"Oh," says Koby, "I'm happy."

"You had fifty. But how do you feel?"

"I can keep going."

An American reporter stuck a microphone in Coondog's face and asked him for comment. Coondog shook his head and muttered, "Coney Harbor."

Meanwhile, Gersh Kuntzman rushed to the phone to call in the results to the *New York Post* city desk. Before placing the call, Gersh brainstormed analogies that might impress the *Post* editors, who lacked a nuanced appreciation of the gluttonous arts. Kobayashi eating fifty hot dogs was maybe like Secretariat winning the Belmont by thirty-one lengths. Or the Jets winning the Super Bowl in 1969. Or a rookie shortstop breaking Bonds's home run record by 100 dingers.

Gersh dialed and demanded space on the front page. Koby's victory, he argued, was not only a watershed moment in competitive eating. It was a singular achievement in all of sports history.

The *Post* desk put him on hold.

3

THE SWEET SCIENCE

BY THE TIME I first spoke to Coondog, in early September of 2004, he'd been eating professionally, if you could call it that, for three years. I'd heard about him from some friends who were making a documentary about eating. Everything they'd told me was condensed to a small line in my notebook:

COONDOG—Villain. Akron, OH. Ex-Marine.* Hates IFOCE.

The "villain" part was why I was interested in him. My magazine had green-lighted a piece on the Philadelphia Wing Bowl, a huge chicken-wing contest attended by 20,000 drunk Philadelphians, and Coondog was the Wing Bowl's greatest heel. When I called him, the first thing he told me was that my hometown "looks like it was washed with a greasy rag," then added, "Put that in there, man." Then he ditched his sneer and admitted that he loved being the center of attention, even if it meant taking beer cans in the noggin. His Wing Bowl exploits had even earned him a mention in Trivial Pursuit: *What did competitive eater Dave "Coondog" O'Karma get disqualified for in the 2002 Wing Bowl after eating 100 wings?*† Coondog said, "You know, I'm a question in Trivial Pursuit, I've been in the *Wall Street Journal, GQ* magazine, I've done Steve Harvey, Sally Jessy Raphael, all this shit, Nathan's twice,

---

* Coondog was never in the armed services. My friends had seen pictures of Coondog in camo pants and jumped to that conclusion.
† A: vomit.

you know, *Battle of the Buffets* out in Vegas for the Discovery Channel, and I'm just a guy, right? I think I've gone a long way with nothin'."

He was in no hurry to hang up. Within fifteen minutes, thanks to what he called his "diarrhea mouth," he'd told me the entire arc of his story. It had the same tragic contours as any downward spiral excluding those that involve heavy drugs. Two months after the 2001 Nathan's, Coondog signed an eighteen-month contract with the Federation. The Sheas used him on TV specials for Fox and the Travel Channel and gave reporters his phone number ("I must have a quick wit . . . not to brag . . . I'm a good quote guy"). George Shea told him he was "one of the bigger stars." Coondog was ranked fourteenth in the world.

Then the contest bookings dried up. As a second-tier eater, he couldn't beat the big guys at the table. Nor could he score the coveted expenses-paid invites to the big contests, usually reserved for the top eaters like Eric Booker and Charles Hardy, whom the sponsors often requested by name (or by a more general description, i.e., *Send me the big black guy*). Coondog could always truck to the contests on his own dime, but he became impatient with having to shell out for the privilege of being a competitive eater. At the same time, he started to worry about Booker and Hardy, whose bodies were inflating along with their Federation rankings. Coondog encouraged them to stop. Think of your little kids. They told him thanks but no thanks. We love you, Coondog, but mind your own business. So Coondog, scorned, went off on his own. He started booking himself on his own talk shows. George Shea found out and banned Coondog from a wing-eating contest in Buffalo. Coondog showed up anyway, incognito in a giant chicken suit. (He was discovered immediately and wasn't allowed to compete, but he did win Best Costume.) After Buffalo, Coondog went officially AWOL from the Federation. He ate in bootleg contests under pseudonyms such as Kid Coney, Lone Winger, Evad "The Inhaler" Amrako, and TEFKAC (The Eater Formerly Known as Coondog). He started helping to plan contests for Arnie "Chowhound" Chapman's indie league instead, at which point the Federation threatened to sue Coondog for breach of contract. By now the Federation had erased all traces of Coondog from its website. He started calling himself "Forkless Coon"—grandiose even in exile—but it was hard to crack jokes when he couldn't even get his longtime gurgitator buddies to return his e-mails and calls. About the only person who still talked to him, aside from the indie eaters, was Takeru Kobayashi, who sent Coondog a Christmas card in 2002. In three short years, Coondog had gone from eating's golden boy to eating's pariah.

Over the one hour it took Coondog to tell me this story, he was so emotionally spastic—rational one moment, passionate the next, then full of wise perspective, then full of shit—that later I had to diagram Coondog's temperatures just to get them straight in my head.

First and foremost, there was a kind of lucid anger. The anger of the freshly scorned. "I'm one of the best eaters in the world," he said, "and they wouldn't let me in!" To Coondog, this was proof that eating wasn't a real sport, it was just a scam ("Do you understand?") to pad the wallet of George Shea ("and I *like* him, and I *like* him!"), this one guy who gets to make all the rules ("and he's making a *shitload* of money")—what kind of sport (he asked) is run by a PR company, anyway? What kind of sport prostrates itself before Internet casinos and grilled-cheese Virgins? Coondog was trying to scorch eating's pretensions, to burn the whole thing back down to its simple, goofy roots, where eating was more manageable and where none of his friends could get hurt.

His friends. Coondog cooled off when he talked about his eating friends. Coondog couldn't blame them, he could only feel sad for them. Sadness brought out his rational, blithely exasperated, introspective, rhetorically provocative tendencies. "If it's gotten so big that there's thousands of dollars," Coondog argued, "and there's money to be made, and people are actually practicing"—and if 400-pounders like Booker are putting on weight and known diabetics like Hardy are competing regularly, as Coondog pointed out—then why not regulate it, like boxing? If eating can't be fun and healthy and occasional and low-key, then shouldn't it swing to the other extreme, so that the eaters can at least secure the protections accorded to other pro sports, like health benefits, pensions, and a players' union? "If it's gonna be a sport," Coondog said, "*make* it a sport. If it's a PR thing, then call it the way it is. And I'm ambivalent. Part of me is in on the joke part of it, and part of me is like a really serious competitor who's like a little looney. And sometimes *I* don't know which one I am. I really don't. I have a hard time going sometimes from my alter ego 'Coondog' to Dave O'Karma. That's where the sickness comes in. The eating disorder."

In moments like this, Coondog seemed normal enough, even wise: just a guy swept up in a weird new crazy-making *thing* that seemed to hover between extreme meaning and extreme meaninglessness, and who wanted, understandably, to slap a name on it—any name—so he could have some psychic peace and wouldn't have to "think *way* too much about this bull-shit," in his words. Right—but no sooner would he drop such calm, clear-headed knowledge than he'd start heating up again. And this time he wouldn't burn with anger. He'd burn with dearer stuff: with wonder, with belief. As badly as he wanted to expose eating's fraudulence, his glutton's heart resisted, because if eating was a fraud, *how could he explain Takeru Kobayashi?* He'd seen Koby with his own eyes. Nathan's, 2001. The Fifty-Dog Day. The day that Koby turned water to wine. *The most fuckin' bizarre thing I ever saw*—and Coondog still had no idea how Koby had done it.

I had only known Dave for an hour. I had never met him in person. But I knew, from this one phone conversation, that he was the guy who could reify the plan I'd been keeping coiled in the back of my brain. The plan was simple. Fly to Japan, interview Kobayashi, ask him how he does it. Buy him a nice lunch and share some tea. Watch him train; maybe go to the gym. I wanted to go because I was fascinated by Koby, just like everyone else, but I also felt professionally obligated. I was writing a book about eating, and Koby was the greatest eater in the world.

Hearing Coondog talk about Koby changed my thinking. I saw that a trip to Japan could answer the crucial questions that I was just beginning to for-mulate and that had been vexing Coondog for years. What's real about com-petitive eating and what's illusory? Is it a sport? Is it a scam? Is it sublime in a hard-to-define way? The key to these questions was the one eater who had taken eating the furthest, into the realm of both legitimate sport and mys-tery. Wild rumors about Koby and Japan had always circulated in the Amer-ican gurgitator corps, thanks to the firsthand knowledge of several eaters who had flown to Japan to tape TV shows and returned with big checks—Hungry Charles got $12,000 for one trip—and hyperbolic stories: *Yeah, big money over there, Koby makes 200 grand a year, there's mobs of actual crazed fans,*

Koby's like a rockstar, he's pretty modest for a guy who brings home $250 grand, man, he can't even go to the grocery store without getting mobbed, the poor kid, but for 500 grand * *a year he puts up with it, he-he.* "They treat it like a sport," Coondog told me, expressing the consensus of the eating community. "They view it differently as a culture. They actually view it as something you're the best at, you know?"

Nobody really knew, of course. Any firsthand knowledge was old knowledge. Nobody had gone in years, not since 2001 or 2002. And Koby was an even bigger enigma. Any attempt to secure a lengthy interview with Koby would be a quest within a quest. If Coondog and I could find out how he did it—meaning, one, how he ate so much, and two, how he had built a successful life around eating—then Coondog O'Karma would know whether it was worth it for him to keep caring about competitive eating, and I'd know if it was possible to find meaning in junk culture.

So I asked Coondog. I asked if he would go to Japan with me.

Hell yeah, Coondog said, not hesitating. "For my own personal knowledge. Fuck the eating. We would like to know *how he does it.*"

Dave was in. Now I had to convince Koby.

If you need to get in touch with Takeru Kobayashi, you do it through his American interpreter, Bobby Ikeda. Bobby is a sunny, second-generation Japanese who grew up on a surfboard in Southern Cal. He's a thick-torsoed fella who speaks Japanese with maybe 70 percent fluency, which is good enough for the pro gluttony circuit. In November 2004, I caught up with Bobby, Koby, and Koby's girlfriend, Nari,† who is at all times inseparable from Koby, at a hamburger contest in Chattanooga, Tennessee. Nari was lithe and fragile, and Koby wore a tight gray shirt that showed off his muscles. "Nice to meet you," Koby said in English, squinting.

I made my pitch. It was my great hope, I said, to spend time with the

---

* This Koby factoid was a standard bit of propaganda commonly unspooled during the half hour prior to a contest, designed to catch the ear of passersby, convince them that eating wasn't just a freak show, and transform them into spectators; the exact dollar figure varied depending on who was doing the barking, George Shea or his brother Rich or a surrogate.

† She asked that I not name her, for reasons Bobby eventually explained had to do with a stalking incident in Japan.

world's greatest eater in his own country. I spoke of Coondog, and Koby and Nari instantly smiled. Nari leaned forward and said, in English, "Coondog— *frennn?*"

Yes, I said, and Koby and Nari laughed, visions of Coondog dancing in their heads. I used this moment of levity to press for an answer. When would be a good time to visit Japan and see a contest? Bobby said he wasn't sure. There weren't any contests upcoming. There had been an accident. A schoolkid. He'd choked on a piece of food and died.

Koby said something to Bobby in Japanese.

"And another one died," Bobby said.

Koby said something else.

"But it's okay," Bobby said. "They'll still have the contests."

Morbid tangent aside, everything seemed cool. I made plans. Over the last weeks of 2004, I booked plane tickets and hotel rooms, and hired an interpreter. Coondog started salting his e-mails with Japanese phrases and calling me "Fagone-san." But as November turned to December, and Christmas came and went, I still hadn't gotten final confirmation from Bobby. I called him on New Year's Eve, which was when Bobby told me that Koby wanted money (which I couldn't give), and I couldn't watch him train (which was the point of going to Japan), and he wouldn't participate if there was anything in my book about gluttony (which there would definitely be).

So, basically: no interview.

I gave Coondog the bad news. He seemed unfazed. "My name's O'Karma," he said. "That means I'm kind of like a descendant of destiny." He paused. "And that means, what? An anachronism?" He was searching for the word *paradox,* but didn't find it, and gave up. "That means I *make* my own destiny," he said. "We're gonna make my own destiny." He must have sensed that I wasn't exactly reassured, so he added, "I've always had a little magic. I still think I have a little bit left."

Four days before our trip, Koby e-mailed and agreed to an interview. We were going to Japan.

On January 11, the eve of our flight, Dave flew to Philadelphia. We'd leave for JFK airport in the morning. He said he was okay spending the night on my nasty red IKEA couch. Before bed, we watched Dave's Japanese eating tape, an episode of *TV Champion*—a popular prime-time show that used to produce elaborate eating contests. This episode included Kobayashi's 2001 trip to New York and his Nathan's world record. The first two segments of the show, which had been filmed in Japan, were just as flabbergasting as the Fifty-Dog Day. In the first segment, fifty pieces of sushi were placed on a wooden board next to a sushi-making robot. The robot created a new piece of sushi every seven seconds. Koby had to eat the fifty pieces of sushi, plus the robot's additional pieces. It was like running a race whose finish line was moving farther away as he ran. Koby caught up with the robot after 104 pieces.

In the second segment, Koby ate 387 bowls of soba noodles in 12 minutes. Nine thousand six hundred seventy-five grams of noodles. Twenty-one pounds of food.

Twenty-one pounds.

The third segment—well, Dave had lived it. It was all there, everything Dave remembered and some things he'd forgotten, like the time he walked up to the Japanese camera and said, "OHIO! OHIO! OHIO!" There was Coondog giving Koby the high five. Koby, pioneering the "Solomon" technique. The look of confusion on George Shea's face. The penciled yellow sheet with the triumphant "50."

We watched silently, making glottal noises of awe.

Early the next morning we set out, boarding an Amtrak train to Manhattan. Dave is super talkative for the whole ride. He keeps talking in Penn Station as we skitter through the crowds, looking for our Long Island Rail Road connection. "I'm just a jazzbo," he says. "A housepainter. Now I'm in a cave, in Manhattan, on my way to Japan. That's a whole lot of nothin'." I'm touched by his enthusiasm, but I need to concentrate since I'm running the show; Dave doesn't seem to get the flow of a train station, and he follows closely behind me as if he's afraid of getting lost. On the LIRR he sits with his back against the window, his feet on the seat, his knees pulled to his chest, and tells me about the time he e-mailed a Cleveland Browns beat writer and asked what the writer thought of competitive eating. The guy sent a two-word reply: FREAK SHOW. Wrong, says Dave. Lebron James is the real freak show. "Multimillion-dollar contracts," Dave huffs as we approach Jamaica Station and the JFK AirTrain. "A nineteen-year-old. To run around and fling a ball and slam a ball in a ring. That's not excessive?" At JFK airport, we find our ticket line. Dave is still talking. I haven't even gotten onto the plane and already I want to punch Dave in his bubbly man-child face.

Finally, we board. We both have to duck—he's six-two, I'm six-five. We walk back to our seats and fiddle with the overhead compartments. Two dark-haired Asian women are sitting in the seats directly behind ours. Dave notices the women and lunges toward them.

"Konnichiwa," he says.

The women crane their necks upward to meet Dave's neighborly smile. One turns to the other, shakes her head, looks back up at Dave, and says:

"We are Korean."

I pull out a notebook and scribble Dave's gaffe. Then Dave nods to the Korean women and says:

"Annyong ha shimnikka!"

I could not have been more surprised if Dave had swallowed the emergency exit door.

The Korean women make "oooh" sounds and start clapping.

Encouraged by his linguistic triumph, Coondog turns to an Asian-looking man to his right.

"Konnichiwa," Coondog says.

"I'm Australian," the man says.

"G'day, mate!"

Coondog sits down in his big reclining seat and piles his Japanese books to one side. He has brought a language textbook, a thick stack of homemade flash cards, and a green CVS spiral notebook that will serve as his journal. Inside his green notebook is a cheat sheet on table manners. "Don't blow your nose," it reads, "no bathroom talk . . . no burping . . . don't say *chin chin* because it means male genitals . . . don't put soy on white rice . . ." He picks up the flash cards and starts flipping through. They include the Japanese words for *gifts, he, she, me* (on this card Dave has drawn a self-portrait complete with mohawk and goatee), *salt, taxi, beauty, well done, long time no see, sweet, fast, cute, bathe, direction, learn,* and *delicious.* An impressive display of fastidiousness, but it's nothing compared to Dave's green CVS notebook. On the cover, in blue pen, he has written, in the Japanese syllabic alphabet—

クン ダ ゲ ヲ カ ラ マ

—which reads, phonetically, "KU-NN-DA-GE O-KA-RA-MA." Inside, a series of Japanese phrases. Each phrase is repeated several times in both print and cursive, so that the notebook resembles a kindergartener's penmanship workbook. *Itadakimasu—Let's eat. Gochisoosama—That was delicious. Ganbare—hang in there.* This forty-nine-year-old college dropout has apparently tried, in his free time between painting jobs, to teach himself one of the world's hardest languages.

We take off. The plane ascends to cruising altitude. I try to sleep, but the plane keeps shifting from side to side as it climbs. My subconscious flashes an image from last night's *TV Champion* viewing: the great Kobayashi, mid-contest, wiggling his chest. The mysterious limber childlike shimmy, signifying what? I'm flying halfway across the world to learn the secret of the shimmy, known only to the great Kobayashi and perhaps, in my half-sleep reasoning, also this 777, now burning fuel in a digestive blaze, its wake of wind and light and oil streaming behind us into the plane-gulped miles of afternoon sky.

Two hours from Tokyo by bullet train, the city of Nagoya is near the world headquarters of the Toyota company. The otherwise peppy *Fodor's Japan* travel guide describes Nagoya as "an industrial metropolis whose appeal is, admittedly, limited." Coondog and I are inside the circular observation deck of Nagoya's train station, fifty-one stories up. From here we can see the full panorama of Nagoya's limited appeal. Planes scuttle behind hills in the distance, their silhouettes dulled by lots of warm haze. The soft-porn burgundys and ochres of the buildings accent a heavy foundation layer of industrial gray. Coondog says, "It looks like it was built in the sixties." The only green is a tiny blotch of lawn surrounding Nagoya Castle. Somewhere in all that gray, tucked into an apartment with his girlfriend and his two dogs, is the world's greatest competitive eater. We think. But we don't know for sure, because Takeru Kobayashi hasn't called us yet.

The first thing we did yesterday, after touching down in Tokyo, was rent two cell phones, so we would be Reachable by Koby at All Times. We used the phones to rendezvous with our interpreter, Marina, and haven't used them since. Marina seems to be okay with the uncertainty and open-endedness of our odd quest. She used to interpret for American rock stars in Japan, such as Moby; she can roll with the punches. Yesterday, after getting the phones, we took the bullet train to Nagoya and Marina helped us check into a business hotel. I logged onto the lobby's wi-fi network, e-mailed Koby our cell numbers, and waited.

Last night, no call. This morning, no call. Dave and I got up early, ate a breakfast of pineapple and hot tea, and walked to the Nagoya fish market. Around his neck, Dave wore a lanyard looped through a laminated photo pouch, in which he'd inserted a snapshot of himself and Kobayashi taken at the filming for the 2002 *Glutton Bowl*. In the picture, Dave and Koby are in a limousine, Dave wearing his customary tank top, looking more like Jesus than usual, his arm around Koby's shoulder. Dave says he won't remove it until we leave. At the fish market, one Japanese worker recognized Koby, but only after Dave prodded him. At lunchtime, we ate in an Italian restaurant, and our maître d' looked at the photo and said:

"Ohhhh. Boofay kink."

"Sumimasen?" I said. *Excuse me?*

"Boofay kink."

"Ahh. Buffet *king.*"

But aside from a few random hits, the photo isn't causing much of a stir. And since Koby doesn't seem to be rock-star famous, it's even more confusing why he's stonewalling us.

We leave the observation deck, go back to the hotel, hang out in the lobby, and call translator Bobby Ikeda for news. Bobby has no news. Dave shrugs and says, "The mysterious Kobayashi."

He pulls out a manila folder with a Japanese postage stamp. Inside is a magazine that Koby and Nari sent him three years ago, along with their Christmas card. Dave opens the magazine and flips to an article about Koby. He has never understood the article's words, only the pictures—one of which is the same picture he's now wearing around his neck. We set Marina to work translating the article.

The magazine, the December 13, 2001, issue of *Josei Seven*—literally, Woman Seven—is a popular women's rag in Japan, roughly equivalent to *Marie Claire*. On the cover are pictures of the Japanese prince and princess and three television actresses. Inside, previews of upcoming movies, as well as pages of infoboxes on the hairstyles of certain Japanese entertainers called *tarento*, or "talent," whose talent, Marina explains, consists entirely of looking pretty on a wide variety of TV shows.

"Like Paris Hilton?" asks Dave.

"Yes," says Marina. "But many of them with less character."

The profile of Koby runs to three pages. In addition to the shot of Koby and Dave, there are photos of Koby lifting a 59-kilogram barbell and Koby holding a cabbage. "From the way he appears," the profile's author writes, "the sweet face and the tight body, they named him Prince. . . . Where does such power reside in this thin body?"

With Marina translating, we learn the following: Koby's blood type is A. He runs a 50-meter race in six seconds. His body fat is 13.9 percent. He eats yogurt, garlic, cabbage, carrots, chicken, and "a lot of leafy things." He first ate competitively in the seventh grade, after hearing that one of his fellow students drank nine bottles of milk. Koby challenged him, drinking ten bottles. In college, while studying economics, he ate about seven pounds of curry—the Japanese can't get enough of curried rice, meat, veggies—in seventeen minutes. His friends pressed him to try out for *TV Champion*, where he won his first televised contest in November 2000. Koby apparently finds it "very offensive when people think of *oogui* as something humorous." (*Oogui* means "to eat a lot," as opposed to *hayagui*, which means "to eat fast.") Koby tells his interviewer, "I want you to understand that I chose this *michi* (way/path) as a profession to challenge my limits. During a competition, I don't stop moving my chopsticks until I hear the gong."

Clearly, one intense dude. Proud. Serious. Prickly. And first among unequals, when it comes to *oogui* superstars. "Shoving things in their mouth," the article's author writes, "it's not a beautiful sight. But, somehow, Kobayashi is beautiful."

"It's nice to know what's in that article, finally," says Dave. "I just think he's mentally tougher than everybody." I find the article reassuring for a different reason: it reveals nothing. The Japanese don't know Koby's secret, either. They are asking the same questions we all are:

"Where does such power reside in this thin body?"

Before you can even ask that question, you need to get past the skepticism, the suspicion that Koby is not in fact hiding any power in that thin body, and what he is really hiding is a set of tricks. Hirofumi Nakajima, a Nathan's champ from the late nineties, was said, half-jokingly, to possess two stomachs, but that's nothing compared to the Koby speculation. In late 2001, when Koby was starting to peak, so were the rumors: Koby was taking drugs. Koby had been surgically altered.* Koby was a stooge of higher powers using him for their own obscure ends. "It was presumed to go as far as the government of Japan," says Mike Bailey, a producer on Fox's *Glutton Bowl*. "I mean, this guy wasn't a sole man working on his own. The conspiracy included elected officials."

Koby has always denied using drugs, and even if he were, he wouldn't be breaking any rules. Many eaters cultivate chemical advantages: Ed Jarvis is open about popping digestive enzymes, and at the *Glutton Bowl*, some eaters lined their nostrils with Vicks VapoRub to block the smell of the more unpleasant foods while also making it easier to breathe. The IFOCE has no drug-testing policy to prevent eaters from taking, say, Reglan or Zelnorm, two of the most likely prescription drugs that might boost a pro eater. Zelnorm, used to treat irritable bowel syndrome, smooths out the gut's motility, or movement of food. Reglan is potentially even more helpful, flooding the body with chemicals that twiddle the body's dopamine receptors, lessening nausea while speeding both peristalsis (the churning of food in the stomach) and gastric emptying (the movement of digested food from the stomach to the small intestine). Another drug, called sumatriptan, normally used to treat migraines, can also be used to relax the fundus—the top of the stomach—so one can get fuller before feeling discomfort. More recently, the eating fan-sites have speculated on the potential use and/or abuse of ghrelin, an appetite enhancer.

---

* Gastroenterologists say this is implausible; any alteration (like widening the esophagus) would create bad digestive problems.

If Kobayashi-level eating prowess were as easy as taking a pill, though, all the Americans would have tried it by now. The difference is something else. Some*where* else.

The maze that runs through you is the digestive tract, or alimentary canal. It's what unbuilds the world to build you. It shuttles food through a Rube Goldberg machine of interlocking muscle flaps and tubes, sucks out the nutrients, and deposits the remains in your septic tank—an impressively complex process even in normal, non-Kobayashi humans. The brainy breed of plumbers who diagnose and repair kinks in this system are called gastroenterologists, and they train for five to six years—in addition to the four years of medical school—for the privilege. Gastroenterology is a subspecialty of internal medicine, like cardiology and geriatrics, and a hot one at that. As our bellies have expanded, so have the salaries and research budgets of our gastroenterologists. The subspecialty has spawned its own subspecialists, so that if you call a swallowing expert, he may be uncomfortable discussing general matters of the stomach, and will refer you instead to a stomach expert, who, if you happen to be calling about competitive eating, will admit up front that whatever gastroenterologists know about the human digestive system—and "there's still a lot we don't know," says Dr. Robert Coben, clinical assistant professor and gastroenterology fellowship director at Thomas Jefferson University Hospital—they know even less about the biomechanics of professional gluttony. "Um, there's not a whole lot written," says Coben. "I looked, too." Agrees Dr. Edgar Achkar, chairman of gastroenterology and hepatology at the world-renowned Cleveland Clinic, "I wish I knew. . . . If there are experts out there, I just don't know who they are." Achkar adds, "You know, this is not something we deal with, you understand?"

From here, it's all speculation and educated guesswork: a plumber visualizing, and then mentally deconstructing, a prolific set of pipes. How can an eater like Koby swallow so much food, and how can his stomach hold it?

Swallowing and stomach distension are the two aspects of digestion that are somewhat controllable. In swallowing, your tongue locks against your upper jaw, the hot dog and bun tumbling behind it. Your epiglottis, at the back of your throat, levers upward to block off the windpipe, so you don't choke. From here on in, it's all involuntary, your gut on autopilot. In peristalsis, esophagus muscle grabs the hot dog and passes it down the pipe at a rate of one or two inches per second. Neurotransmitters signal the stomach to relax in advance of the dog. The hot dog passes through the cardiac sphincter into the stomach proper.

The stomach is a dull, slippery, pinkish sack. Empty, it holds a quart of food and/or liquid. It hangs on the body's left side, below the diaphragm, protected by the ribs. Its shape is fetuslike—an inelegant, supine mass with valves at the top (the cardiac sphincter) and the bottom (the pylorus). The interior walls are flaccid and ridged, like your shriveled hands after taking a bath. When you pig out, the walls, which are made of smooth muscle cells, stretch, making the ridges disappear. Other cells in the stomach then secrete a hormone called gastrin, which stimulates release of the acids and digestive enzymes that churn your food into a slurry called *chyme*. As your stomach fills up with dogs, nerves trigger the neurotransmitters that tell your brain that you're full. Food doesn't completely leave the stomach for at least two to four hours. High-fat foods like Nathan's hot dogs take longer. In the small intestine, where nutrients from the dogs are absorbed into the bloodstream, the dogs might sit for five to six hours before they pass, in liquid form, to the colon. In the colon, where the liquid dogs are solidified into a stool, the dogs remain for twelve to twenty-four hours.

Everything about Kobayashi's digestive process is bigger and faster and more efficient. The only explanation that the eating community has produced is called the "Belt of Fat" theory, and it focuses, like most of the Koby speculation, on his stomach. The gist of the BoF theory is that fat guys' stomachs get trapped by their "belts" of fat and can't expand as much as the guts of skinny guys. Though the doctors I called seemed to think the BoF theory plausible, it's just as likely to be pap, as Tim "Eater X" Janus believes—an ego-softener dreamed up by the heavy eaters to pawn off their losses on science. According to the scientific literature, if you want to expand your stomach, you can. It doesn't matter whether you're fat or skinny. All you have to do is abuse your stomach, repeatedly, until it gives in to your demands.

For while the stomach may lack the heft of the liver, the industriousness of the heart, the mystery of the pancreas, and the transplantability of the kidneys—like other understated valiant things, cops and tollbooths and C-SPAN, the stomach's glory is not aesthetic—it does have a glorious toughness, what Dr. George Triadafilopoulos, a clinical professor of medicine at Stanford U., calls a "tremendous accommodating capability." The stomach is the body's 5-mph bumper, a thing designed to take abuse. When fully distended, the wall of the stomach is only a few millimeters thick, and susceptible to perforation and "gastric rupture"—colloquially, a bust gut. However, reports of rupture due to overeating are rare, and in cases of blunt abdominal trauma, the stomach is less likely to rupture than the liver, spleen, and kidneys; one surgeon named Ritter even tested this proposition by "delivering repeated, forceful blows on the upper abdomen of dogs without producing a gastric rupture," according to a 1941 paper that attributes the stomach's resilience to its flaccidity (as a squishy bag with two pressure valves) and its mobility (it floats, loosely anchored, in the chest cavity). Indeed, there appears to be no category of brutal injustice the stomach cannot, well, stomach—from sharp foreign objects to the ingestion of caustic liquids. A *Pediatrics* article from 2000 details the case of an unfortunate grade-school science experiment in which a thirteen-year-old, after pouring a liquid nitrogen cocktail, decided to drink what his Toronto doctors later called "the still smoking mixture." Amazingly, the child not only survived, he left the hospital after just ten days, presumably with prospects as a comic-book hero. Research shows that the stomach is stronger than metal; stomach acid peels Abe Lincoln's mug straight off of zinc pennies, reducing their weight by 5 to 8 percent in just a week. Indigestible objects are swallowed routinely by schizophrenics (metal tools), children (toothbrushes, pennies, batteries), and the elderly (dentures), but the smaller stuff either sits shiva in the gut, with no ill effects, or passes right through—one whippersnapper in Mumbai even passed a 4-centimeter nail—and the bigger pieces can be dug out with an endoscope. Swallowing a foreign body is only fatal in the most extreme of cases. For instance, a forty-six-year-old schizophrenic woman in Germany died after 422 "mostly metallic" objects were found in her stomach, which had been perforated in two places. But here in the United States, a forty-five-year-old schizophrenic man with 206 firearm slugs in his gut literally shat bullets, and survived.

No less heroic is the stomach's general ability to expand. In 1885, a

French physician by the name of Revilliod removed a stomach from a cadaver, filled it with water, and noted that it burst after he'd pumped in 4 liters of fluid, about a gallon's worth. Hearty eaters, however, can push the one-gallon threshold. In an effort to get a handle on the volume of food consumed in an eating contest, I drove to the Franklin Mills mall in Northeast Philly and bought twenty Nathan's hot dogs and buns. Back home, I cut the dogs and buns into equal bites,* and filled a water bottle with 32 ounces of water, a guesstimate of the amount of liquid needed to wash down the food. I cut the top off a plastic one-gallon water jug and started placing the dogs into the jug. When I'd placed 15, along with 24 ounces of water, the jug was full. I started smushing the dogs like I was compacting trash. With smushing, I was able to fit the five remaining dogs and buns, as well as the final 8 ounces of water. Each frank weighs 2 ounces and each bun weighs 1.5, so the full jug, including the water, weighed about six and a half pounds, which is hardly exorbitant in competitive eating terms. By weight, that's like swallowing a middling Halloween pumpkin or suddenly becoming pregnant with a thirty-seven-week-old fetus. By volume, it's like swallowing a smallish volleyball (1.2 gallons). With more aggressive smushing, I could have packed five or six more hot dogs and buns into the gallon jug, so I figure that if I had bought fifty-three and a half—Koby's world-record tally from 2004—I could have filled two gallon jugs to bursting. A regulation men's basketball holds 1.88 gallons. Every Fourth of July, Koby swallows a basketball, and then some.

Without stretching his stomach, he wouldn't be able to do it. Stomach-stretching is exactly what it sounds like: the repeated ingestion of large volumes of food and/or liquid in order to gradually enlarge the stomach's capacity. Every eater swears allegiance to one of several stretching techniques that tend to come and go like fads: cabbage, water, buffets. Most eaters use a combination of buffets and water training. Stretching is difficult but not mysterious. It works. Even with stomach-stretching, however, it may not be possible for a guy like Tim Janus to approach Koby. Koby may have

---

* But only after realizing that a certain Nathan's fan in my household had eaten the twentieth hot dog and bun, despite claiming to find the smell of twenty (and then nineteen) hot dogs "disgusting," thereby necessitating a trip to the grocery store to replace the twentieth hot dog with a store-bought Nathan's dog and the twentieth bun with a Stroehmann's bun.

other intrinsic advantages that can't be taught. "Everybody's pain threshold is a little different," says Dr. Robert Coben, who explains that the stomach contains nerve cells that "feel" pain, but not in the same sense as the nerves in your arm; when the stomach stretches, discomfort is signaled by a separate but interconnected nervous system called the *visceral* nervous system, a subset of which is the stomach's own *enteric* nervous system: the stomach's "brain." Koby may feel less discomfort than other people. (He once told an MTV crew that because his stomach sits especially low in his body—a phenomenon called "gastroptosis"—he can fit more food.) Or maybe, as Dr. Achkar guesses, he has an unusually robust and quick belch reflex. Or maybe he is able to pass food whole from his stomach to his small intestine without ill effects. Or maybe he's got killer stomach enzymes.

Koby's stomach could, almost literally, be a genius.

Or maybe his genius is located a foot or so higher.

Koby's eating performances have a distinctive rhythm independent of whatever's happening in his stomach. The rhythm is due to his unique way of swallowing. *Phase One:* He's relaxed at the starting buzzer. Initial pace is moderate to fast. He lags behind lesser eaters. *Phase Two:* Koby starts plunging through the food. A hamburger disappears not in five bites but a predatorial two, punctuated by a sudden backward jerk of the head. He is literally whipping the burger—the barely chewed mass of it—back into his throat. He has engaged the Koby Gear. *Phase Three:* The other eaters drop off. Their pace slackens. The Koby Gear remains engaged to the last second if it's close, or if it's a blowout, he shuts it down early.

I first saw the Gear at a Krystal hamburger qualifier in Jacksonville, Florida. Before the contest, Koby sat in the shade with Nari, occasionally taking off his dark sunglasses and posing for pictures. He blinked and blinked, as if his eyes weren't used to the sun of the American South, or Earth. Come contest time, Koby engaged the Gear, tore through fifty hamburgers in five minutes, and shut down the Gear with three minutes left on the clock. Months later, at a TV taping in Las Vegas, I saw the Gear again. Koby was presented with a plate of spaghetti. He picked up his fork, twirled the pasta absentmindedly, took a slow bite. Then he grabbed a second fork and dipped his head. Leaned into the pasta and vacuumed it, his mouth a spaghetti press in reverse. Swallowing became a constant process in his throat, abstracted from chewing just like a jazz saxophonist can abstract breathing from blowing.* Koby seemed to have accomplished what Dr. Achkar describes as the "immobilization" of the esophagus. Studies show that if you swallow, say, six or seven times very quickly, "your esophagus stops responding," says Achkar. "So it becomes an inert tube, and at that point, I guess, you could stuff that tube until it's full, and then from time to time it pulls the food down."

This self-paralysis isn't just a neat trick. It has the potential to be life-changing, according to Dr. Triadafilopoulos, who sees in this ability of certain eaters to "actually override their autonomic system" potential hope for the 60 million Americans who suffer from gastroesophageal reflux disease, or GERD. In GERD, the cardiac sphincter "relaxes inappropriately" and passes food from the stomach back up into the esophagus. The sphincter's activity, along with the contraction of the esophagus itself, seems to be controlled by the midbrain, says Triadafilopoulos—"at least in the evidence we have so far." But he and other scientists aren't certain, so he suggests a study. "An important study." Perhaps under the auspices of the National Institutes of Health. Step one: gather the best eaters in the world. Step two: hook them up to PET scanners, which measure brain activity. Step three: have the eaters eat really fast. Step four: see which brain regions light up on the PET scan. Step five: develop a drug that targets those regions to produce the opposite effect—i.e., contraction, not relaxation—in GERD patients.

The toughest part of the study might be assembling the test group. Judging by the magnitude of Koby's superiority, he's probably one of the very few eaters who can relax the esophagus at will, like a sword-swallower. If other eaters could do it, they wouldn't describe Koby's eating feats with such naked awe, as Sonya Thomas and Charles Hardy did immediately after Koby's pasta-swallowing triumph in Las Vegas. Sonya: "He is soooo fast . . . always, my mouth is full, right? But his mouth is not full." Hardy: "He's eating that pasta like a fuckin' anaconda swallowing its prey."

The anaconda scored thirteen pounds in fourteen minutes.

---

* Tim "Eater X" Janus once tried, with little success, to develop a technique he called "circular swallowing," à la Roland Kirk's "circular breathing."

And did the anaconda then slither to the men's room and vomit up his prey?

Koby always gently denies vomiting. In the 2002 Nathan's, Koby appeared to vomit into his hand after the buzzer. Koby says that "it was misreported that I threw up." He claims to have coughed. "If he coughed," says Charles Hardy, whose good friend Eric Booker would have won had Koby been disqualified, "he coughed through his nose." When Sonya Thomas appeared on *The Tonight Show* in 2005, Jay Leno asked, "You throw up?" Sonya shook her head and said, "No, because I—it doesn't bother me. I'm fine, you know? All kinds of foods doesn't bother me." Even Coondog is uncharacteristically tight-lipped. I asked him once if eaters ever threw up. "Sometimes," he said, and didn't immediately elaborate.

There are two reasons for this reluctance. One, vomiting is seen as a sign of weakness. Real men hold their food. Two, the IFOCE fears that vomiting will scare off corporate sponsors not keen on associating their products with vomit. For this reason, vomiting is grounds for immediate disqualification. It is referred to only euphemistically, as "reversal of fortune" or, occasionally, "Roman methods." The eaters themselves prefer the simpler and more colloquial "launched," as in, "Yeah, Chapman launched at Doodle Burger."

Exercise alone can't zero out the caloric load of a big contest, so if the top eaters aren't eliminating by launching, they must be doing it the other way. Dr. Achkar surmises that in a contest situation, the small intestine will be overloaded—"there's no way the bowel can be trained to absorb all this stuff"—and the rest will shoot into the colon and overload the colon, too, "and the contents will come out liquid and voluminous," says Achkar, in the form of diarrhea. Dr. Triadafilopoulos says the eaters may be triggering a bowel phenomenon called "dumping," which is common to people with weakened pyloric sphincters: food empties from the stomach to the intestine not in a slow stream but in a gush, skewing the gut's internal pressures and flooding it with pints of fluid. Speaking of Koby, Achkar says, "Obviously, he's getting rid of it. And it would be interesting to know how soon that happens." Unfortunately, discussions of shitting lean even more heavily on euphemism than discussions of vomiting, even though it makes as much sense for a professional eater to be coy about his shitting habits as it makes sense for a porn star to blush at insertion. Tim Janus says that certain of his bowel movements are controlled by "the toothpaste effect," likening his colon to a tube of Crest being squeezed from the bottom. "Collard Green" Hughes, a Southern eater, calls it "unpacking the suitcase." Certain foods cause across-the-board distress: cannolis ("like swallowing a cat," says Ed Jarvis, "and it's fighting all the way down your system"), pickles ("you can't even leave the venue, you just gotta wait there and an hour later your colon is like a water fountain"), and, of course, jalapeño peppers. "With the peppers, it's a rough night," says Don Lerman. "You ever see that movie *Altered States?*"

Excretion usually takes up to a day, but eaters, when not suffering from quick-turnaround diarrhea, have a few tricks to speed it up. In 2000, while competing in a twelve-hour, all-you-can-eat box-lunch battle in Japan, Charles Hardy cracked, cursed the Japanese as "fucking crazy," and said he was done. His opponent, "The Rabbit" Arai, took him aside and told him a secret that Hardy keeps to this day, though he hints that it involves "literally eating and shitting at the same time."* Hardy is also known to take "magic water," a type of high-test laxative. Ed Jarvis favors digestive enzymes. At a recent multiday contest in Las Vegas, featuring two rounds of eating per day, Ed ate four pounds of chili cheese fries at 11:00 a.m., then went back to his hotel room, took a shower, put on a new pair of drawers, and consumed the following:

OPC 3 superantioxidants
MegaPack megavitamins (specifically coded to his personal DNA)
2 capsules Isotonics brand digestive enzymes, dissolved in liquid
Tums
2 Advil
3 pieces dark Hershey's sugar-free chocolate (to cleanse the palate)

Back at the contest venue, I sat at Ed's table as he waited to compete. At one point he got up abruptly and left the room, and came back and said,

---

* Later, I had my interpreter call Arai and ask him to reveal the big secret he confided to Hardy. My interpreter summarized Arai's response: "Arai's body constitution changed by itself through the training for eating; his body learned to rush food from stomach to intestine and out to excrete without digestion; in other words, his excrement is in a state of diarrhea and indigestion gives him cramps. He has to fight the urge to go to the bathroom during competitions." So there you go. He's dumping.

"That was an Imodium moment. Those fries? Right through." This was his third movement since morning. He credited the enzymes. "Your system works fast when you want it to." Soon enough, he got up again. When he returned ten minutes later, Ed sat down in his chair and likened his rectum to a Midwesterner waving at a train: blank and happy. He leaned back and smiled. "My ass," he said, "has left the building."

I doubt I could ever bring myself to ask Kobayashi about his bathroom habits, or Sonya Thomas, although they must be as prodigious in elimination as they are in gurgitation. And I am positive I could never ask that question around Coondog. He would consider it rude. As much as Coondog talked about finding Koby's secret, he seemed to enjoy thinking of Koby as a superbeing beyond human comprehension.

"I just think he has nobility," Coondog told me late one night in Tokyo, his legs stretched out on his too-short hotel bed. "Where does that come from in a twenty-three-year-old?"

Coondog paused, considered.

"It's from the gods."

Coondog leaned back, cackling.

"God," he said, "am I throwing out some bullshit, or what?"

4

THE BIG TOMATO AND
THE BLANK SLATE

T HE E-MAIL COMES on January 15, our third day in Japan. "Unfortunately," Koby writes, "I cannot participate in your project." He does, however, want to meet up with Coondog, and suggests a date, January 23, a week away. Has somebody gotten to Koby? A smear campaign against me? Or is his prior sticking point—his aversion to American-style gluttony—still the problem?

I don't understand. I need to call Bobby Ikeda. Coondog and I walk upstairs. Coondog unlocks his room and sits on the bed. I dial Bobby's number and hand Coondog the cell. If there was ever a time when I needed that "little bit of magic" that Coondog claimed to possess, it's now. I listen as Coondog speaks (here follows a rough paraphrase, as I was too flabbergasted to take down the quotes):

Uh-huh.
. . .
Yeah.
. . .
But Ed *is* fat.
. . .
Yeah, I know . . .

Coondog hangs up and tells me the problem. Somebody in America read an article I'd written on the Philadelphia Wing Bowl. In that article, I referred to Ed "Cookie" Jarvis, the 400-pound realtor from Long Island, as a "fat realtor from Long Island." Someone e-mailed Koby about it. And Koby thought that phrase—"fat realtor"—was disrespectful. So no interview.

If I were a more experienced writer, less caffeinated on the lobby's hot *cohee,* I would have laughed and thanked the gods of stranger-than-fiction for pulling it off once again. I would have seen this not as a setback but as a gift of sublime comedy. If Ed were a physicist, and I had called him a "fat physicist," I could understand. But Ed is not a physicist, and his girth is not ungermane to his stature as—to take just one of the dozens of eating titles embroidered on the giant cloak he wears to contests—the Russian Pelemini Eating Champion of 2003. Is it possible that a 400-pound dude who maintains a website called HugeEaters.com could object to being called, truthfully, fat? Or else—even weirder!—is Ed okay with being called fat while Koby is *not* okay with Ed being called fat? A principled stand from a man who is, in Bobby's words, "really serious about this being a sport more than anything else, not just fat guys at a fuckin' country fair goin' at it," yet has himself eaten cow brains on *Glutton Bowl* and once ate against a Kodiak bear, for cash, on *Man Versus Beast?*

But I'm too angry and confused to notice that in this one turn of events, the glutton's tortured psyche has been splayed out in front of me. I just look at Coondog and say, in a wounded voice:

"Ed *is* fat."

Coondog nods and looks down. I repeat the phrase to myself, changing the emphasis each time. Ed *is* fat. Ed is *fat.* Ed is *phatty-boom-batty.* Ed is a *fuckin' fatass fuck.* It feels nice, like I'm back in a place where people say and do things that make sense. I have my power back.

I ask Coondog what I am *supposed* to call Ed.

Big?

Coondog sheepishly informs me that, yes, "big" is an acceptable synonym, as are "huge," "enormous," and especially "gargantuan."

Except for Coondog, these people have fallen down the donut hole. Except for Coondog, these people are fucking crazy.

For hours I mope alone on the bed in my room. Then I join Dave across the street at a beerpub, and a few beers later—I do all the drinking— we walk back to the hotel. Before saying goodnight, Dave says he has an idea.

"You wanna meet Koby? I'm gonna get him to come to the States, to come to Akron. We've got a big fish-eating contest there."

Dave can't even arrange a full day with Koby in the kid's own country. Now Koby is going to fly to the States to eat at Dave's fish contest?

In Akron, Ohio?

Oh *really?*

"Yeah," Coondog says. "They just named the smallmouth bass the state fish. I think we should rock it in with the world fish-eating championship." He traces a marquee in the air with his hands. He pauses, says "No!" and then traces an even bigger marquee. "The world *smallmouth bass*–eating championship."

These people are all fucking crazy. Coondog included.

I am not the first journalist to reach this conclusion about Coondog. That distinction belongs to a columnist for the *Akron Beacon-Journal* named David Giffels. For years, Giffels wrote about Coondog regularly, but he has since sworn off that particular beat, for complicated reasons.

Giffels is a youthful forty-one, with red curly hair and the quiet voice of a onetime hipster who reads modern fiction. His entanglement with Coondog began with a 2001 voice mail left on Giffels's machine. It went, "Hi. My name's Dave 'Coondog' O'Karma, and I'm a professional competitive speed eater, and I think you should write a story about me." Sight unseen, Giffels agreed. He visited Coondog's home, ate hot dogs against Coondog, and wrote a column about the experience. The column generated more feedback— both positive and negative—than anything he'd done with the exception of his work on Akron's charitable response to 9/11. From then on, Giffels says, "He latched on to me. He was just calling me all the time."

The Giffels columns proliferated and spawned other media hits— Coondog reviewing hamburgers in the Food section, Coondog speed-eating donuts on the Channel 19 news—until Coondog was a solid B-list celebrity in his own town. In 2002, the only people in Akron who bested Coondog's twenty mentions in the *Beacon Journal* were the mayor (290 mentions) and native hoops prodigy LeBron James (222). In fourth place, after Coondog, was Melina Kanakaredes, the Akron native and star of *CSI: New York*. Coondog was also *NewsNight Akron*'s Most Trivial Celebrity two years running.

("Fuckin' honor. All I can say is, threepeat.") A threepeat would prove difficult because, by 2004, Coondog had saturated whatever market existed in
Akron for light stories about competitive eaters. Giffels decided "to extricate myself from the Coondog situation" for Coondog's own good. "The
best thing for him would be to stop doing the Coondog thing," reasoned
Giffels. "The smart thing would be to *write* about it."

Coondog had been trying to do that for thirty years. As a teen, he left
Ohio, briefly, for Hollywood, shlepping a screenplay called *Casey and the
Worm,* about "an alcoholic young cowboy" and his "semi-retarded" buddy
who "ended up robbing a bank." One day Coondog bluffed his way into the
offices of Universal, was directed to another office, and got lost on the studio
lot. He came back to Ohio, where his writing career got forestalled by, well,
life, which he once described for me in a breathless paragraph:

"I was born in Akron. Grew up in Cuyahoga Falls. Went to Catholic grade
schools. Went to Kent State High School in ninth grade. I was a really good
swimmer and they recruited me to swim for 'em. Didn't like it so I went
back to Falls. I was a pretty good swimmer there but then I became Coondog and became more interested in being a star." He sighed. "Aaaaaaaand,
dated a high school cheerleader, got her pregnant, I was a freshman at Kent
State, she was still in high school, she had the baby but supposedly her parents never knew she was pregnant, and then they moved to Arizona and left
her here, and I filed for custody of the child, there was a big long court battle
and I got custody, she moved to Arizona and I've never seen her again. No, I
was never married. Uh-uh. Ahhh, and had a little girl, lived with my parents.
Till I was twenty-five. Moved out to a couple places. Eh, just a bunch of
crap. My daughter went to live with my sister. Then my dad died, I met this
girl, got her pregnant, got married, got the house and kids, got divorced. Got
custody of my child. Your basic human tragedy."

In between the tragedy, he'd occasionally submit a piece to obscure
online humor magazines, like this George Shea parody titled "Riots at
Indian Cow Eating Contest":

"A cow eating contest in India may seem slightly insensitive,
but it really shows that India is progressing past the ancient
cultural restrictions of caste and religion, and positioning itself

as a true cosmopolitan player in the global environment," were the words of master of ceremonies George Shea . . .

The author is listed as "Kilgore O'Karma," a reference to Vonnegut's lonely, Christlike scribbler, Kilgore Trout. The rest of Coondog's adult output is in the form of poetry, written under the name "D. M. O'Karma." The poems are as serious as the byline suggests. The more than four hundred bite-sized aphorisms in *Wit and Whimsy of a White-Trash Jesus* are total sincerity and bared soul. Each one has a short title in bold type followed by from two to seven lines, like so:

> **Believe It**
> *Like words on paper*
> *that can be erased*
> *People, too*
> *can be replaced*

The poems' style is a bit E. E. Cummings, a bit Ogden Nash, a bit Shel Silverstein. They're the best kind of unpublishable—guileless and autobiographical. They have titles like "Man, I'm Tired," "This Shitty Poem," "The Perch of Eroded Youth," and "The Starving Children of Africa." *Ointments* is rhymed with *disappointments*, *decay* with *pray*, *clod* with *God*. Some poems are sweet, like the one about his daughter's smile; some are playful, like the subgroup of poems about animals: dalmatians, termites, turtles, lions, horses, rhinos, flamingos, zebras, and ducks. But most of the poems are dark and sad and bitter. Even one of the animal poems ends with a *duck* getting run over by a *truck*. One poem, about drugs, is called "They Eventually Kick Your Ass." Two poems describe Dave's "high highs" and "low lows," and the fact that he's "sick to death of both of those." A poem called "Desperate Voice" is literally a cry for help. There are even poems that describe the pain of having to conceal his pain by "putting on a show," so that "no one will ever know":

> **I'm Soooo Boring!**
> *I gave up*
> *all my favorite vices*

and now I'm suffering . . .
an identity crisis

Then, in late 2004, Coondog caught a break and sold his first magazine story: a memoir of his early Akron eating antics and his first Nathan's hot dog contest. *Cleveland* magazine ran it at 3,000 words. It was funny. It had voice and style. The *Cleveland* piece was proof of what Dave Giffels had been saying all along—that Coondog could actually do it. "And for some reason every time I hear from him it's, Oh, I'm goin' off to Chicago where they have this thing where if you eat a 24-inch pizza, the whole thing, you don't have to pay for it . . . It's meaningless."

So Giffels tried to force Coondog to retire. In a 2002 column headlined "Coondog's Hotdogging Has No Bite," Giffels described Coondog's recent back-to-back losses in hot-dog qualifiers, writing, "It pains me to say this, but I think it's time for Coondog to face reality. He's forty-six years old. He still has some dignity left. It's time to walk away."

Coondog thought Giffels was joking.

Giffels told him he wasn't joking.

"It kind of crumbled," says Giffels.

Not long after, Giffels received, in the mail, a picture of Coondog dressed up as Giffels—as if Coondog were schizophrenically obsessed with the journalist who had been covering him. "And I'm sure he was joking," says Giffels, "but not positive."

The Big Chuck and Lil' John Show, which used to be called *The Hoolihan and Big Chuck Show,* is a Friday-night movie show produced by WJW-TV, Cleveland's Fox 8. The movie's hosts are "Big" Chuck Schodowski, age 71, a soft-voiced man with the bearing of a kindly innkeeper, and "Lil'" John Rinaldi, age fifty-eight, a midget with a bushy black mustache and a toothy grin who owns a jewelry store with his wife in a Cleveland suburb. Big Chuck and Lil' John are beloved for the skits they perform during breaks in the movie: lighthearted ethnic gags and pop-culture parodies with such titles as "The Kielbasa Kid" and "Cuyahoga Jones and the Castle of Doom." According to Dave Giffels, "If you grew up around here, and you are within the age range of Coondog, you grew up watching Big Chuck and Hoolihan." And if you were Coondog, you didn't just watch. *The Hoolihan and Big Chuck Show* is where Coondog made his pizza-eating debut, back in 1972, against the formidable Mushmouth Mariano.

In 2004, Coondog helped revive the Pizza Fight after a decades-long hiatus. He quickly established himself as the new champ, the Mushmouth of the modern era, and started taping the Pizza Fight every Tuesday night, taking on a new opponent each week.

My trip to Akron—a three-day visit in May 2005, four months after Coondog and I returned from Japan—was planned around the Pizza Fight. I had been telling Coondog for months that I wanted to see him eat against somebody with a good shtick: a cage-fighter, a mime, some kind of large animal. Coondog e-mailed me and said no, no, he wanted to eat against *me.* I said no thanks. I feared I'd be dull TV. A few days before I was set to drive to Akron, Coondog sent me an e-mail: "My opponent for next week's match is billed as, The Writer." He had ignored me completely.

When I got to Akron, Coondog said, "I'm going to so totally crush you. I'm going to humiliate you." He dialed the official restaurant of the Pizza Fight to order me some practice pies, which were doughy and mediocre. He plopped them on his kitchen table, poured me a glass of water, and timed me. I finished my first piece after thirty-nine seconds. Coondog's record time is twenty-seven seconds for the whole pizza.

"It's a little harder than it looks, isn't it?" he said.

"Oh, shit," I said.

"Some of us are gifted," said Coondog. "The doctor told my mother I had the biggest tonsils he ever saw."

Lisa, his wife, came home a few hours later and prepared dinner. "So here we got big-shot writer, right?" said Coondog. "Tell 'em what you did."

"One piece in thirty-nine seconds."

"One piece, huh?" said Lisa. "Woooo!"

At dinner—salad and chicken parm with low-fat dressing—Dave told stories about the Pizza Fight. One story started with "So I'm eating against the bear, right?" and ended with "Not the smartest thing I ever did." The bear, a 900-pound grizzly who may have acted in *The Jungle Book* movie, beat

Dave easily. Before the contest the bear had tried to bite Coondog. It missed him and bit through his pizza box instead. This was not broadcast on Fox 8.

"He was nice. He was clean," Coondog said. "And he had really really nice, healthy-looking fur. And he didn't seem to be drugged."

At around six, we left for the Fox 8 studio, twenty minutes away, where Coondog, pulling into the lot, rolled down his window and said to the security guards inside, "It's pizza-eating champion of the world Coondog O'Karma here for Big Chuck."

"Oh, okay, come on in."

Coondog wore a calico beret. Walking into the studio, he was immediately greeted by twenty or so people standing around eating pizza. One of them was Tony Rizzo, Fox 8's sportscaster. "He's my man," said Rizzo, his hands shiny with grease from the free pizzas over on the counter. "I'm here every week to watch him. He's the best. Last week, twenty-eight seconds. Twenty. Eight. Seconds last week. I mean, you know what? I can appreciate somebody who can hit a curveball 415 feet. I can appreciate a ninety-five-yard touchdown. There's nothing quite like watching a guy eat a small pizza in twenty-eight seconds." I left Rizzo and was ushered onto a stage that resembled a boxing ring, with bleachers on both sides, facing the camera, and a small table in the ring's center. On the table was a single pizza. Chuck tested his microphone and I arranged my water. "Eye of the Tiger" came on. "Stand by," said Chuck, "this is for real." Lil' John took the mike and screamed:

"Ladies and gentlemen! And welcome to another Big Chuck and Lil' John Pizza Pan Pizza Fight of the Worrrrrrld! And in this corner, from Philadelphia, a writer . . ."

I held up my pen and tried to look menacing.

And in this corner, "at six foot two inches, 185 lean mean pounds, it's the champion pizza eater of the world, it's King Coondog O'Karma!"

Coondog held his fists up like a prizefigher. He was joined at the table by a tall man in a tuxedo. This was "Spiffingham," Coondog's "butler" and, in real life, one of Coondog's painting buddies.

"Ladies and gentlemen," barked Big Chuck, "this week as always we will abide by the Marquis of Queensberry rules. The winner is the first man to completely eat all of his pizza and show me an open mouth . . . I want a good clean fight, so shake hands and when you hear the bell, come out eating."

The bell rang five times.

Twenty-eight seconds later, the bell rang five times again.

"Winner and still champion, King Coondog O'Karma!"

"Goll-ee," said Coondog.

The TV cameras powered down. Coondog's fans walked around in a happy daze. They cued the tape on two nearby monitors and watched the contest again. Rizzo clocked the time on his watch, confirming twenty-eight seconds. "Sorry guys," said Coondog, apologizing for needlessly drawing out his final sip of water. "It was the last stutterstep move."

He walked out of the studio with Spiffingham, who lit a cigarette. Coondog was loud and happy. "The people are proud of me, man, they're proud of me," he said, and climbed into the car to drive home. He said he only had two regrets. One was going for that last sip of water. The other was that he hadn't asked Big Chuck to wheel him out in a cage and handcuffs and a face mask, like Hannibal Lecter. "I could have beat you with my hands behind my back and had somebody just feed it to me," he said. "That would have been funny."

For a long time, I thought Coondog's humor was *sui generis*. If his shtick seemed wacky to me, I assumed it was because Coondog was a wacky guy. I didn't understand where the humor came from, or what it meant to him. For that, I had to meet the Big Tomato.

One evening while I was visiting Coondog in Akron, Coondog said we needed to go see the Big Tomato. Coondog sat in the back of my car and directed me out of downtown Cuyahoga Falls, where he lives, and through the hillier parts of greater Akron until we pulled into an attractive one-level home just a few miles from the house where Jeffrey Dahmer grew up.* A man came out to greet us. He was squat, with whitening hair, glasses, and a round head; he looked a little like George Costanza and a little like Dick Cheney. Coondog introduced the man as the Summit County tomato-eating champion of 1970. Ergo: the Big Tomato.†

"Do I have to go through my shtick to be the Big Tomato?" asked the man, laughing.

---

* Coondog calls Dahmer "Akron's most famous eater, after Coondog."

† Also, said Coondog, "He was just such a big old dago."

His real name is Phil Angelo. He is Coondog's best friend. Like Coondog, Phil is a self-employed construction contractor. He's fifty-eight, nine years older than Coondog. The two of them first bonded back in the eighties, when Akron's rubber factories closed, the painting work dried up, and Phil and Coondog spent months driving through West Virginia looking for jobs. They've been working together off and on ever since. "[We're] acting all the time," Phil said. "When we're painting we'd be so bored we'd take on a persona. Of course sometimes it wouldn't be fake because his"—he gestured to Coondog—"emotions are like this." He flopped his hand around wildly. "There's some kind of sugar imbalance. And Lisa told me the same thing."

"Aw, shut up," said Coondog.

I asked, "So you guys are the painters who aren't really the painters?"

"I never *really* committed to painting," said Phil, who has been in construction for thirty years. "As I look back, I don't know what else I would do. I'd *love* to be a writer. To get it all off your chest? That would be tremendous."

But Phil had no aptitude for writing, and Coondog had aptitude but no outlet, so they had to find other ways to keep their minds fresh. At work, they impersonated their crewmates. They made up silly songs like "The Akron Cleveland Screwin' on the Glove Compartment Blues," which was both a pithy blue-collar lament (one verse went, *wife's kinda bitchy / the kids need shoes*) and a sendup of old workingman's dirges like "Sixteen Tons" (*it ain't right, lawd knows it ain't right*). Over the years they built up a library of routines, a set of goofy pratfalls and jokes. Shtick as survival skill: a way to cram some distance between themselves and their circumstances.

Thanks to Coondog's eating career, they could take their shtick to a larger audience, starting in 2001, when Coondog needed an audition tape to send the Fox producers on *Glutton Bowl*. He set up a camera in his backyard and invited Phil and his stepdaughter, Juanita, to "interview" him. Juanita froths in a valley-girl dialect—*Omigosh I'm here with Coondog O'Karma! So how's California! Anywayhowarethehotdogs! Howmanydidyoueat!*—forcing Phil to step into the Burgess Meredith role and introduce Coondog properly: "This is serious bidness here. This is the jam-peen-chip of the world . . ." Even better was the Pizza Fight, because it was weekly, and local, and all their friends watched it. One week, Coondog ate against Phil, who dressed up in a red felt suit that was supposed to make him look like a tomato but really made him look like a Christmas elf. During filming, Coondog took a slice of pizza and waved it in front of Phil's head in a circular motion until Phil's eyes went all googly, having been "hypnotized." Coondog told the referee his move was called "the hypno slam." Phil, after his star turn, moved into a producer role, helping Coondog recruit—and develop—Pizza Fight opponents. Recently the two of them had approached a 300-pound African-American painter named Deion.

"I want to call him the Black Hole, though," said Coondog. "Do you think that sounds racist?"

"I was thinkin' Hoodbilly," said Phil.

The comedy is proudly simple. Coondog told me, "We laugh at ourselves," and Phil told me, "We laugh at pretentiousness." In a sports town like Cleveland, home of the Dawg Pound, pretension is death. Better to be unfunny than pretentious. Nuance has to be smuggled into the joke like heroin through airport security. To see the inner payload you need some serious rays, but if you've got the rays, then Coondog and Phil want to know you. At one point, Phil walked me back to his bedroom where he showed me a pile of clipped editorials plus a stack of books by Ralph Nader, Lester Thurow, and Thomas Frank. He picked up *The Blank Slate* by Steven Pinker and said, "I disagree with what he says but his framework I guess you could say of how we think and why we think is tremendous." Phil led me back to the living room and asked if he could read me something out loud. I said sure. Phil disappeared for a minute and came back holding one of his letters to the *Beacon-Journal*. It was a Swiftian defense of Ebeneezer Scrooge as a model capitalist. "If Cratchit were a good father," Phil read in a stentorian voice, sitting next to Coondog on the couch, "he would have instilled in Tiny Tim the idea of pulling oneself up by the bootstraps—or in Tim's case, crutches." The letter's concept had been Phil's, but the words were Coondog's. "My mind is too helter-skelter," said Phil, "so he'll pick up the idea and say it better than I was even *thinking* it."

Coondog appeared uncharacteristically embarrassed. He started talking about the Pizza Fight. "The last two weeks I've been in the zone," he said. "The pizzas look really small. The pizzas look like Doritos." This is the kind of quote that unfurls into multitudes once you give Coondog credit for being at least as sharp and complicated as the reporters who cover him.

In the zone: cliché sports-guy talk. *The pizzas look like Doritos:* suggesting a state of grace, of deep communion with the universe or possibly a God, a God that is aware of Doritos. This is what Dave Giffels means when he says that "it's almost like he's manipulating the press and they don't even realize it." My favorite example is an *Action News* clip from 2002. A blonde anchorette interviews Coondog about appearing in a recent issue of *GQ.* "So what's next for Coondog?" asks the anchorette, looking into the camera. "Well, to first of all become world champion, one bite"—and here she bites into her own chocolate donut—"at a time." Chewing, the anchorette holds up the issue of *GQ.* The cover is a naked male posing as a classical Greek athlete. Then the camera pans to show Coondog, a chocolate donut in each hand, mimicking the cover model's discus-throwing pose. Coondog's mouth is frozen in a rictus of terrible joy: a seething caricature of crapulent celebrity that's too overblown to be accidental. Also Coondog just really, really enjoys being on TV.

After an hour or so in Phil's living room, we walked over to Phil's second, larger living room. It was getting dark. Phil's yellow lamps coated the furniture like a layer of varnish. Phil sat down at his piano and started pounding out blues-scale fifths. He leaned into a microphone, attached to an amplifier, and sang "Whole Lotta Shakin' Goin' On":

> *Come on over baby baby*
> *Baby got the bull by the horn*

Coondog was stretched out on the couch, preoccupied, as always, with Coondog. "I'm almost fifty years old," he said. "People don't want to hire me . . . I have to have a shtick going, and this stuff is keeping me out there . . ."

Phil dismounted from the piano. I listened to Phil and Coondog tell stories, which grew more and more personal. Phil asked if Coondog had ever told me about Coondog's father.

"He's real quiet," said Coondog. "Nothing like me, right?"

"You tell him how he got screwed?"

"Nah. It's too sad."

Coondog told the story anyway. He said his father, John, was a longtime clerk at the Cuyahoga Falls post office. One year Coondog's father, along with several other clerks, came up a few bucks short in his yearly accounting. It happened to be a year that management wanted to thin the ranks. They fired him after twenty-eight years of service. He lost his appeal. A week later he had a heart attack and died.

"Think of the stress," said Phil.

"Twenty-eight years, you know?" said Coondog.

"*Think* of the *stress*," said Phil, louder, indignant.

"His funeral, from his casket all the way outside, down the block, for three solid hours, people were lined up for my dad."

"You ever heard the term 'going postal'?"

"It broke his heart because my dad was an honest guy."

During the appeal process, Coondog's dad tried to get other work. He even asked Phil for some painting work. Phil blew him off. Coondog's father was fifty-four at the time, and slow; Phil and Dave were young and quick. "It would take him a week," said Coondog, laughing softly. "I didn't want my dad to be humiliated like that."

"But now I can relate to him," said Phil, grinning. The more worked up he got, the wider he grinned. "Because now I'm fifty-eight and I know what it *means* to really not be that physically able and to realize *I can't go back to school*, and to be a dinosaur. And it's shocking . . ."

"That's why," Coondog said, "when people say, 'How can you be Coondog at such an age?' I'm thinking, like, I'm not ready to become invisible. As Coondog I'm still visible. As a painter, I'm just nothin'."

"We're *nothin'*," said Phil, with glee.

"I'm not ready to become invisible," said Coondog.

In Japan, he'd be visible. Oh yeah. You kidding? The six-foot-two *gaijin* with the redneck hat and the loud nasal voice and the goatee and the screwy, off-balance walk? That guy? The one hopped up on vending-machine *cohee*, ducking when he boarded the subway cars and laughing, just roaring his glutton's guts out every time he saw a salaryman conked out against the glass? Nah, you couldn't miss Coondog once he got to Japan. Or so he imagines in the weeks prior to our trip. He's so excited that when he does errands around Akron he wears the photo of Kobayashi around his neck, just to provoke questions he'll answer by saying, *That's Takeru Kobayashi. You know, the hot-dog champ? Yeah! Yeah, I know him—hell, he knows me. He's my little buddy. I'm going to see him next week. I am going to Japan to seek the Great Kobayashi.* He tells everybody. The ladies at the drugstore. The guys at the paint store. He even e-mails Dave Giffels, even though he doesn't need Giffels anymore, because now he has a new pipeline to copy and attention, a new enabler.

Me.

I am now confessor to a forty-nine-year-old man in midlife crisis mode, validator of his odd pursuits. So I have to listen to rants like the one Coondog delivers at 4:57 a.m. on Sunday, January 16, in the lobby of our Nagoya hotel, with me hung over from drinking away my Koby-related depression. "It's not a fitness sport," Coondog tells me, "but it's a sport. And I'm fuckin' good at it." He is too awake for 4:57 a.m. His tone is too urgent. His logic is a pummeling logic. If eating is a sport, it's as worthy of respect as any other sport, and if Coondog is fuckin' good at it, then Coondog is an athlete like any other athlete. QED. "And I am *YUUMEI!!!!*" he says, flexing his biceps. "Famous!"

Of course, Coondog is demonstrably *not* famous in Japan. Even Koby is barely famous here. This is the whole problem. I can't get access to Koby, and I can't use Coondog to score interviews because nobody knows Coondog, or cares. Our translator, Marina, has been sending torrents of e-mails to addresses on *oogui* websites, but the few eaters who write us back demand money. Is this standard practice in Japan? What am I supposed to do?

And how do I get Coondog to chill out? I mean, it's not so bad, Coondog pummeling me with his logic, because on a quixotic reporting trip like this one, anything bad is good. Anything bad is just material for the eventual story. But just because it's entertaining as material doesn't mean I understand it. What always impressed me about Coondog was his self-awareness, the fact that he was part of eating but above it, too. A pundit-philosopher. "To be up on stage," he'd say, "shoving food in your face, beats everyday existence for most people." He was a character but also a real human. And now that our dead ends have exposed all this real human drama—the tension of coming face to face with the limitations of one's own influence, effectiveness, fame, whatever—Coondog is reacting by becoming even more of a character. It's confusing. Is this what I'm going to find as I keep digging into this world? More funhouse distortions?

I have to get out of this hotel, this city.

So we leave. We decide to get a pension room with a weekly rate in a cheap outskirts of Tokyo and move our operation there. Since most of the eaters live in Tokyo's outskirts, if we get a break and finally score some interviews, at least we'll be close by. Shiinamachi, our new "home," is nice enough. There's a coffee shop, a newsstand, a rice bowl shop, a ramen stall whose chef plays reggae on the stereo, a pachinko parlor, an Internet café, and a hundred little huddled food stalls arranged in a warren of crisscrossing alleyways. Our room itself is crap: maybe nine feet long and six feet wide, with a single fused-plastic bathroom, a small TV with six or seven channels, and a tiny window that overlooks the alleyways. There's just enough space between the beds for Coondog to do push-ups.

This first night, we ride the subway into Shibuya, a neon-happy slice of innermost Tokyo. After four days in a quiet business hotel, talking mostly to ourselves, the lights and the noise are gloriously refreshing. In a journal, Coondog writes:

> an Orgasm of humanity!
> strawberry shortcake
> prostitutes . . .
> A city where cute
> is buxom steroid
> cartooned God
> where creativity is stamped
> packaged & franchised
> to a thirsty uncreative
> glutton
> I feel raped—but kinda like it

And then, at an expat bar, the orgasm is over as soon as it starts.

The culprit is Yuko, age unknown. Our very first interview. The only interview we can get. Yuko, who is in her mid-twenties, declines my offer of a drink, adjusts the collar of her white sweater, looks down at her shoes, and clasps her hands. She is tiny and nervous, with short black hair. In between my questions she wipes her nose with a white handkerchief dotted with little hearts. During the week, Yuko does paperwork for a factory that makes door hinges, but I am interested in what she does at night, which is to manage a website called "Y.I. Kiss." It stands for "Yukihiro Iteya Kiss." Yukihiro Iteya is an eater from Nagoya. And Yuko, shy Yuko, is in love with him.

Why Iteya? She can't explain. She suddenly brightens and pulls an album from her purse and flips through two dozen photos of a tall guy with dark hair like Nic Cage in *Raising Arizona*. Iteya. Yuko is in one of the pictures next to Iteya, both of them giving the peace sign. As soon as she puts the photos back in her purse, she tucks back into herself and won't look at me. She ferociously rubs her pendant, which is inscribed with Iteya's initials. It feels like I'm having a conversation with Marina, my translator, about somebody who isn't sitting next to me:

—What does she think about when she's watching Iteya?
—*Sugoi*. (Cool.) Fantastic. Wow.
—And the *sugoi* is like other feelings of *sugoi* or is it different, better?
—There's nothing she can compare it to. It's really *sugoi*.
—What's her favorite thing about Iteya?
—Everything. He's her type.
—Is there any possibility she'd fall for another eater?
—No.
—Does she think about Iteya when she's at work?
—When she's not really busy.
—How does she picture him?
—[blushing] Just like any other fan, she pictures him when he's eating.

In early 2002, she had to suddenly start working much harder to picture Iteya. At a school in Aichi province, a fourteen-year-old boy, mimicking his *oogui* heroes, staged a bread-eating contest at lunchtime. "Suddenly the victim took a sip of milk and rushed out of the classroom," the *Asahi Shimbun* reported. "He collapsed in front of a drinking fountain." The boy died, and the *oogui* shows shut down. Two and a half years later, when the shows were about to start back up, a thirty-eight-year-old housewife died after choking on a piece of wheat rice cake at a contest in Hyogo prefecture. Yuko has now been Iteya-less for three years. Marina says, "She is very sad about that . . . even if she wanted to write fan letters, they don't know where to send them."

Yuko doesn't know it, but this is her lucky day.

"Tell her she's eating with the world donut champion," says Coondog, pounding his chest.

"Sugoi," says Yuko, and goes back to rubbing her pendant.

It's like hitting golf balls off the edge of an ocean liner. Coondog's shtick drops into a void. As we say good-bye to Yuko and walk back to the train station, Coondog seems angry. "She's in love with a competitive eater," he says, shaking his head in disgust. This is supposed to be the promised land of competitive eating, and all we can find is a sad little girl with a sad little photo album. The Yuko incident—which Coondog thinks reinforces that eating "is a pretty weird cult here and in the U.S."—throws Coondog into a minor depression that's exacerbated by our circumstances. Over the next few days our pension room starts to smell like feet and noodles. We have nothing to do. Coondog takes long meandering walks while I lie in bed drinking lobby Sapporos and reading *Dogs and Demons*, a nonfiction jeremiad by an American, Alex Kerr, who fell in love with Japan and spent the last decades watching its countryside fill with concrete and its cities become choked with the flimsy architecture that Coondog described so well in his journal:

> *Erector set*
> *cities that*
> *are so*
> *ugly*
> *you are just hoping*
> *Godzilla*
> *will come*
> *in & crush*
> *them*

It's reassuring to know that Kerr feels as bewildered by his wack country as I do about mine, but mostly the book makes me homesick. Coondog has it even worse. He has never been away from Lisa for this long. He misses his kids and his dog. It's a bad combination: Coondog mopey, me anxious. The very real prospect of failure, of flying back home with no Koby interview, puts me on edge. Seeing me on edge puts Coondog on edge. One day he's so moody I have to take him to the Imperial Palace just to get him near some grass and trees. Whenever we have to hump our bags on the trains, he grumbles about having to do it himself, then apologizes; he says he's used to getting chauffeured, which sounds strange until I realize that for a competitive eater, this is half the reason to do a talk show: the talk show picks you up in a limo. On the train, Coondog is either obnoxiously loud or grumpily withdrawn. He'll look out the window and ask me something like:

"How many times smarter do you think we are than ants? A million, maybe?"

"Why don't you ask an ant?"

"That's what this trip has made me realize. We are all ants. This is an ant country. Koby is just the ultimate *nihonjin*. He knows how to make use of every bit of available space."

Koby. The white whale/white rabbit. The more frustrating our trip becomes, the more our thoughts turn to Koby. He looms larger as we grow smaller. "I am an oddity here," Coondog writes in his journal. "Some things Coondog . . . no matter where on / earth / never / change." Coondog is turning out to be a more localized phenomenon than he hoped. Coondog came to swallow Japan, and Japan has swallowed him instead.

One night I break down. I'm in bed. Can't sleep. Two a.m. I can hear Coondog breathing. I can either listen to Coondog breathe, or I can type something on my laptop.

I take out my laptop and start typing.

I find that I'm typing a small parable. My protagonist is an obscure Belarussian pro golfer who shoots a final-round 49 at the golf Masters tourney, stealing the Green Jacket and throwing the PGA pros into disarray. Coondog hears me typing and wakes up. "Hey," he says, groggily. He grabs his own journal and starts scribbling. I find out later what he has written:

I am tired & my eye hurts
the light burns & Jason
calmly writes he has
become Japanese I might
as well not be here the
pitter patter of his fingers
across the comp pad is
annoying I think he
may be writing about
me . . .
I think I will murder
Jason
THE END

"What are you typing?" Coondog asks me, finally. "You writing about me?" So, to allay his paranoia, I read my parable out loud:

> . . . In the clubhouse, bedlam. The lone TV anchor from Belarus ululated wildly while the American journalists swarmed the Belarussian, demanding to know how he had done it. The Belarussian beckoned to his interpreter, squared his shoulders, and smiled. He started speaking in hard, unintelligible syllables. The PGA pros leaned in, holding their breath. "I train very hard," said the Belarussian's interpreter in clipped English, "and keep a positive mental attitude."

Coondog shoots upright, fully awake.
Exactly, he says, laughing; *exactly.*
The Fifty-Dog Day.
He asks me to read it again, and I do. He laughs even harder the second time. Nothing I've ever written has had such an immediate and positive effect on somebody. Coondog's instantly all loud and goony, gesturing, excited, now he wants to tell *me* stories, and does—he tells me the story of the Fifty-Dog Day for maybe the fifth time, start to finish, from the press

conference all the way on through to the part when his son, Adam, looks at Coondog and points over at Koby, trying to clue his dad in—the same story that Coondog, in the years after 2001, would tell and retell whenever Adam became sullen or distant and Coondog needed an icebreaker to reach him. Coondog would lean over and speak four little words: *How'd he do it?*

And it would work.

I think this is why my dippy little parable makes Coondog so dispropor-tionately happy. For the first time, I've shown him that I can have fun with the idea that there is a Japanese man out there who can eat fifty hot dogs in twelve minutes. And Coondog is showing me that it's possible to go a step further than just having fun. It's possible to *share* the idea of the Japanese man: to make it part of your own private language, to integrate it into your own sacred jokes; to use it to connect with your kid, or your friends, or maybe to bond with an inconsiderate American reporter who has woken you up with his typing, until the both of you, you exhausted strung-out souls, are cackling together, past 2:00 a.m., like idiots.

5

"MISTAH COONDOG—HE FULL"

THE MORNING AFTER his run-in with Yuko, Dave wakes up thinking about her. "I'm ashamed," he says, sitting on the edge of his bed, "to be a part of a humanity that created someone so desperate and docile." He smiles. "That's a fuckin' great line. Write that down. I'm pollinated, you know? Tokyo has pollinated me. I mean, fuck the Coondog shit. I'm seeing things as a writer now. Everything's so clear. Maybe this is what I needed."

Dave's newfound clarity lasts eight hours. Because that afternoon, as soon as Japan has killed Coondog, a twenty-nine-year-old weatherman in a charcoal suit comes along and resurrects him.

Kenji Aoki. I e-mailed him weeks ago, after I came across his meticulous *oogui* website that described, in great detail, his attempt to eat a giant Japanese pancake. More important for our purposes, Kenji's site made it clear that he often staged his own informal contests. He called them "Sushi Battle Clubs" in homage to the popular Japanese eating show called *Food Battle Club*. I asked Kenji if he might stage a Sushi Battle Club with Coondog, and he said yes. Now we're meeting him to work out the logistics.

At a coffee shop in Harajuku, Kenji orders a tomato juice. Unlike Yuko, he seems normal and high-functioning, with his flawless charcoal suit, pale blue shirt, and Gucci watch. He says he works for a company that produces weather reports for the government. Kenji explains his enthusiasm for *oogui* with a nonchalant half-smile. "It feels good to eat a lot," he says, simply. "Doesn't it feel good when you eat a lot?" He makes *oogui* seem as unthreatening as hot cocoa on a winter afternoon, and he couldn't be more deferential to Dave.

"I didn't know you would be such a famous eater," Kenji says. "I'm feeling . . . not quite up to that level."

"No, we are here for fun," says Dave.

"You have a nice build," says Kenji.

"Tell him I'm an old man."

There's some minor haggling over the format of the Sushi Battle, owing to Dave's reluctance to eat raw fish. Somehow this isn't a deal-killer. Coondog pounds his chest: "Tell him that Coondog has come to Nihon to bring back *oogui*. I am an ambassador."

Kenji says, "Mmmm."

But we can tell he is excited, if not as excited as Coondog. Leaving the coffee shop, Coondog tries to push the door open instead of pulling it, meets resistance, and trips. "I'm pumped now," he says. "It's great, because win or lose, I'm bringing them together." In the night air of Harajuku, cutting a wake through streams of schoolgirls in striped leggings and knee-high boots, Dave makes a solemn promise to no one in particular. "I'm gonna shake this country up, man. Loosen 'em up a bit. Give 'em back their appetite."

He adds, "Watch me choke on a piece of sushi."

I expected the sushi, the pachinko, the fast trains. I didn't expect the bakeries. The Japanese bakeries as majestic as Jack Kerouac's vision of the "shining glazed sweet counter" of the 1940s American cafeteria, "showering like heaven—an all-out promise of joy." The Japanese bakeries in train stations and the low-slung warrens of inner Tokyo, displaying, through wraparound windows, multitiered racks of glowing buns and croissants and twists and crullers so moist they look as though they'd dissolve on contact with your tongue. Reflecting light like the bald heads of the U.S. Senate, like they'll pop and leak fluid if you squeeze. But they're just bread. Every morning we eat at a bakery just across the train tracks from our pension room. For lunch we walk to an alleyway lined with cheap delicious food on both sides, like the 90-yen batter-fried potato pancakes I buy three and four at a time—greasy, but not like a fat man's sweat. Greasy like a fat angel's breath.

Japan is food-crazy, like America, but its mania is different. A 1999 study in the journal *Appetite* suggests how. The study's authors—among them Paul

Rozin, professor of psychology at the University of Pennsylvania—surveyed students and adults in America, Japan, Belgium, and France, asking people about how they perceived food. One survey question, which was part of a series of questions designed to figure out whether people saw food as a "culinary" experience or a "nutritional" experience, asked respondents to "circle the word you think is most different from the other two: carbohydrate, bread, butter." The least "culinary" country turned out to be America, and the most "culinary" was Japan: just 16 percent of Americans circled "carbohydrate," as opposed to 36 percent of Japanese. This makes sense: Japan's food culture is more highly aestheticized than America's, more focused on food's beauty, even when quantity factors in. Japanese gluttons aren't slobs. They eat clean.

You see this in the Japanese competitive eating shows. In the heyday of Japanese *oogui*—from November 2000, Koby's debut, to April 2002, the date of the first fatal choking accident—two competing shows aired on rival networks: TV Tokyo's *TV Champion* and Tokyo Broadcasting System's *Food Battle Club*. Of the two, *TV Champion* seems far less alien to my American eyes. It's a prime-time variety show that uses empirical means to crown Japan's greatest whatever—dog trainer, bread baker, home remodeler, bubble blower, eater. A typical episode of *TV Champion* is the April 2001 "All Newcomers Battle," on which the host—a slim, excitable fellow with a goatee and faint black mustache—guides a crop of *oogui* virgins through four gluttonous rounds. The show begins with a shot of thirty or forty hopefuls at a cattle call, standing in line outside a sushi restaurant on a cold day. They shuffle to the door, pick up a marathon-style bib, and take a seat at the sushi bar. The host bangs on a traditional drum and the eaters tear into the sushi, stacking piles of tiny colorful plates to the ceiling. Twenty-six minutes later the top six eaters advance to the first round. We are introduced to the eaters in a quick montage, beginning with Nobuyuki "Giant" Shirota, a genial six-foot-four fellow with acromegalic features who can stuff an entire coffee cup in his mouth. The Giant attempts to eat the camera. The lucky six contestants are then flown and bussed to four restaurants across Japan, from Kyushu to Tokyo, where they eat pot stickers, boiled eggs, breaded pork cutlets, and, in the final round, ramen noodles. Iteya—Yuko's Iteya—beats the Giant by a noodle. The restaurant employees stand and clap. Iteya tells the host that it feels good to be number one because in high school he wasn't popular. Then Iteya starts crying. "I feel really full," he says. The host crowns him with a garland of leaves. Cut to a TV studio, where a set of golden double doors opens to reveal Iteya silhouetted against a halo of yellow light and blue flashing strobes.

"You must feel so super!" says the host to Iteya.

"I am very happy," Iteya says. "I'm going to continue to eat like a champion." As the audience applauds, the studio's flooded with the power-ballad strains of some *nihongo* Michael Bolton, and the bleachers begin to slide apart from the center, exposing a lighted stairway that pulsates in pink and leads upward to a plush throne plated in gold. Iteya, bowing to the crowd with each step, ascends and takes his rightful place on the throne of *oogui* kings.

"Is it good to become a champion?"

"It's good! It's super!"

Blue strobes, Michael Bolton, plush thrones—I fear that I'm making *TV Champion*'s production values sound impressive. They're not, especially compared with the other eating show, *Food Battle Club*, or *FBC*. If *TV Champion* is *The Gong Show, Food Battle Club* is *American Idol. FBC* is bigger in every way—more glitz, more prize money (10 million yen, about $100,000), a more elaborate tournament structure, and epic, expensive-looking sets. In *TV Champion* the clock counts down in seconds; in *FBC* the clock is accurate to hundredths of a second. In *TV Champion*, an eater raises his hand when he's done eating; in *FBC*, an eater slams a red button that sends a plume of fire into the air. Consider *FBC King of Masters*, a two-part special that aired in 2001 and 2002. On a long horizontal stage, twenty-four eaters, wearing tuxedos, stare ahead with grim faces as the camera zooms slowly on a distant cage—all else is darkness—that snarls with blue laser beams. An announcer says, in English, "FOODA BATTA CLUB! THE KING OF MASTERS TOURNAMENTO!" as the camera zooms into the laser light. The tournament proceeds in stages. The stages have names like Scramble Break Out, Hang Over, Burst Attack, and Shoot Out. The most dramatic stage is Hang Over, a cross between a game of chicken and an auction. A certain food is brought out (say, strawberries) and a time is listed (five minutes). The eaters raise their hands to offer "bids." Bidding stops when Kenji Oguni, with the aid of a calculator, decides that he can safely consume 146 strawberries, about six and a half pounds, in five minutes.

Each stage pares down the field and ratchets up the martial tension until, by the Finals, you are not at all surprised to see a very large man wearing full-body armor and a white executioner's mask summon the three eaters, who ascend on pneumatic lifts. A waiter emerges with a large silver platter holding the secret ingredient, curry rice. Giant Shirota finishes his curry first and smiles sickly. The executioner shakes his hand. Shirota is $100,000 richer.

In early 2002, just a month after King of Masters, America's very first eating show debuted, on the Fox network. Dubbed *Glutton Bowl: The World's Greatest Eating Competition*, it lagged slightly behind *Fear Factor*, which debuted in 2001 and proved to NBC that there was money in the sort of misogyny—enticing models to eat mealworms for cash—that would cause any softcore porno to be reclassified as hardcore. (Men compete, too, but are hardly the focus.) In *Glutton Bowl*, thirty-two male competitors and two females pound hard-boiled eggs, butter, beeftongue, hot dogs, mayonnaise, hamburgers, monster sushi rolls, cow brains, and something called "Rocky Mountain oysters"—a euphemism for bull testicles. The sole bit of drama involves the introduction of each round's food, which is stored in a large oil drum, painted red, white, and blue, hovering high above the eaters on a mechanical pulley system. The producers press a button; the drum tips over and showers that round's food into a giant glass bowl below. The food makes wet plosive sounds as it stacks in a gooey heap. It is the only time you will ever see a hamburger spatter. For the eaters, the aftertaste of cow brains and bull testicles can be tamed with toothpaste and Listerine. But for you, the viewer, a more appropriate cleansing act might be to volunteer at a homeless shelter. *Glutton Bowl* feels just that dire—as if the culture, and you, are hitting bottom together.

Why don't Japanese eating shows feel like this? Why is *Glutton Bowl* degrading and *TV Champion* a lark? Is it the difference in respect paid to the food itself—the aesthetic contrast between an oil drum and a silver platter? Is it the contrast between the eaters? The Japanese eaters, after all, are mostly young college-aged men, and skinny. Their rude health is unspoilable even by 10 kilograms of curry rice. They've got no wives to embarrass, no kids to disappoint. They've got time to recover, which means the aura of desperation that makes the American shows such train wrecks—the whiff of the ticking clock and the midlife crisis—is absent. Paradoxically, the very hyperseriousness of the Japanese shows may protect them from this fate. The imperial overtones and laser beams and explosions and inconceivable quantities of food all combine to convey the *opposite* of seriousness: the feeling that *oogui* is still, despite the high stakes and athleticisim, a *game*. Schoolyard. Innocent.

Thanks to Kenji Aoki's ad-hoc contest, I see this firsthand. The Saturday of the contest—Kenji's calling it *Sushi Battle Club 2: The Speed*—Coondog spends the morning preparing his outfit. He takes a blue Ballpark Franks T-shirt (GRILL OR BE GRILLED) and rips off the sleeves. Then he rips the sleeve material into long strips and ties them to the bottom of his shirt, making a fringe of blue knotted tassels. Underneath the blue T-shirt he wears a bright orange tank top, matching the orange bandanna on his head. He ties the leftover blue strips to his ankles. His intent is to look like the sumo warriors he's been watching on TV, but the effect is somewhere between punk-rock bassist and homeless person. When we arrive at the restaurant, Coondog sees Kenji and his friends, points to his chest, and says, "sumo," then walks in back, saying, "You will all win. My stomach is not ready for sushi."

Kenji introduces Coondog to his opponents. One of them, Tazawa, has competed on *TV Champion*, finishing sixth, but the rest are novices. Kenji didn't know them until he started his website, but now they are all friends. Yasuharu Kimori is the twenty-year-old who'd come all the way from Osaka that morning; Sadao Kakei is the thirty-two-year-old office worker; "Koaten" is the middle-aged guy with big glasses and overalls; Shinya Taniguchi is the twenty-nine-year-old food-company worker with the Gap hoodie; Koichi Tazawa is the twenty-four-year-old machinery student. They all seem excited to meet Coondog.

"Excuse me, Mistah Coondog," says Sadao. "Would you like to take picture with me?"

"Yeah!" says Coondog. "How do you say hell yeah! *Mistah Coondog*. I like that."

The *oogui* entourage moves to the back of the restaurant, where Kenji has reserved three tables. Two girls with eating websites have stopped by. One is

Yuko, shy Yuko, snapping pictures. The other asks me to identify her by her online screen name, "toro umiyamada," because she works at a Tokyo bank that she describes to me later, in an e-mail, as "very conservative."* Also here is Kenji's girlfriend, Minori, a tiny woman with fake pearls and tall fuzzy boots; she tells me that she met Kenji at an eating contest a year ago after reading his website, thought he was cute, and now they are engaged to be married. "I try to support him," she says. "He tries hard. He is competitive. . . . As a girl, I can't eat very much. So it is good to see people eat a lot."

Waitresses start bringing out plates of food and Kenji directs traffic, ushering each eater to the one table he's reserved for competition. *Sushi Battle Club 2: The Speed* is to be a series of one-on-one contests, culminating with the Coondog-Kenji fight. As each eater competes, Coondog gives him a nickname based on his eating style. Sadao becomes the Pelican. Shinya becomes the Grouper. Tazawa is the Snapper. Tazawa is the most impressive. He can swallow two pieces of sushi at a time without chewing. He eats thirty pieces in a minute and eighteen seconds.

"Subarashi!" says Sadao.

"Wonderful!" says Marina.

"I knew that one," says Coondog. He shouts *"Subarashi!"* and pounds the table, shaking the sushi. "I like the way they eat," Coondog says. "They're very rhythmic."

Now it's Coondog's turn. The waitress brings the plates of nontraditional sushi he specifically requested—hamburger, boiled shrimp, scallop, and a bean curd dish that the Japanese call *inari* but Coondog calls "donuts"—and the Japanese all say, "Wow, it looks tough." Coondog touches the burger with his forefinger and licks it, frowning. "It's cold," he says.

"If he does well with that menu," says Kenji, "it will be really *sugoi.*"

"I appreciate that he realizes that," said Coondog. "It means he really knows eating. Kenji-san." He bows deeply to Kenji. *"Itadakimasu."*

It's close at first, neck-and-neck in the middle. Coondog falls behind when he hits the burgers, and Kenji methodically plows through his salmon. The "donuts" prove overly chewy and destroy Coondog's chances. Kenji

---

* "Maybe it feels unpleasant that one of its staff thinks about *oogui* very much while the company is very busy at this important situation."

wins. Coondog pops off about his "donuts" but remains gracious in defeat, pulling off his blue GRILL OR BE GRILLED shirt and handing it to Kenji. Kenji bows and puts on the shirt as Sadao tries to console Coondog. "The type of sushi you were eating, to eat that fast was very impressive," he says.

Coondog suddenly grabs Marina and says he has a question for Kenji. "When do we do hot dogs? Ask him ... My turf. How do you say 'my turf'? I am really hungry for a poisonous American hot dog."

We're about to leave when I see one of the most lasting images from my time in Japan: Minori, Kenji's girlfriend, wearing Coondog's sumo shirt. It almost comes down to her knees, like a dress. Kenji has given it to her like a varsity jacket. She looks down at her hips as the shirt hangs loosely on her small frame, tassels ringing her legs. As I gawk at Minori, Coondog gawks at Kenji's friends, who are sitting together at a table, chatting and laughing, picking at the leftover sushi.

"They *enjoy* it!" he says. "Look at 'em. They're not pissed off."

There is craziness here, sure, but it's sublimated; it feels like we could be watching any group of friends enjoying any shared activity, salsa-dancing, bird-watching, playing Halo on XBox. The Japanese have safely slotted *oogui* into the rubric of "subculture," which is to the larger Japanese culture as a sidecar is to a motorcycle: attached at the hip, along for the ride. There's no existential component to a Japanese eating contest because there's no void behind it—no real danger of losing yourself, of not belonging, because in Japan everyone is the same race, with the same schooling. Everyone belongs. There are no weird corners of Japan, only momentary sweeping fads. The Japanese could put *oogui* on TV and in their manga,* but it could only get so big before it cracked its skull against the edges of the box called "subculture." America is different, because in America there is no subculture anymore (as the *New York Post*'s Gersh Kuntzman told me once), just groups of people who haven't yet been made into reality TV shows, one big

---

* While we were in Japan, a popular manga weekly aimed at college guys was running a story called "*Kuishinbou*—Gourmet Fighter" (*kuishinbou* = "glutton"). We didn't have to dig around for it or anything. The manga was on the complimentary reading rack at our Nagoya hotel. I had it translated: a ponytailed rebel eats a massive bowl of ramen noodles. People cheer. His chopsticks make little "zzz zzz zzz" sounds. I figure the whole thing is just an excuse for the artist to draw ramen noodles.

mass culture with millions waiting for their shot in a centrifuge that's spinning everyone out to the edges, to weirder and weirder corners, so that the News of the Weird, for a lot of people, is just The News—spinning some of them so far, so violently, that they find themselves flung, at age forty-nine, with a wife and kids and a dog back home, into the back of a sushi restaurant in Harajuku, looking at a table of sushi-munching guys, wondering why the sushi-munchers seem so damned happy.

"What state are you from?" asks Sadao.

"Ohio."

"Was that you on stage, shouting, 'Ohio, Ohio'?"

"Yeah!"

Coondog has to think about this for a second. Sadao is talking about a hammy slogan Coondog shouted in 2001, at the Nathan's contest in New York. Incredibly, Sadao remembers a two-second clip from a four-year-old episode of *TV Champion*.

"He remembers!" says Coondog.

Here there are no grudges, no lingering tribal resentments. Here there is only a meticulous young weatherman—Kenji—who has used eating to find a group of friends and even a wife. Kenji's vision of *oogui* is so organic, so laid-back and human, that he makes it easy to forget why we have come. Takeru Kobayashi doesn't exist here except as an urban legend, a disembodied stomach of myth.

Which he is—up until the pinch-me afternoon when we stand in front of him, staring at his very corporeal stomach, at last.

"KOBAYASHIIIIII! KOBAYASHIIIIII!!!!!"

Coondog's screaming it, in homage to the *TV Champion* host who wailed like a Brazilian soccer announcer when Koby broke the hot-dog record.

"KOBAYASHIIIIII!!!!"

Here in the Nagoya train station, our agreed-upon meeting place, Koby ducks his head, puts his finger to his mouth, and shushes Coondog. Koby doesn't want to get noticed. But he's not angry. He's smiling. He's laughing.

Jesus, he's huge.

I saw him only two months ago, but now his face is much thicker, sparsely dotted with protuberant freckles or mild acne on his cheeks near the ears, and I can tell that his shoulders are more muscular, even though he's wearing a zippered sweater that ought to hide the bulk. Beneath the sweater is a long-sleeved beige jersey with a picture of an elephant and some vaguely Hindu designs. His wool hat makes him look like a kid from *South Park,* all grown up, which I suppose he is, since he hails from snowy Nagano, the Colorado of Japan. Nari has one or two inches on him and is easily the more striking of the two, with her slender frame and porcelain features and pink press-on nails and glittery turtleneck.

Coondog reaches into a plastic bag and removes his first *omiyage,* or gift: a red Ohio State football hat. Koby puts it on and says, in English, "Cooool." We find an Italian restaurant inside the train station and wait for a table while Coondog empties the rest of his bag's contents onto Koby's lap: two mugs painted with caricatures of Coondog (the goatee is emphasized, along with a very severe mohawk), plus a white chef's hat for Nari overprinted with the same caricature, and for Koby, a yellow Superman T-shirt and a white LeBron James jersey.

"Do you know LeBron James?" says Coondog.

Koby shakes his head.

"Yokozuna." A champion sumo wrestler.

Koby laughs. "That is an interesting comparison."

We get a table on the restaurant's outer balcony, overlooking Nagoya's picturesque Sanyo billboard. It's cold and gray. The conversation is awkward and tentative in the manner common to reunions.

"Where'd you get those big muscles?" asks Coondog. "You used to be skinny."

"I have been training for the past four years."

"I don't think you could beat Coondog."

Coondog anchors his right elbow to the table and opens his palm in classic arm-wrestling stance. Koby smiles. He straightens his back, skootches closer to the table, and cracks his knuckles. His smile fades. The size of the muscle awakened beneath his jersey is not lost on Coondog. "Wait," says Coondog, "be easy. Tell him that I am getting old." They lock hands and engage, but Koby is too strong. He wins easily. "One more," says Coondog, and loses again. He shakes his head. "Coondog is finished, man. Tell him Coondog is finished."

"You look exactly the same," says Koby.

"You look happy," says Nari.

"I am seeing my friends," says Coondog.

COONDOG: I am banned by eye-eff-oh-see-ee. George Shea wouldn't let me in any contests.

KOBY: You've been kicked out?

COONDOG: Punished. Punished . . . I am for the eaters to make money, like athletes.

KOBY: I don't think any of the money is going to the participants.

COONDOG: *Chotto.* [A little.] And I don't think that's fair. [To Marina.] Tell him that I think eaters are like athletes and should get paid like athletes.

KOBY: A lot of the player-participants can't concentrate on both things because the rules aren't really made.

COONDOG (in Japanese): My stomach is hungry.

NARI (in English): Hungry Hippo? Remember Hungry Hippo?

KOBY (in English, making hippo-chomping motion with his hand, smiling): Hungry Hungry Hippo.

Koby and Nari pick at their salads. Nari's has prosciutto on top.

We ask how he trains.

Koby says, "If you try to overcome the wall every single day, you will become drained."

We nod, murmur.

Koby says, "After the competition, if you stop training for a while, it is true that you can't eat as much. But if you compete again, you can go over your maximum."

Coondog says he worries that his friends eat too much.

Koby says, "If you eat, of course, you're going to gain weight, so you have to think about losing that weight."

We nod and nod.

Koby says, "I'm not interested in how many titles I have. It's more important to overcome my goals."

We are getting nowhere.

Koby shows Coondog a pic on his cell phone. "That's when I was really fat," he says. The picture shows a fat Japanese man retaining water—a close-up of the face, cheeks puffy, mouth hanging open. Koby adds that Nari says there is a big problem in the United States with obesity, so maybe there are some issues with that, but the way Koby trains, "I have in mind how to lose weight, so it's healthy, not unhealthy."

We try switching topics.

Baseball.

Koby says he used to play baseball, left field. He was a good batter, known for his strong throwing arm. Koby says he likes Matsui and the Yankees. "I like the home runs," he says. "That's anyone's baseball dream, to hit a home run. Once they hit a home run, all they have to do is walk slowly around the bases. There is no doubt about it when you hit a home run."

Koby smiles.

You know what this is like?

It's like making a long, grueling pilgrimage to the top of a sacred, faraway mountain, and instead of finding the wise man of legend, or even the wise man of a *Far Side* cartoon, finding a bureaucrat from your county water department.

If we learn anything useful from our Koby interview, it's that Koby is an aberration, even in his own country. Other top *oogui* stars are less stilted and more forthcoming. We know because we have met some already, and will meet others.

Yesterday, for instance, we met with Rabbit Arai, the two-time Nathan's champ who gave up his crown to Koby, and the Rabbit's comrade Toshio Kimura. Toshio was a big, jolly guy who tried so hard to talk to us in English that he started sweating. He used to appear in the way-back *oogui* shows, early on, doing shticky pratfally gags before the gags were nixed in favor of dark violins and flame. The Rabbit dressed in dapper black velour and told stories about his distinguished eating career; my favorite was about a TV show on which he ate bananas against a chimpanzee, watermelons against an elephant, and beef against a lion, beating them all except for the lion, who was given raw meat while the Rabbit had to eat cooked meat, which the

Rabbit thought was an unfair advantage. Nowadays the Rabbit was working in his relatives' meat shop in Saitama until the *oogui* shows came back on TV. Toshio and the Rabbit, who were both thirty-seven years old, were part of a different generation of Japanese eaters, and they blamed the younger folk they called the "pretty boys"—the Kobys, the Iteyas, the Giant Shirotas—for becoming so good, so fast, that it led to the hyper-intense shows like *Food Battle Club* that led in turn to the choking incidents and thus ruined *oogui*. "Tell the Americans that this happened," Toshio told us in a dire tone. "The balloon is getting inflated, but in order to keep it from popping, it needs control." The Japanese, Toshio had said, have a historical tendency to get carried away. (Yes, Toshio was comparing the collapse of *oogui* to the Japanese military experience in World War II.) As serious as they were about eating, Toshio and the Rabbit reminded me more of Coondog than Koby: strident defenders of their chosen hobby/sport, but not so strident as to lose sight of eating's goofy side. When it came time to leave them, they were only too happy to take pictures with Coondog and yell, "One, two, three, mothafuckaaaa!!!"

Tomorrow, we'll meet one of the "pretty boys": Nobuyuki "Giant" Shirota, whose head is so large it looks like he's wearing a jack-o'-lantern on top of his real head (Coondog's words). Shirota can fit an entire rice ball in his mouth and can wedge a lollipop vertically between his upper and lower lips. He beat Koby three times in *Food Battle Club*, and can make a valid claim to be the greatest eater in the world, greater even than Koby. We'll buy Shirota dinner at a dark Shibuya restaurant, and Shirota will grin and joke with us right off the bat as he orders five plates of appetizers and five big beers, daring me implicitly to keep pace. He'll smoke Lucky Strikes and marvel at Koby's incredible devotion to *oogui*: "Koby, he does it with his life. His life is at stake, competing so much. He could die if he overate or had an accident." Shirota will add, in English, "Fantastic. Wonderful." As for himself, though, "I have other dreams and goals."

Right now, in a second restaurant here in the Nagoya train station, Koby is finally loosening up, but only a little. Maybe it's the milk tea he's drinking, or the handful of chocolaty brown protein powder he pounds into his mouth, mixing it *in camera*, mouthwash-style, with a gulp of water. We ask about his family—he grew up the younger brother of two sisters, in what he calls "female" surroundings—and he tells us a joke about his hometown, where his family name is famously common: "In Nagano, there are lots of *baka* [stupid morons] and Kobayashis." And when he's not joking, or pounding protein, or showing us cell-phone pictures of muscle-rippling bodybuilding poses, he's looking at Nari between questions to make sure he's answering correctly; he's ultra-sober, talking about the league he's trying to start (the United Food Fighter Organization, or UFFO), talking about how he's always been afraid to accept offers to do TV commercials or appear as a *tarento* host, because to be a *tarento* "you don't have to have anything special . . . a *tarento* doesn't make you feel anything." He is at his most oracular when he speaks of his own sporting idols, especially Lance Armstrong. "He's like the God among all the sports," Koby says. "No matter what kind of sport it is, it all comes down to your heart. And he's got heart." Koby says that he wears a yellow Livestrong band, but only on the days when he feels worthy of Lance's example.

And he means it.

Boy, Coondog loves that.

Koby draws us the kanji character for his name, Takeru, and says it means "respect."

Coondog loves that, too.

This is the stuff of a Matt Christopher sports novel. Heroism and heart. Personal goal-setting and goal-breaking. It's not the language of Japanese sports. Koby carries himself like an American, with an American's sense of individualism mixed with a Japanese person's sense of propriety and politeness:

Does he make any money in Japan?

Koby says that the most he's made is $100,000, from winning *Food Battle Club One.* There's not much money for winning *TV Champion,* maybe a tenth as much. He deposited his *FBC* winnings in the bank to use them to buy weightlifting equipment and dietary supplements, which are expensive.

What does he do for a job?

He eats. He hangs out with bodybuilders at the gym. He draws down his winnings to buy protein powder, and Nari supplements the bank account with her own steady job. And he waits for the shows to come back, and plans trips to America.

What will he do after his eating career is over?
"Still thinking."
What would he be if he wasn't an eater?
"I like animals, especially dogs." So maybe a dog groomer.
What is that mysterious wiggle?
Koby laughs and says something short.
Marina translates:
"I'm dancing."

In the beerpub back at our hotel, Coondog and I ordered tempura and wound down, sharing our favorite Koby quotes from the six-hour interview. "You know how I think he does it?" Coondog asked. "He just *does* it." Coondog was elated, hopped up. He had found what he came to Japan to find. "He's a throwback," Coondog said. "I'm thinking, this is the kind of sports story I loved when I was a kid, and then you find out it's all bullshit. And here's this twenty-seven-year-old hot-dog eater who has every sports-hero cliché that I used to eat up when I was a kid. *And it's for real.*"

Honestly, I was happy too, even if my happiness was only a form of profound relief. Coondog and I had fulfilled our quest's objective. I could go back home and tell my friends I'd met the Skinny Japanese Guy. The mythic man. We spent six leisurely hours with Takeru Kobayashi—ate with him, hung out in his hometown, joked around, taught him a little English ("I eeet eet to defeet eet"), posed the burning questions, saw him perform feats of upper-body strength. He spent six hours talking, and we spent six hours oohing and ahhing, but what felt like wisdom dissolved into banality a few hours later, when I looked back over my notes. They amounted to a handful of jokes and a few overbroad statements of purpose. I still didn't know how Koby ate as much as he did, or why. I didn't know how he trained or what his apartment looked like. I didn't know what his toilet looked like after he took a dump. I didn't know why he and Nari weren't married. I didn't know whether he used drugs or popped Flinstones vitamins.

I had jack.

Moreover, what little I did learn from Koby tended to complicate Coondog's preconceptions, not validate them. Japan wasn't the promised land of competitive eating, for one. America was. America had the better eaters and the higher-paying contests. Japan's *oogui* culture had imploded, and now all the eaters—Koby, Shirota, the Rabbit—wanted to eat in America. Nor was Koby some mystical innocent or "throwback." As much as Americans liked to infantilize him by calling him "little buddy" (Coondog) or "the kid" (George Shea), Koby's genuine kidlike qualities—like his love of the Nickelodeon cartoon *Hey Arnold,* the theme to which he sang while making jazz hands: *Heyyy Ahnuld, Heyyy Ahnuld*—coexisted with an extreme adultness. Koby, after all, is a guy who's gone off on his own in a culture that values conformity, building his job description as he goes. He's a guy who had the courage and vision—or, alternatively, the ego and obstinacy—to stand up to the TV bookers who wanted to make him a mere *tarento* and thus dilute his special-ness. Yes, Koby is a great athletic performer. He's also an entrepreneur, as any modern athlete must be, and doubly so because he's breaking fresh tracks in weird woods.

Does he make a living from *oogui* alone? Pay his rent, support Nari, take her to a movie every once in a while? Yes. I had to find out later how much he makes and where he makes it. It turns out that Koby makes his money in America. When Koby flies over for the Krystal Square-Off and the Nathan's hot dog contest and the Alka-Seltzer U.S. Open of Competitive Eating, each sponsor pays him an appearance fee in the low to low-mid five figures, on top of whatever prize money he almost certainly will win. According to Koby and his interpreter, Bobby Ikeda, Koby's contracts are negotiated by a Japanese sports lawyer, who acts as a de facto agent. Yearly, then, Koby flirts with the low six figures—not the $500,000 of George Shea's imagination, but enough that he doesn't need a day job.

So Koby is real, as Coondog insists, if "real" means "athletically success-ful" and "financially viable." Is he real in the sense of being a rounded human presence? I had more fun in six minutes drinking beer with the Giant Shirota than I did in six hours with Koby. Don Lerman is more real to me. Cookie Jarvis is more real to me. Koby is a nice person, *but not interesting.* Even his training secret is not so interesting, when you get down to it. This is the closest thing in competitive eating to blasphemy, but I think it's true. We already know how he does it—or the broad outlines, at least. One, he's stretching his stomach with enormous quantities of food. Two, he's somehow making his esophagus go limp. What we're missing are the fleshy details, the exact composition and volume of his training meals, the exact regimen of vitamins and weightlifting reps and (perhaps?) muscle relaxants. As much as I'd like to know all those details, I have to believe that if his secret were ever revealed, it would be disappointingly mundane if it wasn't incriminating. Weren't we better off with Deep Throat, the shadowy power broker, than with W. Mark Felt, the nonagenarian in the ugly blue shirt? Better that Koby remain Deep Esophagus. The mystery is the best thing going.

I think Koby gets this—which is why he's so coy—and Coondog gets it, too. All along, my American blowhard companion was more interesting than the faraway mythic man, and what's more, the American blowhard *knew* he was more interesting. ("I think I'm more interesting," he would tell me a few months later.) The trip, for Coondog, was never about verifying or debunking Koby's legend. It was about sustaining Koby's legend and adding to Coondog's own. That's why Coondog was full of answers while I was close to an existential crisis. A middle-aged man, having laid out a small child's fantasy—*I'm gonna go meet the hot-dog man and we're gonna arm-wrestle and then we'll be best friends forever*—saw his fantasy granted, serving not to reinforce the fantasy's essential absurdity, but to imbue it with the force of a higher calling. Destiny and all that. *Karma.*

Now Coondog was headed back to a roiling country, ego unpunctured, the wrong lessons learned—but maybe his wrongheadedness contained a lesson for me, his very imperviousness a hint to my own riddle, the one I came to Japan looking to solve. Trash culture: how to confront it, conquer it? How to master it instead of the other way around? Maybe the answer was contained within Coondog's willingness to power through the setbacks and see what he wants to see. The American mythmaking impulse is strong enough to overpower any source material, no matter how cheap, tacky, crappy, shitty. Norman Mailer talks about ego being like a shell. Ideally it's thin enough to let you stay connected to other humans, but thick enough to protect you from harm. Coondog's shell probably needed to be thicker just to deal with the increased toxicity of competitive eating. No matter what else Coondog did in his life, he'd always be the guy who went to Japan and met the *oogui* greats. That gave him a mythic power of his own. Now he could tell whatever tale he wanted. He could even tell me, his own chronicler, that he'd land in JFK Airport a changed man, purged of his impulse to eat competitively:

"When I get back, I'm out, I'm done."

I knew him well enough by now to know better.

Coondog won the hot-dog contest in Harajuku. He ate against Tazawa and Kenji, who had agreed, like the gentlemen they are, to give Coondog his rematch. Coondog consumed eight Nathan's dogs in just shy of three minutes, beating Tazawa by thirty seconds and Kenji by even more. He seemed happy. Facing the small crowd that had gathered at the Tokyo Nathan's restaurant to watch him eat, he raised his arms high above his goofy *gaijin* head—Coondog O'Karma, self-appointed kick-starter of foreign appetites—and then uttered his last public statement before flying back to appetites that needed no such assistance:

"God bless America," said Coondog.

A boast, a prayer: God bless America.

part two

THE BIG MAN
FIGHTS BACK

Bill "El Wingador" Simmons, Wing Bowl's
greatest champion. (Bill Walsh)

1

WING BOWL

THE THREE GREAT psychic preoccupations of the human race are sex, death, and eating. Freud missed one. He explained human behavior—"the clash between our biology and society"—in terms of our sex drive, but "it seems to me," writes Paul Rozin, professor of psychology at the University of Pennsylvania, "that he would have had a stronger case with eating." And why not? Eating, like sex, is a vile, animal act. Every bite is a risk. Food can be poison. Food can be infected with tiny devouring agents. Also, eating involves an orifice, which is gross. The anus is an orifice, too. These are truths we choose to forget in order to munch our potato chips in peace—except, of course, when we organize competitive eating contests, and choose instead to flaunt every dumb-animal impulse we've invested 40,000 species-years in civilizing.

Paul Rozin is an expert on the psychic gears that control our food drive. He's got brown, curious eyes, a professorial gray beard, and the kind of academic credentials and reputation that allow him to safely be seen in public with a guy writing a book about competitive eating. On the day before Christmas in 2004, he met me over lunch. He glanced quickly at the menu, ordered a salmon burger—"That's simple"—and, when it arrived, dug in with gusto. I had read some of Rozin's papers and was particularly interested in his stuff on cross-cultural food attitudes. In that seminal 1999 paper in *Appetite*, Rozin and his coauthors had quantified how Americans derive far less pleasure from food compared with the French, the Belgians, and the Japanese—and I had also looked into a separate track of his work that concerned the origins of disgust. Rozin writes that when we encounter a disgusting thing, such as a piece of rotting food, we're forced to acknowledge that "we are animals." And animals die. And humans don't want to die. Therefore, disgust is a defense mechanism, a way to distinguish us from the animals and hence "a way to suppress concerns about death."

An eating contest does not exactly distinguish us from the animals. Once, at a hamburger contest in a New Jersey diner, I chatted with a retired nurse named Kathy Stelnick. Kathy was there because of her daughter, nineteen-year-old Kate Stelnick. Kate was an honorary official at the contest. She had recently become famous for being the first person to eat a particular eleven-pound cheeseburger ("Ye Olde 96er," whose beef patty alone weighs 96 ounces) at a particular bar (Denny's Beer Barrel Pub in Clearfield, Pennsylvania,) in under three hours. The only reason Kathy approved of Kate being at this burger contest was that the proceeds were supporting the troops in Iraq. Kathy said competitive eating "is disgusting" and assured me that Kate "doesn't want to be a professional or anything."

Not even if she could make money?

"No amount of money to exploit yourself in front of people like that, like *savages*," Kathy said, adding, "We're very religious. Katie is, too."

"Good one," said one of Kate's friends.

Kate walked over and said, "Buddhism. Ever heard of it?"

But an eating contest isn't savagery, exactly. Rozin pointed this out between bites of his salmon burger. At an eating contest, "people are eating like animals, but in a very complicated constrained human environment," Rozin said. "One of these great contradictions in the ways humans deal with stuff." There's death lurking in an eating contest, and yet death is conquered by it; the contest, while it breaks taboos, imposes new rules of its own: rules of safety, rules of decorum (no "reversal of fortune"), logistical boundaries like time limits. Encase gluttony in bulletproof glass; display it in the public square. Have your cake and gorge on it, too.

In my year on the circuit so far, I had seen mostly death avoidance. I'd seen people like Coondog O'Karma, who were using contests to outrun death in an existential sense—"I'm forty-nine, I figure this is my last chance"— and eaters like Sonya Thomas and Takeru Kobayashi, who seemed to make death disappear by creating an ethereal world of food. Gluttony without consequence, gorging without fatness.* I'd even met a woman in New Orleans, Tootie Williams, who wondered if Sonya's superhuman control over her own stomach might not be a boon for civilization more generally. "The pharmaceutical companies are always tryin' to figure out how to get this magic pill," Tootie said. She pronounced "pill" like "peel." "If you can channel into their minds, figure out what kind of chemical is firin' in their minds, to make them be able to do that," then Big Pharma could make a pill to make you skinny, to cure your cancer, to make you live forever.

So, it was easy to find death avoidance, but not so easy to find death-embrace—unless I looked in one special place, and at one special contest.

Luckily, that place was quite close.

Philadelphia, my hometown.

Wing Bowl, Philly's epic chicken-wing contest.

By the time of my lunch with Rozin, I had been researching Wing Bowl for six months. I had interviewed all the principals and written an article about it. Still, Wing Bowl eluded me. It was too crazy, too big and confusing—so my hope, in meeting Rozin, had been to throw a hail-Mary, to offload my head into his, and perhaps even to persuade him to attend Wing Bowl 13 himself. Fortunately, Rozin was fascinated by the idea of Wing Bowl. Right off the bat, he asked me a string of detailed questions about Wing Bowl's history, its rules, personalities, controversies, finances, pageantry. Rozin had never been to Wing Bowl, but he had seen a hot-pepper contest once, and had chatted with the pepper champ, Don Lerman, and the experience had persuaded him that pro eating, in a broad sense, was "this great lark" that fused Americans' love of big food, our passion for competitive sports of

---

* Sometimes an eater would make his death-avoidance explicit. "My understanding of gluttony is having something in excess," e-mailed a young born-again Christian eater named Hall Hunt. "As far as I can tell I am not eating in excess because I am using every single calorie I am eating." And Hall Hunt gave me an example. He started with the number of calories he had consumed in a Nathan's hot dog quali (6,285), then estimated the number of calories he burns in a day (2,550), giving him a weekly caloric burn of 17,850, meaning that during his Nathan's week "I could consume 1,652 calories every other day to break even at 17,850 calories consumed and burnt," which is "not too hard to do"—eating just 1,652 calories every other day—"since my normal diet consists mostly of chicken, vegetables, fruits, nuts, yogurt, oatmeal," etc. . . .

every size and reach (Rozin grew up a Brooklyn Dodgers fan, and his son is a professional juggler), and our mania for ranking every human capability in hierarchical lists (a tendency that always flabbergasted his French colleagues).

If Rozin couldn't explain the idiosyncrasies of Wing Bowl, who could?

We talked for fifteen minutes. I told him everything I knew. Then he pulled out his scheduler and made a note in the box for February 4, 2005, five weeks hence—the date of Wing Bowl 13.

Rozin smiled and looked up.

My pen trembled.

"What a crazy species," is what Rozin said.

In the simplest terms, Wing Bowl is a radio promotion. It may be the largest pure radio promotion in the country. Wing Bowl is owned, trademarked, and produced by 610 WIP-AM, a sports talk radio station in greater Philadelphia. WIP is itself owned by Infinity Broadcasting, a division of the Viacom, Inc., media empire: CBS, MTV, VH1, Paramount, Simon & Schuster, etc., etc.* In 1993, two of WIP's deejays created Wing Bowl as a stunt to boost ratings for their *Morning Show.* Today the show, which airs from 5:30 to 10:00 a.m., Monday through Friday, is one of WIP's flagship products—it's the show on WIP with the most listeners and the fifth most popular morning show in the Philadelphia market—owing in no small part to the fact that *Morning Show* deejays talk about Wing Bowl every single day for two and a half months, starting in November and ending on the day of Wing Bowl. The date changes from year to year. Like Easter.

Wing Bowl season begins after Thanksgiving. That's when the *Morning Show* deejays, Al Morganti and Angelo Cataldi, start trolling for eaters. Anyone who wants to compete need only call the station and propose an eating "stunt"—a promise to consume a certain quantity of a certain food or non-food item in a certain period of time. If the *Morning Show's* producer, Joe Waechter, likes the stunt, he patches the call to Al and Angelo for final approval, then Waechter schedules a day for the caller to visit the WIP studio,

---

* Viacom would later split into separate broadcast and cable companies, with the radio stations accruing to the new broadcast entity, CBS Corp.

on the seventh floor of a nondescript office building in Bala Cynwyd, Pennsylvania. On that day, the caller brings his food to the studio and signs a release form saying he won't sue WIP if he chokes and dies. (Occasionally an eater signs the form *after* the stunt.) Then he eats, on-air, while the WIP deejays time him. If he succeeds, he wins a slot in Wing Bowl. There are about twenty-five slots total, sometimes more, sometimes less, and the last slot goes to the winner of a "Wing-Off" held in January. The returning champion gets a bye. On Wing Bowl Eve, WIP holds a "weigh-in" ceremony attended by all the eaters. WIP staffers give the eaters a handful of VIP passes, and the eaters rush off to Kinko's and make stacks of counterfeits.

The contest itself is held on the Friday before the Super Bowl. Doors open at 5:00 a.m. Admission is free. By six, the Wachovia Center, where the Philadelphia 76ers play, is 20,000 bodies heavier.

The event officially begins as soon as WIP's overnight deejay, Big Daddy Graham, parades a live chicken around the arena while wearing a thong, trailed by a cadre of strippers in fat suits. What follows, for the next hour and a half, is the real meat of Wing Bowl—not the contest, but the gladiatorial procession of eaters and their "entourages," which can number anywhere from four to fifty, depending upon on their success at Kinko's. Some eaters walk and some ride on floats, the best of which are the product of hundreds of man-hours. If an eater's float is elaborate enough, it may win the Waechter Cup, named after the *Morning Show*'s producer: a jockstrap pinned to a piece of plywood.

Another important part of Wing Bowl is the breasts. Wing Bowl breasts have two types of owners: average girls in the crowd, who flash them to great acclaim; and the eighty or so "Wingettes," working for WIP, who present them in as alluring a fashion as possible without drawing the wrath of the FCC. Some Wingettes are strippers and the rest are fans. They stand on the Wachovia stage during the eating portion of Wing Bowl, which starts at eight.

The eaters sit at tiers of long tables on the stage, with the top eaters on the topmost tier. Wings are distributed on paper plates of twenty wings each. Wing procurement is the job of the Wingettes, who are assigned to monitor specific eaters. The first eating period is fourteen minutes long. The eaters gorge, and when they run out of wings, their Wingettes bring a new plate. "Judges"—including the chief judge, former National League umpire Eric Gregg, who was so famously overweight that baseball officials once gave him a leave of absence to ship off to a weight-loss clinic—pace in front of the tables to make sure no one's cheating. This is necessary, because the prize is substantial enough to make cheating worthwhile: a car.

At the end of fourteen minutes, the judges count the wings. If an eater has left meat on the bone, he may get docked. Gregg eliminates all eaters except the top ten. There's a second fourteen-minute period, then another round of judging to determine the top five, then a final two-minute eat-off.

The winner is crowned with a rubber chicken.

There are other wing-eating contests in other cities. The official IFOCE wing championship is held each fall in Buffalo, attracting several thousand. Smaller events have sprung up at radio stations in Pittsburgh, Columbus, Austin, and Denver, and at prep schools in the greater Philadelphia area. These bootleg wing bowls—some of whose promoters have received threatening letters from WIP attorneys—are but flecks of gristle on the massive tumescent bone of the One True Wing Bowl, whose live audience is the largest in all of competitive eating, worldwide, period.

Of course, competitive eating is a small pond. In the larger pond of Philly sports events, Wing Bowl barely registers. The Eagles average 67,674 per home game; the Phillies draw 33,316. In thirteen years, Wing Bowl's cumulative attendance can't be more than 100,000 to 150,000. The Eagles crack that in a month. Wing Bowl's radio audience is hard to estimate. WIP's ratings swing dramatically. In the summer, the station has dipped as low as sixteenth overall in the Philly market, but in the winter, thanks to football (and now Wing Bowl), WIP can go as high as tenth—and, with its key demographic, as high as third. Its key demo is the coveted "P1" listener: male, age twenty-five to fifty-four, cash to spend. In the winter of 2004, 300,000 or so listeners tuned to WIP every week, most of them men. You can certainly live and work in Philadelphia or its suburbs and stay ignorant of Wing Bowl. In the grand scheme, it's not such a big deal.

That is a rational argument.

But Wing Bowl is not rational.

•   •   •

"I would like to think that Al, who came up with the original idea, has a blueprint," says Cataldi, one morning after wrapping his show. "But you had no blueprint, right, Al?"

Al, sitting on the windowsill, looking bored, shrugs. "No," he says. "I don't even have a pen."

"It took on its own life," says Cataldi. "You know, it put us on the map a little, but that wasn't even the intent. The intent was to fill some time on what we figured would be a rather dead week."

Cataldi credits Morganti with being the idea guy. Morganti credits Cataldi with being the genius promoter. Cataldi is the manic one, the one with the broad Italian nose and the thick body, the charisma, the loud deep voice. Morganti is the misanthrope: sartorially grubby, introverted, loves animals but hates people. Both are in their fifties. Both are former sports writers at the *Philadelphia Inquirer*. These are the men responsible. One day in January 1993, Morganti mused, on-air, that since the Philadelphia Eagles were such losers—and since the Buffalo Bills, though they'd lost two Super Bowls in a row, were at least getting to throw fun citywide parties—WIP ought to sponsor its own party, in Philly, featuring a chicken-wing contest in honor of Buffalo's signature snack. It was cynical and pointless and self-hating, and the callers loved it instantly. Within minutes, Morganti had a line on free wings and two willing competitors. One moment, a slow, barren sports month in Philly and a lot of dead air; the next, Wing Bowl.

WIP planned the first Wing Bowl in a week and a half, quick and dirty. At the time, the *Morning Show* did a remote broadcast every Friday from the lobby of a midscale hotel. The deejays scheduled Wing Bowl for a Friday. They didn't even bother to run their plans by the hotel, thinking no one would show. They were wrong, by 150 bodies. The two competitors were Doc, whose real name is lost to history, and New Jersey's Carmen Cordero, an overweight chain-smoker with a dirty mustache who showed up wearing a ratty old white T-shirt on which he'd written, in crude letters, BEAST FROM THE EAST. Carmen ate 100 wings, looked over at his opponent, realized he was far ahead, leaned back, and lit a cigarette.

He won a small barbecue grill.

"Carmen," the referee said, "you just won Wing Bowl. What're you going to do now?"

"Go to Wing Bowl Two," Carmen said.

"We were all like, 'I guess we're having a Wing Bowl Two,'" says Dave Helfrich, WIP's former promotions manager.

This was smart strategy. Kindle, don't smother; let the listeners stoke the fire, then get out of the way of the blaze. Wing Bowl 2 took place in a bar, Wing Bowl 3 in a midsized nightclub, Wing Bowl 4 in a large concert club. In four years the crowd had grown from 150 to 6,000. Local TV morning shows caught on, dispatching anchors to do live shots. Around Wing Bowl 4, WIP recruited Wingettes to help handle the plates. "It was THE best thing we did," says Cataldi. "It was THE defining moment." Cataldi affects a look of shock. "They were glorified waitresses! Who's gonna do that wearin' a bikini? We had no *idea* so many people would want to."

"You should have a section for Wingettes alone," said Mitch Blackman, owner of the Rib Ranch and official wing supplier of Wing Bowl. I was interviewing Blackman at his restaurant. "That's really the only reason we do it. If there were just twenty-five eaters there, you'd never get 25,000 fans in the stadium. It's all about Wingettes. You need any pictures?"

He pulled out a two-inch-high stack of three-by-fives. Most were beef-cake shots, flashlit, of Blackman standing next to Wingettes and smiling like a proud tourist in front of the Grand Canyon. The topmost photo showed an attractive blonde wearing a bustier that exposed the aureole of her right breast.

"I think I can see her nipple," I said.

"Oh, are you kidding me?" said Blackman. He turned around and reached behind his TODAY'S SPECIAL slate and pulled out three more photos. He plunked them on the counter. "These I have to keep in the back 'cause they're extra-risqué," he said. "Katie." I was looking, apparently, at Katie: a red-haired woman, pushing thirty-five, shot from a distance of maybe six feet, wearing a sequined American flag tank top and a black skirt which she was peeling aside to expose, for the camera, her shaved pubis, above which she had painted an American flag.

The next two shots were extreme close-ups.

"She's great," Blackman said. "Katie is great. She is so nice. Shaving Katie."

"Is she a stripper?"

"No, no." Blackman seemed offended. "Works in a doctor's office."

A lot of the Wingettes were professional strippers, but lots weren't. Lots were like Shaving Katie. *Workaday* girls, not working girls. The same phenomenon was visible with the corps of Wing Bowl contestants. As the event jumped to the Spectrum for Wing Bowl 6, drawing 10,000, it was clear that Wing Bowl was no longer just a blue-collar drinkfest. Yes, Wing Bowl still spoke union hall, its native language; it still attracted a robust corps of eaters who considered themselves classic Philly guys. Guys like "Tollman" Joseph Paul, who took a day off from his New Jersey Turnpike Commission job to win Wing Bowl 8. Guys like the Mize, whose crowd-pleasing ability to smash beer cans over his forehead, blood no object, is the reason why an EMT is present at Wing Bowls of today. The Sloth. Big Rig. Belly Donna. Damaging Doug. Yao Bling. Hank the Tank. Flexx. The Tuna.

But there were also middle-class eaters. Bruce "The Norseman" Wulfsberg, an orthopedist, rode into Wing Bowl 11 in a twelve-foot-tall Viking ship he built with the help of his friends, who included a vice president at Campbell's Soup, a deputy director of the Environmental Protection Agency, a city planner, and the school board president of Moorestown, Pennsylvania. One of Wulfsberg's opponents that year was Ira "Dr. Kugel" Thal, a Jewish internist who had separated from his wife. "I needed to do something outrageous," says Thal. "I always wanted to do that and didn't want to have to ask anyone's permission." Thal entered the arena accompanied by a techno version of "Hava Nagila."

Wing Bowl had learned some new languages. It was now fluent in the Pennsylvania Rules of Civil Procedure. It knew how to repair a broken humerus. What's more, Wing Bowl now had some powerful friends. The fourth or fifth most powerful man in the country, Senate Judiciary Chairman Arlen Specter, attended one year, spritzed into the Spectrum through a back door. Then-mayor Ed Rendell had given out trophies to the Wing Bowl winners for several years, and the interesting thing was that nobody at WIP asked him to do it—Rendell just showed up. I myself have discussed Wing Bowl with a sitting U.S. congressman. It happened the Monday night before Wing Bowl 13, at a large sports bar in South Philly. I was there with a notebook, drinking a beer, mingling, when I spotted Bob Brady, the rotund, wavy-haired eminence representing Pennsylvania's first district. Nationally,

Brady is a senior Democratic whip, and locally he chairs Philadelphia's Democratic City Committee. He's the guy whose ring you must kiss, slobberingly, if you want to run for office in the city of brotherly love. Reputation: C-minus legislator, A-plus power broker, profane and ebullient, not to be underestimated. And there he was, sitting at a sports-bar table with his wife and two buddies, wearing an Eagles jersey. He looked like he didn't want to be interrupted.

I interrupted him.

He looked down at the table, rubbed both of his eyes, and mumbled hello.

I told him I was writing a book about Wing Bowl.

Brady lifted his head and looked at me for the first time. He was smirking. "You're going for the Pulitzer, then, huh?"

Brady, to my surprise, went on to recite a factually correct capsule history of Wing Bowl. It's possible that Brady was humoring me, as any smart pol would—*yes, Event X is a wonderful addition to City X's vibrant cultural life,* etcetera—but then I asked Brady if he had ever attended Wing Bowl, and he said that he had. Twice. He pointed to a small white envelope sitting on the table, which he said contained his VIP passes for Wing Bowl 13.*

Brady invited me to sit down at his table, because he was rolling now. Not only had Brady gone to Wing Bowl—he had stories. Funny ones. "Amazing," he said, describing his first Wing Bowl. "We were in line at five in the morning. We had to step over all the beer bottles. We finally figured out what was going on. People had been drinking all night!" He laughed heartily, enjoying the memory. Brady said that, once inside the arena, he'd taken a seat near the hockey penalty box when suddenly he heard people screaming and pointing in his direction. Brady looked up at the Jumbotron, where he saw his face, mega-sized, and instantly understood the source of the commotion. "The girl next to me was goin' like this," said Brady, and he mimed a breast-flashing motion. "I ran and hid!"

I laughed, thanked Brady, and walked away. It took me months before I

---

* I don't know how Brady got his passes, but I do know that Wing Bowl had become such a hot ticket that pols could credibly dole them out as perks to their patrons. According to Dave Davies of the *Daily News,* the mayor's office handed out fourteen Wing Bowl passes in 2003, including two to City Council, two to Democratic City Committee, and four to Shawn Fordham, who ran the mayor's reelection campaign.

could look back and recognize how truly weird it was that we had talked about Wing Bowl for ten full minutes—the congressman and I—as if it were the most natural thing in the world. This was unique. This wasn't happening with any other eating contest, anywhere. Wing Bowl was being integrated into the cultural life of a major American city. A grotesque spectacle was becoming, as improbable as it seemed, a civic institution.

2

EL WINGADOR

RIOR TO WING BOWL 12 in January 2004—which is the year the foul beast evolved from a shallow spectacle into something stranger and darker, less controllable, *realer,* in a fit of punctuated equilibrium that provoked an identity crisis felt citywide—the rubber-chicken crown had been placed eleven times upon seven separate heads. Eleven Wing Bowls, seven champions. All seven were from the greater Philadelphia area, if greater Philadelphia can be seen to include South Jersey. Five men had won once and never repeated. One man, Kevin "Heavy Kevie" O'Donnell, a mortgage banker from Williamstown, New Jersey, won it twice. And one man stood alone. Bill "El Wingador" Simmons, a 322-pound truck driver from South Jersey, had been crowned Wing Bowl champion no fewer than four times. In any Wing Bowl hall of fame, Wingador's bronzed bulk would grace the lobby, his four crowns and four rubber chickens framed reverently in glass, his eyes pointed, like the eyes of all male visitors, toward the Hall of Wingette Polaroids.

Bill's dominance is clear from the newspaper clips, which I started searching in July 2004. They painted a picture of a gentle, highly quotable giant. I learned that in 1999, Bill won his first Wing Bowl with 113 wings. The next year, at Wing Bowl 8, Bill lost to "Tollman" Joe Paul, but Wingador claimed he had been weakened by a case of the stomach flu. Wingador went on to win the next three Wing Bowls easily, finally blasting through the 150-wing barrier at Wing Bowl 11 with 154 wings.

And then, in Wing Bowl 12, the unthinkable happened. Simmons ate just 151 wings, three short of his previous year's total and two wings short of the

top two finishers: Ed "Cookie" Jarvis, the runner-up, and the eventual winner in overtime, ninety-nine-pound Sonya "The Black Widow" Thomas.

Outsiders.

In the news clips, Wingador was noncommittal on the crucial question:
Would he return in 2005 to defend his title? One afternoon in July, five
months after his loss, I got a cell number for Wingador and asked him.

"It's a secret," he said.

Then Bill started talking very quickly, as if he were trapped under a giant
rock high on a mountain somewhere and his cell-phone battery was dying.
As he free-associated, I tried in vain to keep up:

"The wings are cold," he said. "They're hard to strip the meat from.
That's why I was pissed off."

"Why were you pissed off?"

"I was pissed off, because I was beatin' her, and here I'm three wings
behind her, she never finished a plate before me . . . I'm like, Al, how the
fuck—excuse me, how are we tied? I was up six wings . . ."

I typed as fast as I could:

"I just think that they kind of screwed up somehow, big time . . . it was just
all mysterious to me, but, ah, I'm not gonna throw any sour grapes out
there . . . I think it's all political, see, they'd asked me to stay out of it . . . the
local sponsors didn't want me to do it, they were losing money . . . I was
kicking everybody's ass . . . I can understand how the world works, I'm not
stupid, it's a free event . . ."

Apparently Bill was charging 610 WIP-AM, the radio station that runs
Wing Bowl, with robbing him of his rightful prize at Wing Bowl 12, for
"political" and "money" reasons. I tried to get Bill to slow down, to no avail:

"Everything's cool, it's just eating, man, that's all it is, really, I was a great
athlete growing up, I wish I was on ESPN, knocking somebody out, or in a
ring . . . I got shunned on the New Jersey state wing challenge . . . They said,
we don't want you in it—well, why not? . . . They told me I was a ringer. I'm
starting to get shunned . . . It's tough being me . . . I'm not a fat guy, I work
out three times a week . . . I was All-South Jersey in baseball, football . . . I'm
a good athlete, yeah, and I like to win, that's just the competitiveness in me,
and the love of food . . ."

The next day I found myself in Wingador's kitchen.

Like the human stomach, it has two valves, one that connects to the hall-way leading to the front door and the family room, and one that connects to the dining room. Floor space is not ample enough for Wingador to stand and cook and not block traffic. Some of the yellowish wallpaper is peeling. The dominant motif is Pillsbury Doughboy. Wingador considers the Dough-boy his mascot. There is a Doughboy spice rack, a Doughboy clock, a stuffed Doughboy, a Doughboy ceramic plate, and two Doughboy calendars, one of which is four years old. Three wooden chickens hang from a hook above the table near a framed photo of Wingador that was snapped at the moment of his victory in Wing Bowl 9. In the photo you can see, through a scrim of confetti, Bill's hands, upraised, his mullet ably supporting his rubber-chicken crown.*

I compared Bill in the picture with Bill in the flesh, and it seemed that he was even bigger now than at the time the picture was taken. He stood about six-five, with big limbs and a big torso, and broad, leonine jowls sagging from a fleshy face. His hair was short on top, where he'd frosted it blonde in the manner of a Los Feliz skater kid, and longer in the back, terminating in a mass of curls at the neck. You could tell that at one time he'd been drum-tight, but now it almost looked like he was melting.

Bill walked me out to his deck, which overlooked an octagonal above-ground pool. Beyond that, ten yards behind the edge of his backyard, cars throttled past on the New Jersey Turnpike. The noise, he said, never lets up. The vibrations shake the china. I asked if he ever considered moving. "Nah," he said. "Unless I hit it big." He started walking back inside and clucked his tongue skeptically. "You think *that's* gonna happen?"

Bill opened his refrigerator and said I could help myself. "I'm a juice freak, man," he said. "I'm not a soda drinker." I said I liked cranberry juice, so he grabbed a big jug of cran by the handle and poured me a drink. In the fridge, the first thing I saw was a bowl with two marinated chicken breasts, ready to pop on the grill if Wingador got hungry. There was also a three-pound tub

---

*   Bill later took the photo down because he thought it made him look fat. He replaced it with another Doughboy.

of I Can't Believe It's Not Butter and a gallon jug of a brown viscous liquid that turned out to be Wingador's own eponymous "specialty sauce," which he sells to local grocery stores and hawks on a website, elwingadorsauce.com. Bill opened the freezer so I could see the several additional boxes of chicken parts. Later in the interview, when I would ask Bill about his two daughters, Bill would reply, wistfully, "They are the love of my life, man. That, and chicken." Bill's gratitude for the vivid and reliable pleasure of chicken can seem a little nutso. "Chicken, chicken," he said, closing the freezer. "I'm a chicken freak. I have chicken everywhere, man. Well, it's my lobster of the land, you know what I mean?" Bill spoke this as if it were a folk saying. It sounded Steinbeckian: *lobster ulla lan'.*

Bill took me on a short tour of the rest of the house, starting with the garage, where he walked up to a large heavy bag and punched it twice, quickly. He pointed to a stand-alone freezer. "You could put a couple bodies in it," he said, and flipped open the lid to let me see the frozen meats. "We go through so much stuff," he said. We walked back into the kitchen and Bill asked how old I was.

"Twenty-six."

"If I was twenty-six I'd be comatose," he said. "I used to party all the time. Now I've settled down."

In the kitchen, Bill pulled out a bottle of El Wingador Sauce. "I'd give you a bottle, but I have to mail these two out," he said, holding the bottle delicately, label facing forward, like a spokesmodel on *The Price Is Right.* He dug a taco from the fridge and told me to put some sauce on the taco and crunch it down. I did. It was delicious.* "There's no butter, no oil," he said. "It's got honey in it. It's made with a vegetable puree. No carbs. NO carbs. Don't think so."

---

* I say this not to shill for Bill's sauce, but to point out, perhaps, the prejudices that complicate the plight of a competitive eater who wants to cross over into the culinary arts. At first I assumed Bill's sauce was a gimmick; then I tasted it, and was surprised at its complexity; then I felt guilty for thinking it was a gimmick; then, to appease my guilty conscience, I proselytized the sauce's virtues to everyone I met. I think this is why Philadelphia is full of powerful people who will not shut up about Bill's sauce. In interviews, they mention it often and early. "I like Bill. Bill's a good guy. He makes a good sauce, too."

He looked at the label to make sure. On the front, it read:

> In 1999, El Wingador, famed Wing Slayer, won his first WIP Wing
> Bowl . . . long famous for his wing sauce, El Wingador now makes
> his sauce available to you.

"Let me see," he said, checking the back. "Oh wait. Total carbs, five grams, which is nothing. Four percent."

At this point, Debbie walked into the kitchen wearing a softball uniform. Athletic and pretty, a tough chick with a Jersey accent and straight, shoulder-length brown hair, Debbie is Bill's second wife, twelve years younger than the big man. She listened as Bill talked about the sports agent he'd just retained. "He thinks the Wingador name should be doing something locally," Bill said. "At least locally. At least. Because everybody knows who I am, you know? Because I don't care if I sell furniture, you know what I mean? If you put the name up there. Now, I'm not trying to sound greedy, but I worked hard to get this name to where it is, but, you know—and it's not like I'm out to get stuff just for me me me. I'm trying to take care of my family, trying to establish something good." Bill listed his charitable activities: donating toys to the children's hospital, feeding the homeless—"all that crazy stuff," he said.

I asked Bill and Debbie how they had met.

"Hot and heavy," Bill said.

"A friend of a friend, I guess you could say," Debbie said.

"Six years [ago]? Seven? That long?"

"Yeah, that long," said Debbie, laughing.

"And she fell in love with me and that was it," Bill said.

"Yeah. I had a stalker."

"STALKER? I didn't stalk you."

Debbie laughed.

"I stalked you?" said Bill.

"Yeah, you were bangin' on my neighbor's—"

"I didn't bang your neighbor!" laughed Bill.

After a few minutes, Debbie left for a softball game. Bill's cell phone had been ringing this whole time, and every time it rang, he would answer it and tell the caller that he couldn't talk because he was doing an interview. Now it rang again. "My phone never stops ringing, as you can see," Bill said, picking it up and checking the incoming number. "This is Gervase from *Survivor*," he said, then held the phone in front of my face so I could see he wasn't lying. The caller ID read: *Gervis*. Gervase Peterson, a youth basketball coach from Philly, was a cast member of the inaugural season of the CBS reality show *Survivor*, where he distinguished himself through aggressive laziness. Gervase got kicked off the island and made a soft landing on the Philly celebrity bartending circuit, which is how Bill met him.

Bill answered on the third ring. "Gervase!" he said. "This phone call is gonna put you in the *Philadelphia* magazine article! They're right in my kitchen! I said, 'This is Gervase calling,' they said, 'Get out!' Now he's writin' stuff down. So you're gonna be in an article. Whassup my man, how you doin'." There was a brief pause. "Tomorrow night?" Bill exhaled. "Nothin'. Why, what's up?" Another pause. *"Where?"* Bill's voice was hushed. "I'm there," he said. "I'm there. What time?"

Bill hung up and told me that Gervase had invited him to tomorrow's release party for the 2004 Eagles Cheerleader calendar, at the Eagles' NovaCare practice facility in South Philly. All the cheerleaders would be there.

"Sometimes it's *nice* being El Wingador," Wingador said.*

We'd been talking for more than an hour. I was getting ready to leave, but I still didn't have an answer to the question I had asked him on the phone. Would Wingador return to Wing Bowl 13 in 2005? It seemed impossible that he could say no.

He seemed to be saying no.

He explained that he suffered from heartburn so intense it kept him up nights and doubled him over in crashing pain. "What I've eaten in my past has just kind of screwed up my belly a little bit," he said. It was so worrisome, in fact, that Debbie had lobbied him to stay out of last year's Wing Bowl. To retire as the four-time champ. But five was such a nice round number. With five titles he could retire with some dignity. With a little bit of

---

* Out of fairness to Bill: there isn't a straight male Eagles fan in Philadelphia who wouldn't have reacted the same way.

grace. He could open a sports bar or something. He could stop driving a truck, finally, after nineteen years.

And then Sonya ruined everything.

When Cataldi announced the final tallies at Wing Bowl 12, Bill looked up at the stands and saw his two daughters, and they were crying, and his wife, Debbie, was yelling at the security guards, and the reporters started crowding around him until he had to swipe his giant mitts at the cameras to get them away, and he felt a flash of what could only be described as rage. To his credit, he wiped his sauce-smeared mouth, walked over to his conqueror, and kissed her on the cheek—but the loss "really took a lot out of me," Bill told me, there in his kitchen. "It kind of devastated me at first. And it's not just me, it affects [people] all around me, you know? I go to work, I gotta hear people. 'Oh, you let her beat ya.' And no, she *didn't* beat me. But then I gotta explain it. It gets me aggravated. That's where the stress kicks in." He laughed hugely.

It looked like I wouldn't get an answer at all. Bill had just spent an hour telling me that it didn't matter, it's just a wing contest, what are you gonna do.

Then Bill leaned forward and crushed his hands together.

"To be honest with you," he said, "I want to fuckin' get in there and beat that bitch."

3

BIG COUNTRY

IP-AM DEEJAYS discussing Sonya Thomas:

> —Last year, we had a ninety-nine-year-old woman who—
> —Ninety-nine *pounds*.
> —Can we *get* the ninety-nine-year-old woman?
> —Wow. That would be spectacular.
> —It was shocking.
> —She's really like the carnival freak show.
> —When Al and I were up that close, it was scary to watch.
> —She's amazing. She's fuckin' like a cell phone. [Size-wise.]
> —I'm tellin' you, it's like watching a magic act.
> —Yeah. There's no meat left on the bones.
> —You're watching it and you can't believe it. I don't know how—
>   it's *so clean.*
> —She can suck the chrome off a bumper.

Sonya is thirty-seven years old, but you only believe it if you get very, very close. If you don't, she looks eighteen. That black scrunchie holding her ponytail. Those star-shaped barrettes where devil's horns would be. Halos of blue eyeshadow. She speaks in clipped English punctuated by an immigrant's tics—quick laughs and question marks to make sure she's being understood. "I like action movie," she says, describing her taste in American pop culture. "Like, real action movie. Not, like, funny action. Sometimes war movie. I like that. War movie. Real war, right? I like that kind of movie.

Comedy, too. Comedy?" Movie-watching is her hobby. Her other hobby is driving. She takes long drives to nowhere in particular. She owns a red Pontiac Grand Am, and she drives it very, very fast.

The luxury of a long drive in a red Grand Am was not available to Sonya in her native country of South Korea, where Thomas was born with the name "Son Kyong" and lived until she was in her twenties. Her home was Kunsan, a hilly, churchy port city of 300,000 on the Yellow Sea, next to a U.S. military base housing the 8th Fighter Wing, nicknamed "the Wolf Pack." When Sonya was five, she spent Christmas day with an American military couple at the urging of her mother, who wanted Sonya to "have a chance to experience another culture—and a full meal, for a change," says Sonya. Much has been made of the fact that Sonya and her siblings grew up poor: her mother a maid, her father a carpenter. At least as crucial to her hunger, however, was the stifling nature of South Korea. She worked as a typist for a shipping company. "In that time I was a little bit heavier," she said. "Forty pounds heavier. I don't eat any meals. I just eat all junk food . . . typist, sitting down, answer the phone, sometimes get sleepy. I don't like that job so I change it." When she put herself through restaurant school and looked for new jobs, men told her, "Oh, you are a woman, you cannot do this." So she moved to America.

Sonya worked at an air force base in Maryland managing a Burger King. She worked ten-, twelve-, fourteen-hour shifts and saved her money. In 2002 she watched the Nathan's contest on TV. She had always wanted "to show my face on TV," she says. "I want to be there. Really! It's an honor to be on TV." She decided to practice. "I bought a hot dog from 7-Eleven and try to eat one hot dog, right? But I couldn't finish one hot dog per minute!" Sonya laughs. "Yeaaaah! I couldn't swallow!" Eventually, after more practice, Sonya entered her first contest: a 2003 Nathan's qualifier at the Molly Pitcher Travel Plaza, a rest stop on the New Jersey Turnpike. Sonya ate 18 hot dogs in 12 minutes. She felt "sooo, soooooo happy . . . They think I'm just this woman, walked in and did this hot dog! Nobody paid attention to me!"

Sonya's Molly Pitcher performance earned her a spot in the finals, where she broke the women's record with twenty-five dogs consumed. In August 2003, she took third in the U.S. Chicken Wing–Eating Championship in

Buffalo. In October, despite never having eaten a pulled-pork sandwich in her life, she ate twenty-three in ten minutes to win $1,250 and the world title. She did not shimmy like Kobayashi or puff her cheeks like Eric Booker, nor did she apply post-contest makeup like Carlene LeFevre or wear funny hats like Dale "Mouth of the South" Boone, which is perhaps why Sonya, despite her immediate dominance, attracted little national attention until late 2003, when her friend Coondog O'Karma told her about a little wing contest in Philadelphia.

Coondog, in a mischievous mood, e-mailed Angelo Cataldi and said he knew a ninety-nine-pound girl who could beat El Wingador. Cataldi knew a great storyline when he saw one, and gave Sonya a bye into Wing Bowl 12. She beat the Big Man, but the Big Man accused her of dropping her chicken on the floor. Witnesses were procured for both sides. Wingador was seen both cleaning his bones (judge Eric Gregg) and doing such a poor job that "I could have an entire meal off the meat that Bill left on his bones" (*New York Post* scribe Gersh Kuntzman).

But a few months later, Sonya beat Bill in a hot-dog contest, and she kept winning other contests, too. Brian "Yellowcake" Subich, a top-twenty eater, tells a story about a baked-bean contest from summer 2004. The field included Sonya, Subich, and Cookie Jarvis. After just two and a half minutes, George Shea announced that Sonya was almost done with her 8.4 pounds of beans. "I said, 'You have to be freaking kidding me,'" says Subich. "What does she do? Pour 'em down her shirt? Put 'em into a plastic bag?" Jarvis lifted his head, glanced at Sonya, registered what Subich calls "the most crestfallen look you could ever imagine," and vomited beans through his nostrils.

Sonya quit Burger King and lived off her savings so she could concentrate on contests. (Eventually she got antsy and went back to her old job.) She was forcing a realignment in American eating, and none of the newspaper feature writers now flocking to the Black Widow and filing long profiles could unpack her riddle. They only got so far before Sonya would flash them a wink of that blue-haloed eye and describe, as if it explained everything, her earnest love for her adoptive country. The contests, America, freedom—it was all, to Sonya, intertwined.

"In America," she says, "if you have desire, you can do anything. Is big. *Big*." She holds her hands out wide. "Big country!"

"Sonya Thomas, she's so small, it looks as though she could not eat a tin of cottage cheese, Eric Booker's so large it looks like he has his own ecosystem, with an El Niño underneath his arm, and roving around the orb that is his body . . ."

This is George Shea, riffing on size differential, one of the great arrows in his promotional quiver. The thrill of contrast. Before they were usurped by scrawny folks like Sonya, the great eaters were people like El Wingador: big men. The "Big Man"—it deserves to be capitalized—denotes a certain type of competitor that has dominated American eating contests going all the way back. El Wingador is one in a great heaving line of gargantuan dudes, mostly ethnic Italians and Poles and Irish and in recent years a few African-Americans, who've racked up the lion's share of the titles and trophies and cash. The 320-pound Frank "Large" Dellarosa, the first great capacity eater, downed twenty-one-and-a-half Nathan's hot dogs in 1991 (the famous "21 in '91") despite having no discernible neck; Ed Krachie, the six-foot-six enormity from Maspeth, Queens, won the Nathan's contest in 1995 and 1996, sometimes rolling up his shirtsleeves to display the tattoo on his left bicep that said MASTER OF DISASTER, perhaps referring to his ability to throw down thirteen, fourteen, sixteen beers in a single sitting. Within the Big Man genre are several flavors. Eric Booker's bulk is planetary—solid and evenly distributed around a dense core—whereas Ed "Cookie" Jarvis, who usually weighs less than Eric, is amorphous, like a cloud of hot interstellar gas. Ed often wears a fanny pack that rests snug against his belly's front and gives the impression of being an auxiliary stomach, a stomach annex.

Citizens "of enormous physical stature," as George Shea calls them.

You know. Big Men.

And not just Big Men. *American* Big Men, descendants of a long line of Big Men originally lured from Europe by the smell of the New World's dinner table. They came to see if the stories were true: stories of the "gross plenty" written about by Americans like Washington Irving ("meats, poultry, vegetables, excellent bread, pies, puddings—food seems to be wasted—as if of no value") and European travelers like Isabella Bird, who wrote

rapturously of New England apples, "huge balls," she gushed, "red and yellow, such as are caricatured in wood, weighing down the fine large trees.
There were heaps of apples on the ground, and horses and cows were eating
them in the fields, and rows of freight cars at all the stations were laden with
them, and little boys were selling them in the cars..." A riot of food: the
very land edible, apples *paving the damn ground*—this was food porn to the
Euro-hungry. Not the starving; the starving couldn't read, were too far
gone. But the working-class hungry salivated, wondering if the New World
lived up to all the hype—not just about food, but about wealth and opportunity and justice and equality, too.

So they came, 30 million in the century starting in the 1820s, and found
war, and child labor, and discrimination, and anti-Semitism and slavery—
The Man's greatest hits—but they stayed, because they'd also found the
food. The other stuff was, to put it kindly, a work in progress, but the food
was real: abundant, available even to the working poor, a normal weekday's
meals equivalent to once-a-year feasts back home. The immigrants appreciated American abundance the most, and their glorying in America's tricked-
out table spread ushered out the earnest Puritan palate—the idea of food as
mere fuel, like hay to a horse—and ushered in an earnest indulgence. Immigrants were the first American gluttons. "Don't you remember," recalled
one Italian from New York, quoted in Hasia Diner's *Hungering for America*,
"how our *paesani* here in America ate to their heart's delight till they were
belching like pigs and how they dumped mountains of uneaten food out of
the window?" Charles Dickens visited America in 1842, and wrote this dark
scene in *Martin Chuzzlewit* in which the protagonist sits down to dinner
after arriving in New York:

> The poultry, which may perhaps be considered to have formed
> the staple of the entertainment—for there was a turkey at the
> top, a pair of ducks at the bottom, and two fowls in the middle—
> disappeared as rapidly as if every bird had had the use of its wings,
> and had flown in desperation down a human throat. The oysters,
> stewed and pickled, leaped from their capacious reservoirs, and slid
> by scores into the mouths of the assembly. The sharpest pickles
> vanished, whole cucumbers at once, like sugar-plums, and no man

winked his eye. Great heaps of indigestible matter melted away as ice before the sun. It was a solemn and an awful thing to see.

Dickens understood the grotesque side of the American appetite, but he didn't acknowledge that, in George Washington's formulation, the "Lords and Proprietors of a vast Tract of Continent" needed a similarly vast appetite to tame it. There was a moral component to all that feasting that wouldn't have made sense in the Old World. The American glutton wasn't just a fat guy. America nurtured him on the fat of the very land whose taming demanded the kind of energy that only a capacious stomach could provide. America needed the Big Man to tame the frontier. The Big Man went west, spawning real-life heroes like Davy Crockett and tall-tale heroes like Paul Bunyan, whose logging-camp cook used bacon skates to grease the outsized flapjack pan. From America's primordial soup of plenty, the Big Man had finally oozed, jaw clacking, ready to devour the continent.

Bill Simmons eats the fried green tomato. He eats the eight-inch pizza. He eats the goopy seafood ravioli appetizer, he downs the Caesar salad, he chugs two Cokes in five minutes. And the entrees haven't even arrived.

Oh yes, Wingador is just getting started. Here at this Knoxville restaurant, in the lull before the main course, Bill looks across the table at his five-year-old daughter, Felicia. She's clutching a crayon, using it to color a picture of a hamburger on her paper place mat.

"Did you color that?" says Bill. "*Ooooh.* You used all the right colors and everything. The bun, the lettuce . . ." Bill trails off, shakes his head. He says, with no trace of irony, "It's makin' me *hungry.*"

The waitress brings our main courses. I watch Bill checking all the entrées out, and I realize that we're all in trouble—Bill's wife, Debbie, his daughter Felicia and eight-year-old stepdaughter Ashley, and me. Not content to be lord of his own "Chicken & Things" plate (a football-sized chicken breast smothered with cheese and breakfast ham, a scoop of mashed potatoes, a dollop of broccoli), Bill is doing recon on all of ours. Over and over, his fork stabs into enemy territory as we relinquish our dinners, bit by bit:

"I'll steal some of Mommy's butter off her potatoes," says Bill. "She don't need alla that." He swabs the butter on his broccoli and lets out a muffled sound of awe. "We're huge vegetable eaters," he tells me, staring at an entrée with a ten-to-one meat-to-veggie ratio. "How much broccoli do we eat, hon?" Debbie agrees they eat lots of broccoli. The waitress comes over and asks if Bill wants dessert. "Oh, you're killing me," he says. "I'm on a diet." He orders a "regular portion" of Oreo pie regardless, then turns toward his daughter Ashley, who's still working on her personal pizza. "How is it? It's good, isn't it? I'll take that crust when you're done." Ashley gives him her pizza crust, which he chomps with an "mmph." He repays her with a piece of his cheese-and-ham-crusted chicken. "Taste that," he says. "That's, like, smoked or somethin'."

Bill turns to Felicia.

"Yes, pig?" says Felicia.

"What'd you call me?"

"You eat *evewyfwing*," lisps Felicia.

"Well, there's a lot of starvin' fathers out there," says Bill.

"So you make up for them?" says Debbie.

Bill turns to me. "I don't normally eat like this," he says.

"Who are you kiddin'?" asks Debbie.

Unlike the Kobayashis and Sonya Thomases of the world, who make a show of eating noncontest meals mincingly and describe their workout routines in loving detail, Bill is a proud gastronome in the simplest sense of the word: he loves food sensually, loves being surrounded and enclosed by the best of it, the stuff he remembers eating when he was growing up. He ate lots of cornmeal. Cornmeal, every meal. Bill's parents weren't poor—dad a salesman for Aramark, mom a housewife—but they lived with little cushion, hence the cornmeal, which Bill's mom whipped into the most filling formulations her Puerto Rican culinary lineage could muster. Cornmeal: that's why he thinks he's so big. No steak, no shrimp. "Pizza was like a holiday." To escape cornmeal, he busted over to his cousin Alexis's house, where Bill's aunt cooked *pollo guiso*, chicken stew with red sauce, peppers, and onions. "That was something he didn't get a lot of," says Alexis. "He'd come over and eat whatever was at the bottom of the pan. He taught us how to eat chicken. He'd pick up the bones and say, 'You didn't eat this right. Suck the marrow out. Pick the bones.'" The gristle and everything. "I can tell ya," says Alexis, "one Thanksgiving we had to have *two* turkeys because of his ass."

At the restaurant, we pay the bill and shove off. Bill packs his family into the big black Winnebago-converted van and steers it onto I-40 for the ten-mile drive to the Tennessee Valley Fair. Tomorrow, Bill will speed-eat hamburgers against Knoxville's hungriest at the fair. He's been invited by the IFOCE to play the role of the out-of-town ringer. Tonight Bill wants to get a feel for the fairgrounds before tomorrow's contest. Scope it out a little. Maybe hook up Felicia and Ashley with a couple of Ferris Wheel rides. This is Bill's primary justification for the trip: he says it's a cheap, fun vacation for his family, although when I talked to him on the phone a few days ago, he didn't believe it would be cheap—the IFOCE wasn't reimbursing him for his gas or hotel. If Bill wins tomorrow, he'll move on to the November finals in Chattanooga, some expenses paid, with a chance to win a few thousand bucks. "They're expecting me to win in Knoxville," he told me, "but you never know. There might be a fuckin' hillbilly who comes up with big fuckin' suspenders, you know? Some hillbilly that lives in a fuckin' port-o-pot, you know what I mean?"

We pull into the fairgrounds around 7:00 p.m. It's still light out. A warm, sticky-sweet halo of smoke hovers above the rows of barbecue stands, and the fairgoers seem content to stroll lazily and suck up the food smells. On a day like today, it feels like every barbecue maestro within 100 miles has gathered here at the fair to conduct a symphony of aromas into the Knoxville air. This, as Bill likes to say, is what gets his tail wagging. Walking along a line of tightly packed food stalls, he pauses at a metallic barbecue shack that looks like a stiff breeze could tip it over.

"Deb!" he says. "It wouldn't be that hard to make something like that. Could call it 'El Wingador's Chicken Shack,' go around the city and sell chicken . . ."

A few minutes ago Bill was itching to leave. Now he's walking slowly. He wanders by the carousel and says, apropos of nothing, "Ah, I wish I could be a kid again." Debbie and the kids want to go, but Bill's stuck in a reverie of sense memories of the great meals of his youth, memories triggered by all this bounty—apple dumplings, pulled pork, frozen cheesecake, frozen bananas, hot dogs, corny dogs, tootsie dogs, stromboli, funnel cakes, elephant ears,

Polish sausages, turkey legs the color of an open wound, red continents of beef ribs, fried pickles and green tomatoes and Oreos, all of it beckoning Bill so strongly that he can't think straight, can't stand still while his daughter loses a quarter to a carny worker's rigged game. Bill turns to me, spreads his arms, and says:

"It's all there for the taking."

For a few decades, at the turn of the century, the Big Man ruled the world. You could find him peacocking at the finer hotels and nightclubs of New York City, heavy with old-school bling, shoveling oysters by the bucket. The Big Man had a different name then: *trencherman,* a "man of the plate," connoting the sort of fierce appetite that commanded, at the Gilded Age dinner table, respect. The king trencherman was Diamond Jim Brady, who ate public dinners so lavish that he'd start off four inches from the table and would only stop when his belly touched wood, according to a biography by H. Paul Jeffers. Brady was called Diamond Jim because he kept a bag of his namesake rocks in a miner's belt at all times. As an Irish kid growing up in his dad's immigrant bar in Lower Manhattan, Brady'd weaned himself on the remnants of big satisfying saloon meals; he'd learned the city's caches of fresh eel and penny oysters, and he'd grown fat, his fatness signaling, to a certain kind of moneyed man, ambition. His appetite for food kept pace with all the other appetites—money, fame, respect, all of it—a one-to-one relation. He became a millionaire many times over. Railroads. Kept the trains pushing west, making cheaper the abundant supplies shipped back east: the Big Man, growing the country that grew him, repaying the debt.

It didn't last. The era rotted before Wingador's parents were even born. Something terrible overtook the Big Man, each American decade a bite from his self-conception and stature, until finally the Big Man had flipped sides: a minion, not a master, in an age when "most of the robber barons have gastric ulcers and lunch off crackers and milk at their desks," argued the food writer M. F. K. Fisher in 1949. As the buffet spreads got steamier, and the food more toxic, the Big Man only sank farther into the pleather booths of the proliferating strip-mall All-You-Can-Eats on the horizon of every exurb. Food was the Big Man's sanctuary, his last vivid pleasure, and could easily have been his swan song—if not for competitive eating, which promised to turn the bug into a feature; to reframe the Big Man's sad exile in toxic buffet-land as a form of athletic discipline; to unstick the Big Man's thighs from the pleather booth and bring him into the light; to shower him with money and media attention; to restore, at long last, the prestige that was his American birthright.

I didn't get this, viscerally, until the Passion of the Toast grilled-cheese contest in early 2005, when I had a run-in with Booker and Hardy, two of the Federation's most venerated Big Men. Until then, I had been indiscriminately referring to eaters as "fat," as in my Wing Bowl article—Ed Jarvis, "fat realtor from Long Island"—which, in Japan, came back to bite me in the ass. The Big Men wouldn't talk to me, partly because of my own careless verbiage and partly because George Shea was warning them not to.* I had been blackballed, and wanted to know why. So, before the contest, I approached Hardy. He had just gotten a fresh tattoo on the boardwalk; his right bicep now read "IFOCE," in black letters, arching over an older tattoo that said "Big Cee," another of Hardy's nicknames. I asked for an interview. He said he'd have to think about it. Then I tried Booker. Booker said he'd heard I was writing a negative book about eating.

"I heard the title is 'fat' something," Booker said. "The big fat American dream?"

At that moment, Charles Hardy, who had been listening in, spread his arms and pointed to his puffed-out chest. "Dream?" Hardy said. "You think this is a dream?" He stepped back and looked at me aggressively, his mouth half open, and pulled a diamond-studded cross from under the neck of his shirt.

"Nine carats," he said.

He pointed to his large gold watch.

"Six and a half carats," he said.

He was also wearing a $10,000 bracelet. He may have also called this to my attention. I don't remember.

I was too surprised to do anything but gawk.

---

* Shea was throwing his support behind a competing book about eating, written by one of his employees.

"I walk around with a thousand large," Hardy said. "You think this is an American *dream?*"

And I stood there, stammering, as these two enormous men turned and walked away.

Later I bought Eric's hip-hop record, read the lyrics, and felt like an idiot forever being confused about the chip on the Big Man's shoulder. Booker is an unironic rapper of songs about competitive eating. There are shout-outs and guest appearances and everything. His lyrics are all about bulk and enormity: *some call me the big hulk / huge and imposing in the fit of a rage.* His track "Lightning in a Bottle" is even more direct:

> *I rise every morning from a plus Posturepedic*
> *Stretch arms, back, and yams how I greet it*
> *Stepping to the bathrooms, like walking on rose petals*
> *Hear the ocean every time I stream the mellow yellow . . .*
> *Every day feel taller, thinner, stronger, faster*
> *Throwing on my jacket like I just won the masters*
> *Hopping in the SUV, star spangling*
> *Like 'O say can you see the piece dangling*
> *Dawn's early light wonder who that be?*
> *But by the twilights last gleaming oh Badlands baby!*

Hear the ocean every time I stream the mellow yellow—Booker, in the grand hip-hop tradition, was associating his bigness with power, just like Fat Joe and Biggie Smalls before him, but even more literally, because Biggie, for all his accomplishments, never won the Cannoli Belt at the Feast of San Gennaro. Booker and Hardy weren't trying to erase their fatness, but to make people see it in a different way. They weren't fat guys. They were champions:

> *A Gurgitator, no deposit, no return, no turning back*
> *Never ever do I eat scraps*
> *My ribs is never touching, from straight grubbing*
> *Athletically and competitively, end of discussion!*

*   *   *

Bill lost his Krystal contest in Knoxville. In the final seconds, thinking he was ahead, he set half of a burger on the table instead of stuffing it in his mouth. Bill ended up with twenty-one and a half burgers, but a roofing contractor named Jeff Hicks ate twenty-two. The emcee handed the three-foot-tall trophy to Hicks, who hoisted it over his head as the local TV cameras swirled.

"Hooooooooongry!" bellowed Hicks.

Bill winked at Debbie and smiled. She walked toward the stage to meet him.

"I couldn't put no more in," said Bill.

"You mean to tell me you didn't try because you thought you were ahead?" said Deb.

Bill shrugged and walked over to Hicks. "Good luck in the finals, man," Bill said, patting him on the shoulder.

"I'm feelin' it," said Hicks.

"See, *I'm* fine," said Bill. "I just don't like to eat that *fast*."

He walked back to Debbie and the kids, grabbed Felicia, and bounced her on his lap.

"I thought I was ahead," he said.

"So you slowed down?" said Debbie.

"I didn't slow down."

The Simmons family has come all this way to watch the patriarch get schooled by a literal Hick.

The next day, Bill called me during halftime of the Eagles-Vikings game. He was agitated, worked up. He contradicted himself every fifteen seconds. "I'm the best eater around," he said, but he was also "more dimensional than just being a competitive eater," really "a renaissance man." He talked about the Eagles as greedheads ("why does it have to be about fuckin' money?"), as decent hardworking folk ("they try, they're not bums"), and as ingrates ("I would just love to play one play, you know? These guys, they just don't know what they have"). He admitted that his previous day's Krystal performance showed that "I didn't give it my all," yet insisted that "I think you saw I had some fight in me."

Bill seemed terrified that I was going to write about him as a loser or, worse, as a bum with no heart. To Bill, "heart," not necessarily athletic achievement, is the central ingredient of any good sports story. "I like sports stories," he told me, "especially stories that are true. Heroic." Bill said that on the drive back from Knoxville, Debbie drove the Minibago for a while, and Bill popped into the back and watched *Miracle,* the dramatic tale of the 1980 U.S. Olympic hockey team. "First of all it's a true story," Bill said. "And second of all it was very passionate as far as this guy wanted to win, the coach wanted to win. And then you've got Russia that's been a hockey power for fifteen years, kickin' everybody's ass, intimidating every other team." The Americans are huge underdogs. "And then [the coach] gives this unbelievable speech, about how you gotta get in there, you gotta fight. It's something I kind of base my life on." He added, "That's what I love, the underdog."

Our underdogs are stand-ins for ourselves. Now that signs point to a surrender in the obesity war—and what else is the rise of competitive eating if not wholesale surrender?—we have to know that the Big Man can win a few. We can't get rid of him, because he drives, for better and for worse, the consumer engine of the country. He's our future. He's all we've got. So we've given the Big Man a second chance. When he's a television actor like Jim Belushi or Kevin James, we pair him with an improbably hot sitcom wife. When he's a golfer like John Daly or Jason Gore—the aw-shucks, roly-poly duffer ranked 818th in the world who nevertheless found himself just three shots behind the leader after three days of the 2005 U.S. Open golf championship, and who was said, by an NBC analyst, to be "yabba-dabba-dooing" his way around the course—we frame him with gauzy lenses and sentimental music. And now we've given the Big Man his own special sport, one that lets him apply his great masticatory talent and seems to set him up for victory, except not really, thanks to skinny folk like Koby and Tim Janus and Sonya Thomas. Even at an eating contest, the Big Man's natural purview, he is not automatically the best. Each contest is an underdog story.

Bill's is only different because it's more intense. His hometown produced the greatest underdog story ever filmed: *Rocky,* the sacred animating myth of Philadelphia. Bill, then, has been cast as the protagonist in a bizarro-world cross between *Rocky* and *Miracle,* a sappy underdog flick whose producers are functionaries for a $26-billion company, whose director is an egomaniacal Howard Stern clone, whose PR men are U.S. congressmen, whose extras are drunks and strippers, and whose audience is a healthy chunk of the 5.7 million residents of a major American city and its suburbs. Bill has gotten his heroic sports story, but it doesn't look like anything he expected. It's a second chance, but a Faustian one, because the thing about underdog sports stories is that they demand a sacrifice. "Even when I win, I feel like shit," Bill told me. "What am I doin', throwin' shit down my gullet? Like what am I doin' to my body? Just throwin' shit down my gullet doesn't make me anybody's hero."

For Bill's eventual triumph to have any resonance, he must first be abused.

He seemed to understand this. On the phone, apropos of nothing, he started talking about his own funeral. He said he'd been thinking about the kind of funeral he wanted. "I want a buffet there," he told me. "After you see the body, I want somebody to eat something. [Debbie's] like, 'After the viewing you go to the hall and eat there.' No. You eat right there at the viewing. I wanna be around. And if there's any leftovers, throw 'em in my casket."

The Big Man roared and roared.

4

NO DIPPING, NO DUNKING, NO DESECRATING

THE STORY of the chicken wing is the story of Wing Bowl, the story of an improvisation that became a diversion that became a cash cow. Food writer Calvin Trillin traces the wing's origin to the circa-1964 pub deep-fryer of an Italian mother in Buffalo, New York. At first the wing had as much culinary cachet as beef tongues or chitlins or tripe. It was what was left over once you sold all the in-demand parts of the chicken, like the drumstick and the breast and the thigh. Today a wholesale wing costs more per pound than a breast, and it fluctuates in price with the seasons, like heating oil—cheaper in the late winter months after football's over, pricey in the Fourth Quarter when football kicks in, extra pricey around Super Bowl time. The chicken wing has become what we eat when we watch football and drink beer, period, hence the wing tends to be popular in cities where football and beer are popular, like Philadelphia, which has always been associated with the blue-collar palate anyway. One of the details that Stallone got right in *Rocky* is how Rocky talks about food. In Adrian's pet store, Rocky says her tropical birds look like "flyin' candy." When he invites Adrian to his flophouse apartment, he says, "Yo, Adrian, you hungry?" and then offers her "soda," "some donuts or somethin'," "a couple of cupcakes," and "some chocolate." Since Rocky's time, Philadelphia has in fact become one of the country's meccas of fine dining—we had *Esquire*'s best new restaurant in 2004—but when people think of Philly they still think of soft pretzels and cheesesteaks and Tastykakes, and now chicken wings, thanks to Wing Bowl and thanks also to its staunchest political supporter, Ed Rendell, our voluble ex-mayor who raised wing connoisseurship to a civic duty. This from a 2002 gubernatorial campaign story in the *Allentown Morning Call*:

From the back of the bus, Rendell screams for an aide—any aide—to "bring the wings." [A tavern owner at a campaign stop] had packed a doggie bag—three Styrofoam boxes of wings. . . . [Rendell] sits down and grabs his belly. "Six or seven too many wings," he explains. By 2 p.m., it's "eight or nine too many." By 3, en route to Oil City, Rendell asks his staff for an antacid—any antacid—as it reaches "10 or 11 too many." Someone hands him a Zantac.

Back in the mid-nineties, when Rendell was handing out the Wing Bowl tropies, the wings were provided by a friend of Al Morganti. By Wing Bowl 4, the event had grown big enough to require a pro, which is where the Rib Ranch's Mitch Blackman—he of the stack of clandestine Wingette photos—came in. Blackman buys his wings from Quaker Valley Foods, which gets its birds from Mountaire Farms and Allen Family Foods, both major suppliers headquartered in Delaware with contract farmers throughout the Middle Atlantic states. The wings come in forty-pound boxes of "party wings," which include two portions of bird: the "drumstick," or shoulder joint, and the "blade," which is the elbow. He pays, on average, $1.50 per pound. Each wing gets slathered with Blackman's secret sauce—not cayenne-based, like traditional Buffalo wings, but tomato-based, a barbecue sauce—and deep-fried for 9 to 11 minutes. How many calories in each wing? He doesn't know, but an internist once told a Philly newspaper that each wing was 250 calories with 16 grams of fat, which would make Wingador's winning total at Wing Bowl 11 equal to 38,500 calories and 4,000 grams of fat. Blackman explains that wings are a trend, "like sushi was in the eighties," but from a culinary point of view, wings are the inverse of sushi. The goal of a sushi chef is to present fish unadorned, simply and purely, as a fetish object. But a chicken wing is a paltry squib of meat concealed by a coat of fatty skin. There's nothing pure to drill down *to*. A wing is a mere delivery mechanism for spicy, caloric sauces.

The Rib Ranch wing is smaller than most: about two and a half inches long, like a wing you find in a Chinese buffet. There's a reason WIP wants small wings: the smaller the wing, the higher the totals. The wings are mild, sweetish, wet-looking, ruby-red in color. Drumsticks require less work to eat than blades. A top wing specialist like Wingador—who thinks wings are "a tease" and much prefers breasts—will grab the drumstick with both hands and hold it like the wing was an ear of corn, rotating the wing on its axis and munching in an even rhythm. Blades are trickier, because they contain, essentially, two long pieces of parallel bone hinged together at both ends. A blade must first be split in two, then meat-stripped one half at a time. If the meat is sitting just right, a talented eater like Wingador can strip a blade with a single aggressive bite-and-pull motion, clamping down on the bone and bringing the full weight of the jaw to bear. He strengthens his jaw by chewing chilled Tootsie rolls. Wingador is a relatively clean eater, keeping debris to a minimum; other eaters let sauce stain their cheeks. He used to eat with a rhythm, dictated by the song he sang to himself during contests: Pearl Jam's "Jeremy." He doesn't sing anymore, just tries to focus. When Wingador is eating smoothly and his hands keep up with his mouth, he slips into a groove. He rips a blade, chomps half, *TOSS*, chomps half, *TOSS*, then a bite of drumstick, a quick quarter-rotation, another bite, three, four, *TOSS*, rips a fresh blade—jaw, lips, and hands the instruments in Wingador's film score of wet sound, the sound of earthworms writhing in a bait bucket. The effect is hypnotic. Once, when Wingador judged a bootleg wing-eating contest at a Catholic prep school, the headmaster, who was announcing the contest from a megaphone at the top of the football field's bleachers, asked him to perform a quick demonstration of his technique. Wingador reached into a nearby wing tray. Two hundred students stopped jabbering and leaned forward to watch. Wingador picked up a blade. The wing, with all its mysterious joints and hinges and gristle, vanished in a flash of paw, and less than a second later, when Wingador's hand emerged from his mouth, the wing was only bone.

Wingador held up the naked wing. The kids exploded in a cannon blast of sound, instantly and in unison.

The Catholic headmaster screamed:

"Ohh! Myyyy! GODDDDD!"

For his efforts, Wingador walked away with a thank-you card and $200 in cash.

Bill is often described, by other eaters, as a "wing specialist." They mean this disdainfully, and Bill is happy to return the favor. "I think I'm the world champion wing eater in the biggest event in the world," he says. "What I like is the 20,000 people. I can't waste my time with all this little shit." By "little shit," he means the annual Nathan's hot dog contest on Coney Island. Bill's crack is blasphemy—the gurgitators revere Nathan's like they revere their esprit de corps that Bill wants no part of—but they can't begrudge Bill's eagerness to perform for "the 20,000 people," because the gurgitators are eager, too. Starting with Wing Bowl 10, they made the pilgrimage to Philly and returned with sauce-smeared cheeks and fantastical stories: "It makes Coney Island on the Fourth of July look like a backyard picnic" (indie eater Joe Menchetti); "like no other contest you've ever been in" (Don Lerman); "One word comes to mind: it's off the hook" (Charles Hardy); "It looked like Mad Max's revenge in the parking lot" (Ed Jarvis). Coondog O'Karma was especially effusive. At Wing Bowl 10, he says, he got "the greatest boo in all of Philadelphia." He liked that moment so much, he put a picture of it on the cover of his book of poetry, *Wit and Whimsy*.

One hit of the Wing Bowl pipe and they were hooked, all of them—or maybe the better analogy was George Shea's, the way he described Eric Booker's mass as planetary: *When I'm close to Eric Booker I feel a slight tug into him, into Eric Booker's orbit, one has to pull back, such is his mass, such is his density! His mouth an event horizon into the black hole that is his esophagus . . .*

If Wing Bowl was a gravitational event, two factors best explained the strength of its pull. The obvious one was the crowd. The 20,000. The other was more mundane, and it had to do with Wing Bowl's format. In the balkanized world of competitive eating, there are no contests where the indie eaters can match up against the contractually locked-in Federation bigwigs, to say nothing of the shlubby Philly dudes who ache to wipe the floor with both uppity tribes. Wing Bowl was simultaneously the most aggressively local contest on the circuit and also the most diverse. Wing Bowl, then, engorged all matter, every eater and every organization, and with them their conflicts and vendettas and ideologies—all of it accelerated into Wing Bowl's dark center and flung back out into the world bloodied, distorted, bleating.

Quite a show.

And to pull up a seat you had only to set your alarm, wake up extra early, and catch the morning drive-time radio program on 610 WIP.

On December 10, 2004, thanks to Wing Bowl, I saw the metaphorical begin-ning of one eating career and the literal end of another. My day started early, just after midnight, when I walked into the Port Authority bus station in New York City and met up with Tim "Eater X" Janus. We boarded a 2:30 a.m. bus headed to Philly.

Tim Janus was twenty-seven. I'd been following him for four months. I liked him as much as any eater I'd met because, one, he was puppy-dog earnest when it came to eating, and two, he hadn't yet developed the self-conscious media persona that some eaters wear like a vintage NBA jersey. The first time I called him, in September, I asked why he did it, why he ate, and he said, in a shy monotone, "I like to tell people that I started doing it to impress Jodie Foster." He laughed awkwardly.

Tim said that his first contest was in March 2004—a corned-beef-and-cabbage event in the East Village. "I figured I had to give it a shot just as part of the adventure of living in New York." Janus didn't win, but was hooked. After respectable showings in two hot-dog qualifiers, Tim was contacted by the IFOCE. The IFOCE offered to pay for his hotel and ground transportation to a donut contest in San Diego. Tim would have to buy his own plane ticket. "I got my ticket right away without really thinking twice," he said, because "I was pretty flattered, actually. I knew it could lead to big things." Tim wore jeans and untucked blue shirts and a reversed blue ballcap that said CHEVRON. He was leanly muscular and good-looking in a frat-boy way. Not the frat boy who hazed pledges but the kind who listened to Floyd. He didn't have a shtick, just a habit of painting his face with a kind of polychromatic-sleep-mask design on the day of a contest. After Tim tied the veteran Ed Jarvis for fourth place at the National Buffalo Wing Festival in early September—the IFOCE said Tim's "break-out performance shocked the competitive eating community"—Shea started calling him "Eater X" and introducing him as "a man of mystery whose mask conceals an inner torment ... no one knows who he is ... *he's Tim Janus,* but no one knows who he is ..."

After Buffalo, Tim was ranked thirtieth by the IFOCE. Two weeks later, he took second place in cannolis, bested only by Eric Booker. I started fol-lowing Tim to contests. In late September, I saw him take second to Booker again, at a cheesecake contest in Brooklyn; a few days later, Tim ate 33 soft tacos in 11 minutes, only 15 tacos shy of the winner, Sonya Thomas. By mid-October, when I met up with him in Mississippi at a Krystal qualifier, Tim's IFOCE ranking had shot all the way up to ninth, which struck some as premature. The independent eater "Gentleman" Joe Menchetti had called the ranking a "travesty," writing on his gossip website, "don't you have to win something before cracking the top ten?" Janus was sensitive about the criticism, and spent a few minutes defending his number-nine ranking and then asked, "Did that sound all right about what I said about number nine? I don't want to sound arrogant, not at all. I feel really lucky to be at number nine, really happy. That sounds okay?" Tim lost the Krystal contest to Jim "Buffalo" Reeves, and we spent the rest of the afternoon drinking beers in his motel room. Later we checked to see if he'd made the local news. (He had, barely.)

A week later, Tim had his biggest setback yet, losing to a couple of locals in a baked-bean contest in Florida. He had slept in an airport and lost $200 in travel money. He was sore about that—the losing, not the sleeping in the airport. He didn't mind sleeping in airports or his rental car or staying in hostels, because it was all part of what he called "doing the struggle." Now, in December, Tim was trying to qualify for Wing Bowl. He used words like "adventure" and "experience" to explain why, as in, "I really couldn't put a price on the Wing Bowl experience," even though he had never experienced it and had only heard about it secondhand from his gurgitator elders. On the bus, he told me that he was starting to get noticed by spectators/fans who recognized the Guy With the Facepaint from his photos on ifoce.com. He said he felt like a rock star now, traveling in the middle of the night "on a shitty bus, but it doesn't feel like I'm a rock star. It feels more like a minor-league baseball team." He added, "This is the weirdest travel I've ever done. Who the hell takes a bus at two-thirty in the morning?" He plucked a cranberry-raspberry Diet Snapple from his bag and downed it.

We got to Philly around four. I dropped him off in Center City and put him in a cab heading to the radio station and slept for a few hours. While Janus was in the cab, and while I slept, a very different competitor, an electrician named Fino Cachola, was at a grocery store in Bala Cynwyd. Fino Cachola, aka "Chili Dawg," age thirty-six, from Sicklerville, New Jersey, along with his neighbor Jim Flanagan and two other buddies, drove to the twenty-four-hour ShopRite in Bala Cynwyd at 4:00 a.m., and bought a loaf of Stroehmann's white bread (twenty-four slices), a pound of cheese, a pound of chili, and a tub of real butter. The clerk told Fino his purchases didn't look very healthy. He didn't know Fino was planning to eat it *all* within a ten-minute time span. Fino and his entourage killed time until six-thirty, when they walked into the lobby of Two Bala Plaza and took the elevator to WIP's studio on the seventh floor. Fino wore a shirt that read BULLDOG TOUGH/AMERICA'S UNION/IBEW 351. A large man with stocky arms, a bulging stomach, a dirty mustache, a thin layer of close-shaved hair, and a tattoo across the small of his back that said FINO in Gothic letters, Chili Dawg was immediately told to wait. When I got to the studio around seven-thirty, he was still waiting.

"That's disrespectful," Fino said. "This is my sixth year, man, and I gotta wait around."

"No respect," said Fino's buddy, tossing a football absentmindedly. "The dog gets no respect."

Fino's friends busied themselves making the chili cheese sandwiches, and waited. They had already waited through the successful stunt of Tim "Eater X" Janus (five pounds of cottage cheese in two minutes and twenty seconds) and a stunt by a 340-pounder named Dennis, who requested the removal of one ingredient from each of the five Big Macs he then ate in nine minutes and forty seconds, and that ingredient was *lettuce*. Fino and crew waited through on-air phone calls from U.S. Senator Arlen Specter (who said he called because he had "a little free time" before his upcoming trip to Iraq, where he would be handing out Eagles memorabilia to Pennsylvania troops), Eagles defensive end Hugh Douglas, and U.S. Senator Jon Corzine, who was trolling for gubernatorial votes, and whom Cataldi saw fit to endorse. ("By the way," said Corzine, "that Hugh Douglas guy, does he vote in New Jersey? He sounds like a class act.") Fino and crew had waited through in-studio appearances from the Philadelphia Soul cheerleaders and a twenty-year-old University of Delaware student, "Model Molly," who wanted to be a Wingette (Cataldi: "Oh my God, she reeks of class and sex and perfection . . . if that's a hooker, Al, right, I'd pay five grand").

Finally, a little after 8:00 a.m., Cataldi called Fino into the recording booth, and at 8:19, Cataldi went live. He said that Fino was trying out for his seventh Wing Bowl. (It was either his sixth or his seventh.) "And it is no secret to me that you are exactly the kind of eater I am getting rid of this year, 'cause you are a *loozzzahhh*. Arright?"

"He's one of the best eaters we've always had," said sidekick Rhea Hughes.

"One of the best *loo-zzzeers* we've ever had," said Cataldi. "That's correct. Always a bridesmaid, never a bride. However. The story that brings you here today is a fascinating one, because, well, you're fresh out of the hospital, is that correct, Chili Dawg? Tell the people."

"About two weeks ago," said Fino, "I was in there for about a week with pneumonia. And just last week I went to the doctor for a nose alignment, so they stuck these two sticks up my nose, and cleaned out everything. So. It's going to get probably pretty bloody in here."

"Arright . . ."

"I have no control."

"The nose area's still healing, so you could open up some wounds," said Cataldi.

"Right, exactly."

"And blood could flow."

"Right, exactly."

"Well, all right," said Cataldi, "I'm tellin' ya right now. You're gonna have to drink all the blood you shed."

Fino responded by removing his dental prosthetic—without it, he believed, he could eat quicker—and ripping into his sandwiches. He needed to eat twelve. "Oh dear," said Cataldi. "This is not—ladies and gentlemen, a grilled cheese is gone . . . already you can see, Al, that there's some inflammation in his nostrils."

"Aw, there's some blood dripping," said *Morning Show* co-host Keith Jones, disgusted.

Said Cataldi, "There will probably be rivulets of blood down his—and fortunately, Al, he's worn a white shirt today so it will show up beautifully."

"I don't know how he can breathe," said co-host Al Morganti.

"He can't."

Chili Dawg approached the one-minute mark.

"All I can say," said Cataldi, "is he's ignorant. That's an ignorant man."

In retrospect, the deejays look like monsters, but at the time—to be fair—

it just seemed like they were exaggerating for effect. Fino's breathing was labored, and he was an obviously unhealthy guy, but no more unhealthy than any other overweight Wing Bowl wannabe. His shirt was soaked, but from sweat and mucus, not blood.

Cataldi cut to commercial. Fino kept stuffing chili-cheese sandwiches. Ads aired for the Select Comfort Sleep Number Bed, Ford cars, the U.S. Postal Service, and the AmEx business gold card. Cataldi came back on the air at 8:28, at which point Fino peeled off his tank top to expose the hairy chest beneath. His nose made a noise like a vacuum cleaner trying to suck milk. Fino finished his twelfth sandwich with a time of seven minutes, nineteen seconds. Everyone applauded. He was in Wing Bowl 13. Still chewing, Fino mumbled, "I'd like to say hi to my wife, beautiful wife, and my two beautiful kids, Shane and Devon."

"Boy," said Cataldi, "they could not be prouder.... Yes, that's really nice ... Now *leave.*"

Like many self-designated voices of the people, Angelo Cataldi is not originally from the same place as his people. For years he was a newspaper columnist in his hometown of Providence, Rhode Island. He landed a job at the *Inquirer* in 1983. Cataldi imagined Philadelphia "would be perfect for me," he said in a 1999 interview with the *Daily News.* "Tough, demanding, sometimes obnoxious ... And then I went over to radio, no editors cleaning my stuff up, and I created a dynamic where I matched the image of the city."

That's exactly correct: Cataldi's show—bombastic, crudely self-hating, parochial, blue-collar—matched the image, not the city. The city is not particularly blue-collar, not anymore; the city is more accurately described as *poor.* As of 2004, Philadelphia was the seventh-poorest city in the country by median household income, poorer even than New Orleans before the flood, with pockets of decay as bad as anything in Cleveland or Detroit, and also with pockets of concentrated wealth: an elite professional class of lawyers, doctors, and one in ten pharmaceutical jobs in the country, if you include the suburbs in South Jersey and all the way out to Wilmington, Delaware. At the same time, entire neighborhoods in ethnic South Philly have relocated to Jersey, as if airlifted by enormous helicopters, ceding Rocky's own Italian Market to the Vietnamese. Cataldi's show embodied this schizoid quality of the city. The professional suburbanites were Cataldi's listeners, and the city's surviving blue-collar meatheads were his callers. Cataldi's way of identifying with his callers—the way he carried off the manly ritual of mutual chops-busting—was a source of his reputation, while the buying power and electoral influence of his suburbanite listeners was a source of Cataldi's power. "If I can land a client on Angelo's show, it's a home run," a prominent local political consultant told the *Philadelphia Weekly* in 2003. "It's even better than being quoted in the dailies. Opinion leaders pay attention to Angelo." The *Weekly*'s quote came in a cover story about Cataldi's dabbling in Philly politics. He had become the "unofficial advisor" to Sam Katz, the Republican candidate for mayor. The deejay deigned to advise the politician, and the politician listened, because the politician, being familiar with town halls, must have recognized that the deejay's show was just another town hall. Of sorts. Only the topic wasn't politics. It was sports. Sports, the most democratic of radio formats. "All different walks of life get involved in sports," says WIP general manager Marc Rayfield.

When it came to the *Morning Show*, however, sports was just a jumping-off point. The show wasn't really about sports. It was about the lowest common denominator of sports fandom—"guy talk"—whose LCD was the scatological pranky humor the deejays indulged. And the LCD of the LCD of the LCD was Wing Bowl itself.

In December, when I started spending my mornings at the WIP studio, I couldn't make sense of what I was seeing until I stopped thinking of Cataldi as a wealthy radio deejay—he earned a reported million dollars a year—and started thinking of him as the president of a very large fraternity. His brothers were the hundreds of thousands of WIP listeners across the Delaware valley. "He brings it all on the table," says longtime Wing Bowl official and devoted WIP listener Bob Blutinger. "He'll talk about stuff that happens to him, and it's like stuff that happens to you. You know? And the average person connects with that. And you feel when you're around him, you're around, you know, somebody that's famous but, you know, *like you.*" But better. Smarter. More secure. With a hotter wife. A bigger house. Cooler friends. He was like a benificent God, doling out approval and scorn, and if you were in his good graces, you got to spend time in the ultimate male clubhouse, which was the WIP studio. This helped me understand why a man named Sam the Meatball Man came to the studio one day with a Crock-Pot full of warm, moist meatballs for Cataldi, and why the eaters didn't seem to care that Cataldi and his producer called them "fuckin' idiots" when they were out of earshot, and why Fino "Chili Dawg" Cachola submitted himself to such thorough degradation.

See, the degradation had its flip side. If a person could endure the deejays and earn a berth in Wing Bowl, life was suddenly pretty good. The Wing Bowl eater became the instant center of his circle of friends, the focal point of every activity: float construction, practice eats, sponsorship inquiries, T-shirt design. He became, for a month or two, *the man.* He didn't even have to be good at eating. He just had to show up the day of Wing Bowl and perform—and then take his buddies to the strip clubs for free lap dances after the contest. And if he happened to win? More attention. More respect.

He was live on Cataldi's show. He was live on the *Wally Kennedy Show.* He was live on every morning TV show in Philly. He was in the *Daily News* and *Inquirer* and *Courier-Post* and *Gloucester County Times.* "Makes you feel you're doing something for the community," says "Tollman" Joe Paul, winner of Wing Bowl 8. The smaller the community, the bigger the deal. When Mark "Big Rig" Vogeding won Wing Bowl 6, his hometown of Paulsboro, New Jersey—a small town on the Delaware River dominated by oil refineries—insisted that Vogeding ride in its Fourth of July parade. Vogeding also appeared alongside the mayor on a local-access TV show, and was even honored in separate resolutions drafted by the Gloucester County Board of Freeholders and the Paulsboro City Council: *WHEREAS, Mark "The Big Rig" Vogeding, sponsored by Hooters ... set a new record for consumption of 164 chicken wings in 30 minutes ... and received an all-expenses-paid trip for two to Aruba for eight days and seven nights ...*

Any reckoning was deferred. The eaters pushed the wings through their systems, went to Aruba, and came back tanned and rested. Only then, after the wave of press had receded, did the eaters start to notice Wing Bowl's costs. Some costs were pretty direct, like weight gain, or even an eventual stroke in the case of "Tollman" Joe Paul. Other costs weren't quite so physical. Vogeding, for instance, was approached by the owner of a Wing Bowl–affiliated strip club. The owner offered him a night job as a bouncer. Vogeding worked there for five years before he could extricate himself. Wing Bowl could be unhealthy beyond just lipids and perforated bones. After El Wingador won his first Wing Bowl, he appeared on a local TV talk show and sat in front of a backdrop of human breasts and thighs—the Wingettes, posing—while Debbie, his new wife, sat on his lap in a baggy sweater, answering questions in a soft voice, trying to ignore the breasts and thighs behind her.

It couldn't have been easy, this assaultive rolling of the red carpet that the guys were loving every minute of (don't get them wrong) but which they had very little time to assimilate into their legitimately normal-guy lives. It was a kind of strain most normal guys never have to deal with, and it only got worse as Wing Bowl grew, because the more influential and class-spanning Wing Bowl became, the louder its impresarios talked about the kernel of its essential greatness, which was that it "glorifies the average guy," in Cataldi's words. "That's probably the best thing . . . there are very few events anywhere where the average guy, who has no obvious skill, can feel like a superstar." And as Wing Bowl became more mythic, it needed a character to carry those myths, a broad-shouldered Atlas, a suitable vessel for everything Philadelphians believed about themselves: A Philadelphian loves his sports teams. A Philadelphian is a scrapper, like Rocky. A Philadelphian has heart. A Philadelphian loves to drink. A Philadelphian loves to eat. A Philadelphian has pride in his city. A Philadelphian hates outsiders. A Philadelphian is a big guy. A Philadelphian is an average guy.

In other words, Wing Bowl needed Bill Simmons.

Bill, however, had wised up.

"Angelo wants me in," Bill told me in late November, "but they're gonna have to pay me to get me back in. I don't know if they'll do it. We'll see." His demand was motivated by equal parts pride and pragmatism. His stomach had been hurting pretty bad for a month, and if he was going to aggravate it, he needed to make it worth his while. "It just hurts, man," he said. "Just constantly, pain. I don't know what it is. Could be bleeding in my stomach. Could be an ulcer. Could be lots of things." He had scheduled a doctor's appointment, but said his decision would rest more on WIP's offer than on any diagnosis: "If they give me $10,000 and I decide to get back in, I'll get back in, it doesn't matter if it's stomach cancer or what. It'll kill me not to take the money."

So, on a rainy morning early in December 2004, Bill and his agent came to the WIP studio for a meeting with Cataldi and the station's management. Bill and Cataldi exchanged greetings and Cataldi invited him into the recording booth for a brief interview before the meeting. Cataldi said, on-air, "You have set the bar high. You're the one that made it the BIG event that it is. It was a NICE event, and now we have this Philadelphia guy who came in and showed everybody how to eat wings. And now the question becomes, Are you willing to come back to try to win it back? Where are you right now?"

"I haven't decided," said Bill.

"You have not decided?"

"I haven't decided. I really haven't. It—there's a lot of issues there. I don't know . . . it hurts a little bit . . . I really put a lot on myself . . ."

"Bill, I want you to think . . . your greatest conquest of all awaits you . . ."

"Well, I know, I know."

". . . if you take one more big one home. Take these outside losers, these little Asian girls. [Shaking his upper body, grabbing his nipples.] 'Oooh, I got a tapeworm! I got a tapeworm!' Or this BIG, FAT PIG Cookie Jarvis, why don't you show that it BELONGS HERE! In your town!"

"It *does* belong here."

"It belongs to YOU!"

"But I'd like somebody else to do it."

Bill left, and on the way out he passed Arnie "Chowhound" Chapman—the indie rebel—standing in the lobby with a crate of clementines, sopping wet, hair mussed, having driven all the way from Long Island in the heavy rain, wearing a hat with floppy dog ears and a dog chain that said CHOW-HOUND, waiting to perform his stunt for Wing Bowl 13.

Arnie. I had come to know Arnie pretty well. The first time I saw him in action was in October 2004, when he was in Las Vegas to promote the International Chili Society's World Chili Eating Championship. The contest was a small and relatively insignificant part of the World's Championship Chili Cookoff, which had drawn 300 top chili chefs and 350 judges to the parking lot of the Mandalay Bay casino's convention center, in the shadow of the casino's gold-brick towers. The chefs, having won qualifiers all over the world to get here, had set up their portable chili cookers at small stations under long rows of white tents, prepping their best batches for that day's judging. The entertainment was separate, confined to a large stage fifty or so yards away. Anything that happened on the stage was obviously secondary to the chili judging. Still, to Arnie, the contest was a big deal, a major step for him and his fledgling league, simply because the chili contest had previously been handled by his nemesis, the IFOCE. This year the chiliheads had decided to give Arnie a shot. Now he needed to show that he deserved it.

The day of the contest was hot and hazeless. When I first arrived at the parking lot, Arnie was sweating. He jerked his head back and forth as if searching for someone. The contest was only an hour away, which was a problem, because at the moment Arnie didn't have any chili.

"I'm trying to find the guy with the chili," he told me.

Arnie is a forty-four-year-old vocational rehabilitation counselor from Long Island. He works for the State of New York, connecting blind children with blind-appropriate services. Arnie has a meaty, indistinct face, a paunch, a dirty mustache, a voice that comes out in fits and nasal whinges and snorts, and an unshakable enthusiasm for competitive eating. He is a political refugee from the IFOCE and a passionate detractor of the IFOCE's grand poobah, George Shea. By the time of the chili contest, I had been to Arnie's house for dinner, seen his kid-cluttered living room, and met his long-suffering wife, Debbie, who is also a rehabilitation counselor. Deb has spent twenty-two years working with the mentally ill. "But her *real* training," Arnie said, "has been—how long have we been married?"

Deb laughed. "The last seven years."

At dinner, we all ate a Weight Watchers potato dish that Deb had cooked—he was a pro weight gainer, she was a pro weight loser—and afterward Arnie gave me a yellow AICE T-shirt and a white Frank's Red Hot apron and signed it, "To Jason, Think of me at the Barbecue! Arnie 'Chowhound' Chapman."* Whereas George Shea was P.T. Barnum filtered through a Saatchi & Saatchi two-way, Arnie was your kid's sweaty, excitable Little League coach. Shea, a literature major at an Ivy League school, was a fan of the theater. Arnie, who enlisted in the military after growing up in an orphanage, is a fan of his pit

---

* Technically, I wasn't supposed to accept a gift from a source, but it seemed to make Arnie so happy that I would have felt like a prick to turn it down; later, when Don Lerman offered me a T-shirt, I did turn it down, and, looking at Don's face, instantly regretted it.

bull, Roxanne. Arnie believed that competitive eating existed to exalt goofiness and immaturity, and he structured his own organization accordingly.
For one thing, most of his contests were geared toward raising money for
charity, which allowed Arnie to indulge his do-gooding impulse while also
drawing a contrast between AICE and the Federation that was useful in
pitching new sponsors. (AICE's motto—which you could hear Arnie recite
on the answering machine message of his "food phone," aka his home
phone—was this: "A competitive eating organization with a heart as big as
its stomach!") Also, Arnie made it a point to let his eaters develop their own
identities as entertainers, with no top-down control. "We, more so than anybody, realize and understand this sport better than anyone else, and have a
much more realistic view of it . . . these guys from the IFOCE, all right, they
actually believe that billions of people are actually interested in watching
them shove food down their throats. Okay. Let me rephrase that. Millions."
Arnie said that the only one who really stunned him, athletically, was
Kobayashi. Otherwise, "competitive eating, or the potential of competitive
eating, isn't in, necessarily, the fact that somebody can eat a certain amount
of food. It's also in the personalities of the eaters."

Except—and this is crucial to understanding Arnie—for all of his supposed goofiness, he was more invested in eating's legitimacy than anyone I'd
ever met, Coondog included. Arnie, having decided that eating could take a
pure form or a bastardized form, had devoted himself to maintaining its pure
form. His zeal was as total as it could be without wrecking his marriage. He
often railed against the IFOCE's policy of excluding non-IFOCE eaters
from contests—"dammit, it really is un-American"—once going so far as to
tell Eric "Badlands" Booker that Booker should rise up against the IFOCE's
contract because "slavery was over." Booker, of course, is black. Arnie policed
newspaper accounts of IFOCE contests, zinging off e-mails to the reporters:
*Dear Mr. Sederstrom . . . Your statement that this was "billed as the country's first
Latke Eating Contest" is completely inaccurate. . . . Any amount of research would
have revealed that Latke Eating contests are common during the Chanuka season. . . .
Your lack of research and misstatement of the truth is rather scary. . . .* On the Internet,
Arnie published anti-IFOCE missives on his website. The IFOCE responded
by pretending that Arnie didn't exist. Because the IFOCE wouldn't engage
Arnie directly, the AICE/IFOCE battle raged by proxy on two opposing

gossip sites: speedeat.com, run by Arnie's friend "Gentleman" Joe Menchetti, and beautifulbrian.com, run by a postal worker and IFOCE partisan named "Beautiful" Brian Seiken. On Menchetti's site, IFOCE eaters were portrayed as corporate dupes;* on Seiken's site, AICE eaters were portrayed as pathetic losers. The war eventually escalated with the introduction of an ostensibly† third-party gossip site, trencherwomen.com, whose comments sections quickly devolved into epic flame wars complete with threats of physical violence and rhetorical attacks too slanderous to responsibly reprint here, with, for example—just to give the flavor—Seiken referring to Arnie's *retarded looking dog hat and his copycat eating organization,* and telling Coondog to *Go dig into a couple of 4 inch pizza pies and win a 99 cent trophy in front of your hometown boys in Ohio,* and with Coondog firing back by making a highly personal comment about Seiken's family, adding, *you deserve the sad life you live.*‡ And these were the milder posts. (After Coondog complained that he'd been defamed, the site scrubbed the nastier comments.) It was all really vicious in a way that seemed insane from the outside but made perfect sense from the inside. But whether you were on the inside or the outside, Arnie's jeremiads about the IFOCE contract weren't any more insane than the fact that *there is a fucking contract system for eating contests.*

A system that Arnie, here in the Mandalay Bay parking lot, is now trying to destroy.

Assuming he can find his chili.

And Arnie still can't find his chili.

He goes off in search of it and I say hi to Coondog, who's here, too, wear-

---

* The crux of the "dupe" argument came back, again, to the contracts. From the IFOCE's point of view, the contracts were necessary to keep the sponsors happy; the IFOCE couldn't properly run a business if its eaters were going around promoting brands that might compete with its sponsors' brands. In fact, Menchetti once caught hell for eating in a hot-dog contest sponsored by Boar's Head, a competitor of Nathan's Famous. But Menchetti's feeling was that he'd given Nathan's a bunch of free press already, and ought to be left alone to make whatever cash he could make in whatever eating contests he could find. Anyway, Nathan's still owed him free hot dogs from prior years, he says. "I don't owe Nathan's anything. If anything, they owe me."

† I say "ostensibly" because trencherwomen.com was registered anonymously, fueling speculation that it was actually an IFOCE production.

‡ Meanwhile, Don Lerman was ignoring the flame wars altogether, instead posting a string of misspelled boasts: IM GOING TO WIN SO BIG THE PUBIC IS GOING TO CHEER ME WITH A FERVER THAT THEY HAVN'T SINCE LINDBERG RETURNED FROM PARIS.

ing the same dumb red elf suit—he was supposed to be a hot pepper—that he had lent to the Big Tomato for *The Big Chuck and Lil' John Show*. Coondog had just received a letter from the IFOCE's lawyer, threatening to sue him for breach of his contract if he participated in this contest, but Coondog said he was ignoring it. There's a Girl Scout troop here, a bunch of little kids. Coondog's trying to keep them entertained with his pepper shtick. "You guys wanna hear my rap? I'm gonna tell you who I am, okay?"

> *My hair is green*
> *My face is red*
> *Cause I really dig hot stuff*
> *I'm a chill-eee-head.*
> *I'm MC Pepper,*
> *I know I look silly,*
> *But I come to preach*
> *The virtues of chili!*
> *I LOVE CHILI!*

Arnie, meanwhile, has raced off to the grocery store to buy chili to replace the chili that he says Mandalay Bay has misplaced but that the increasingly worried-looking chiliheads seem to think Arnie has misplaced. He comes back with it, goes into the Mandalay's kitchen himself, opens the cans, heats it up, brings it out in a big silver tub. He enlists his buddies— "Gentleman" Joe Menchetti, wearing a tuxedo, and Eddie "The Geek" Vidmar, a computer programmer who lives near Coondog in Ohio—to help. About half a dozen people are ferrying the bowls from a big silver pot in the wings. It's a disaster. It looks like a sandbagging operation after a flood.

"We need spoons," says Coondog.

Already the contest is running an hour late.

"Can we get some spoons out here?"

The audience members look quizzically at the stage, not sure what's going on. The head of the chili society is in the wings, looking on and clucking her tongue. Last year, she says, when George Shea ran the contest, "He was, 'Ladies and gentlemen,' and the bowls were all filled, and everything was ready to go. Oh, I'm so upset." She taps my arm. "Arnie says, 'Well, I put everything on the list.' Arnie! I am paying you a lot of money! Shouldn't you make sure that there are *spoons?*" She adds, "They do not have spoons. They do not have puke buckets. I tell you, somebody is going to puke and these people are just going to go ballistic." The guy next to her just shakes his head. "This is just not what we're used to with the chili contests."

The contest goes on. Arnie eats in the contest himself, wearing a hat with floppy dog ears and a dog necklace that says CHOWHOUND. He ends up beating Menchetti by a slim margin, staining his shirt. Coondog doesn't eat, he just emcees. Afterward, Coondog comes up to me and says, "Not a bad contest, you think? How did we do? People got into it." He says he's proud that AICE discovered a couple of new eaters. "There was a lot of glitches today but we overcame them and we're just going to keep getting better and better."

After the contest, we drive back up to Boulder City, where Arnie and his AICE guys are staying. In the hotel room, Arnie unwinds, cracking a Corona.

For some reason we all pile into a car and drive to Hoover Dam.

I ride with Arnie. We drive down the hill into the basin and Arnie says, "Would George Shea open cans?"

At the dam, Coondog reads out loud the legal threat he has just received from the IFOCE:

> Mr. O'Karma . . . as you are no doubt aware, you have an exclusive contract with the IFOCE, subsection 2 (a) of which expressly prohibits your participation in any eating event not sanctioned by the IFOCE, unless you receive the IFOCE's prior approval. . . .

He's drowned out by a tourist helicopter that takes people on trips over the dam. Coondog walks down the steps to the dam's base, disappears for a good half hour. Arnie sits with his back to the dam and drinks an Aquafina and lights a dark-colored pipe, the old-fashioned kind. His yellow AICE T-shirt is mottled and stained from the chili. Menchetti wears wraparound sunglasses and smokes a cigarette. "The IFOCE, on some level," says Arnie, "is trying to make this a total professional thing, and that's why it's going to die."

By "professional," Arnie means two things:

First, rules and standards. Wing Bowl doesn't have any professional standards. It is arbitrary by design. Judge Eric Gregg looks at a plate of twenty
masticated wings, yells out "Seventeen," and that's it—the eater gets credit
for seventeen wings. Gregg calls wings like he used to call strikes, and takes
pride that Wing Bowl is a stalwart outpost of what he calls "the human element" in competition. "The day of the fat umpire is history," says Gregg.
"They all look like robots. They're all the same. They're all five foot ten.
They're all white. And they all have no *personality*." Gregg says this like it's
five separate words: Per. Son. Al. It. Tee. Gregg fought hard against the
IFOCE's suggestion, back in 2002, that the wings be weighed on scales, as
they are at the IFOCE's official wing contest in Buffalo, or that boneless
wings be used for the sake of consistency. A professional eater respects consistency and rejoices in numbers. I once heard George Shea introduce Rich
LeFevre as a man who had consumed two 76-ounce steaks, with all the fix-
ings, in 43 minutes. A few minutes later I heard Rich and Carlene grum-
bling about Shea. He had inflated the numbers. The steaks, it seemed, were
72 ounces, not 76, and Rich had eaten them in 58 minutes, not 43. "I'd rather
just stand on my own totals," Rich said. Rich, not surprisingly, is one of the
eaters who refuses to do Wing Bowl until it's "100 percent foolproof."*

Arnie also means "professional" in a more aesthetic sense. Wing Bowl's
aesthetic is one of rampant amateurism, randomness, and chaos, and it's
probable that the reason the indie eaters like Wing Bowl is that it values
everything their nemesis, George Shea, despises. It represents a competing
vision of competitive eating, and a valid one. Wing Bowl indulges an honest
appetite for violence, for blood and guts, things that go splat, the scraping
awesomeness of a car crash. There are those who think the barf-o-rama in
Stand by Me is "the best scene in the movie," as Big Mike, a friend of my new
in-laws, told me at a Thanksgiving potluck dinner, adding, in a softer voice,
"The rest of the movie was kinda gay"—and these people are Wing Bowl's
natural constituency. One of Wing Bowl's hallowed moments is from Wing
Bowl 9, in which an eater named Sloth, having ingested a large volume of

---

* In yet another demonstration of Wing Bowl's attractive power, Rich later reconsidered and
  entered Wing Bowl 14.

Nantucket Nectars, suddenly stood up, grabbed a nearby Wingette for support, and released the liquid in an incredibly crisp-edged stream, as if from a gargoyle fountain. "And it just looked like Niagara Falls," Wing Bowl judge Eric Gregg told me. "And it was orange. And they had the big board that showed it in slow motion. You've got to see it." I think about George Shea, circa 2002 or so, having branded his company and his sport so carefully, watching the Wing Bowl and seeing, in three mad hours, the work of fifteen years undone. Seeing Damaging Doug, his greasy hair like Medusa's locks. Seeing Hank the Tank's float plastered with girlie-mag pictures, and Shaving Katie giving the guys a peek underneath the hood.

So Wing Bowl's aesthetic was anticorporate, just like Arnie's.* But when you really drilled down to what Arnie liked about Wing Bowl, it was what he liked about eating, period, the whole reason he did it: control, and freedom. Freedom to tell your own story. Once, at a cheesecake contest, George Shea had introduced Arnie as "primarily a specialist in sweets," Arnie said. "I was sittin' there goin', WHAT? I don't have a particular love to eat cheesecake . . . I don't think you have the right to somebody's identity that way. I really don't."

Tim Janus is a useful counter-example here. In his motel room in Mississippi, after he lost the Krystal contest in October 2004, he told me that he felt bad that he didn't win because the IFOCE wanted to be able to promote him. "I think they wanted me because I was in theory a white-collar worker who trades stocks," he said. "So when I don't do well, I feel like I let them down, and it just opens the door for them to find someone else, so I feel like I've always gotta do well because I don't want that person to come out of the woodwork and be discovered . . ."

That kind of logic is alien to Arnie and Coondog and Bill Simmons, who aren't young like Tim, who don't have much more time to figure out their path, and who have spent lifetimes anyway under the thumbs of other people trying to tell their stories. Tim Janus doesn't have a shtick because he doesn't need one. But Arnie and Coondog and Bill are different.

---

* Once, when my fiancée offered to get Arnie and Deb coffees and came back with Starbucks, Arnie and Deb gave each other a look and said, "Ooooh, Starbucks—did we give you *enough?*"

Shtick, in competitive eating, is the glue that binds every constituency: Arnie, Shea, Cataldi, Coondog, the pseudonymous Wing Bowl mooks—they may hate each other, but they all indulge in a particular kind of humor, broad American male humor, slapsticky, pratfally, physical, pulling from routines, reliant on ethnic gags, aggressively un-PC. Loving shtick is the precondition of loving competitive eating. Mother's milk. Even El Wingador, who flew solo, above and beyond the herd, loved shtick. He took great pride in his ability to crack up his interviewers. He once described a show he filmed for British TV. He was interviewed by two hooligan puppets, against a set designed to look like an urban ghetto. "They're like, Hey, El Wingador, we'd LOVE to have you back on the show, you really lit up our day. I'm lookin' around, they're like, *What's wrong, El Wingador?*—these two puppets—I go, I'm not comin' back. They go, *Why is that?* I said, 'Because that's my STEREO over there!' . . . and they started laughin', and Adam West was there, Batman, he used to do Batman, he was doin' a pilot before me, and he was laughin' his ass off, and they said [you're] real natural with these two puppet characters, I said, 'Well, they remind me of my friends, two knuckleheads, and I just act normally.'"

Shtick is fundamentally a knucklehead phenomenon. The vanilla of shtick is blue-collar shtick. It comes in other flavors—it can get transmuted into a fine sorbet on one extreme (the corporate ballyhoo of George Shea) or a decadent chocolate cookie-dough on the other (the fratboy wingbowlery of Cataldi and crew). But with vanilla shtick there's a nobility, a complicated spontaneity, a usefulness that's often automatically dismissed the same way that eating contests are dismissed, as simplistic and dumb. When you realize what shtick's being used for, it doesn't seem so dumb.

Because Arnie and Coondog and Bill are guys with crushing regret. Arnie joined the military right out of high school, hoping to learn to be an X-ray technician, and instead was forced to be an infantry weapons specialist. Coondog might have become a writer if he hadn't gotten his high-school girlfriend pregnant. Bill, as a teenager, blew off a tryout for the Philadelphia Phillies because "they said I had to eat, sleep, drink baseball, but I guess I was eating, drinking, and sleeping with my girlfriend at the time." There was no real way to explain self-betrayals so deep; they hung, awkwardly suspended, unresolvable, like malformed equations. (Felicia Collazo, Bill's mother: "He wanted to become a professional baseball player ... but things happened ... he has a mind of his own ... opportunity had knocked on doors for him, but I guess he had not listened to that knock.") Though the circumstances of Arnie and Coondog and Bill were different, the outline of their regret was so similar—chances blown off, whole decades they'd like to have back and do over—that sometimes one of the guys would startle me with a quote I knew I already had in a notebook somewhere, same words, same syntax even, the déjà vu so intense I'd mentally accuse them of collaborating just to mess with me. Arnie: "I screwed up my life." Coondog: "I screwed up my life." Bill: "I just screwed up. My life." Arnie's regret is the least hobbling of the three, probably because he has no career angst and relatively little family drama. Where Arnie's regret vein taps out, Bill's and Coondog's keep gushing. Coondog: "I'm great at beer ... You woulda had a lot more fun with me in Japan when I was drinking ... Oh, I'm not joking, buddy. I'm the life of the party." Bill: "Man, I did some bad shit, too, you know, like, I did drugs and all when I was growin' up. I got high, oh yeah, man, I was crazy. But I don't do it anyMORE, you know?" Bill even had his own personal Big Tomato, a high-school buddy and fellow construction worker named Bob Thomas, who leaned over and asked me, at Bill's 2004 Labor Day barbecue, if I went to college, then blew out a gust of cigarette smoke and said, "You're lucky ... I'm forty-one, you think I want to bang nails? No. But I do it. It's all I know. Billy, he's a truck driver. That's all he knows, so he does it." Gaps in their histories like redacted black in FBI files; family members dangling, semi-estranged, out of their lives but retaining a ceremonial power, like ex-presidents. When Kelly, Coondog's first child, was starting school, Coondog was living with his parents—"I didn't have anything really goin' right then, I had no house or anything like that"—so Kelly went to live with Coondog's sister. I ask Coondog if I can contact his daughter and sister, and he e-mails back that they "want nothing to do with the competitive eating and I'd like to protect their right to privacy." (I call Kelly. She says, "This is hard for me." She needs to think about it. She doesn't return my follow-up calls.)

This is where Bill's story veers away from Coondog's. Both men had messy divorces, but Coondog, unlike Bill, won custody of his son. Today, Coondog has a relationship with his son, Adam. Not so with Bill. In the eighties and nineties, Bill and his ex-wife fought in court over child support. Bill fell behind in his payments, and a bench warrant was issued for his arrest. (The dispute has since been settled. Bill is paid up.) As a result, Bill now has a twenty-four-year-old son he says I can call if I want ("I don't hate the kid, I love him") and an ex-wife he says I shouldn't call because of the "bad blood." Trish Koskinen, Bill's ex-wife, reports that Bill "liked to party a little too much" and had trouble keeping jobs, and he "just wasn't a father" to his son, Bill Witt. Bill Witt remembers his father as "intimidating," a "bully," and "really, to sum it up, pretty much an asshole." Both Witt and Koskinen confirm that the Bill Simmons they knew was "not a good person with substances," in Witt's words.* I run all this by the Bill Simmons of the new millennium—the Bill Simmons with a daughter and a new wife and a folk-hero pedigree and a branded specialty sauce—and he says, "Everything you told me is bitterness." Because everybody has skeletons in the closet, he points out, fairly. Even the president of the United States. *Show me a guy who doesn't. A person changes.* "You know, you're a kid having a kid, you're not responsible. And I wasn't. I was *not. Responsible.* I matured late in life . . . I had my daughter . . . this little girl here depends on me . . . it took me a long time to mature. I don't know why." He laughs. "I don't freakin' know why."

Now, though, all that was over with, and Bill was doing okay. Coondog, too. At times Bill and Coondog were so profusely aware of the relative stability of their current family situations that they couldn't stop giving thanks out loud, they were thankful for their kids and their wives, thankful to be moving forward. To be near Coondog and Bill, then, was to feel their prayerful gratitude and their guilt grinding away inside, generating a frictional heat. Coondog and Bill were two guys trying really hard to live in the present, where they were vastly improved versions of their younger selves, more responsible, nicer, more respectful, deeper, calmer, harder-working, and which attributes were recognized and rewarded by their current families,

---

* Witt's opinions are slightly more conflicted than his mother's. For instance, Witt says he used to smoke pot, and sometimes, when Bill was 18 or so, he and his father would smoke pot *together*—which was "the only time we got along." Witt also says that, unlike his mother, he can't bring himself to cheer for the Black Widow at Wing Bowl. "In my heart I kinda want him to win, even though he's an asshole," he says. "You know, I really wish I didn't have those kind of feelings."

these women and kids they loved, these homes they'd made together—all the happy realities for which Bill and Coondog were trying so hard to be thankful, to be satisfied, *and failing*. Because the experience of figuring everything out, only twenty-five years too late, generated a guilt of its own. It only enhanced their already well-developed sense of wasted potential, only reinforced that their whole lives to date had been this stupid, wasteful battle against their own selves, as if every morning they'd woken up and put on an 80-pound backpack, and now that they'd finally ditched it they felt light, and needed some way to fulfill this newly sprung ambition and self-conception— they wanted to win, and be seen, to have their new flowering gloriousness validated (especially Bill, who from a young age "wanted to be known," according to his friend Bob Thomas, and who used to tell his ex-wife that "one day he'd be a millionaire")—except now the options were winnowed way down. It was like waking up in a Holiday Inn at 10:55 when the continental breakfast ends at eleven. No more croissants or good cereal, just dregs, just some crappy donut. All that's left are these stupid eating contests. . . .

Which is where shtick comes in. Shtick compensates for existential oversleeping. Blue-collar shtick, in its purest and most desperate form, is an act of imaginative will. It's a personality projection, a way to wiggle out from the body you're stuck in: a way to appear more slippery than you are. Bigger, more dangerous. Perhaps even as big and dangerous as you ought to have been. The unsquandered you.

Arnie, though. Arnie was a tough case. Arnie had his own special way of taking shtick to an extreme. Using shtick not to expand his world, to build a psychic annex and decorate it, but to twin it with his well-developed sense of justice and moral outrage, and direct it as a weapon against his enemies. In late December, right after he qualified for Wing Bowl, Arnie took a bunch of his AICE gurgitators to Tempe, Arizona, for a Ball Park Franks hot-dog contest at a tailgate party for the Tostitos Fiesta Bowl. The day before the contest, all of us—Arnie and his wife, Deb, Coondog, and four young college kids who were making a documentary about Wing Bowl and whom we called the Wing Bowl Nerds—walked from our hotel into downtown Tempe, just to sightsee. Arnie, who had qualified successfully for Wing Bowl 13, and who had greatly impressed Cataldi by pretending he was a dog having a seizure—the "Chowhound Chomp," he called it—chatted about Wing Bowl with Coondog the whole time, but Arnie did almost all of the talking: *Watch this kid. Just Don. Forget the Jarvises, forget the Wingadors. There is some new talent in this year's Wing Bowl that's rising to the surface. I tell ya right now, man, I can do 175 wings, I can do 175 wings, I'm willing to show you TONIGHT I can do 175 wings. I want Debbie to have a camera at Wing Bowl. I'm gonna clean and strip those bitches like junkyard dogs. If they screw me on Wing Bowl, it's gonna be documented. I can knock down fifty wings in seven minutes no problem. Big wings. Not bullshit little wings. Big wings.*

Coondog grabbed an orange from a tree on somebody's lawn and ate it. We walked past downtown and out to the stadium. We climbed Hayden Butte, a small hill next to the football stadium. The Nerds lugged their digital cameras. It was a gorgeous day and we watched planes flying overhead and landing at Phoenix airport off in the middle distance. A plane would periodically drown out Arnie's tirades about El Wingador—who, according to Arnie, didn't truly love eating like Arnie loved it because Wingador only did one contest a year—and George Shea.

Arnie, who was being filmed, said, "Debbie will tell you the time I put into it. The preparation. The distractions. The heart. The emotion. The time I spend with my friends. And my colleagues. At the cost. To my family. To my friends who are tired of me just talking about competitive eating. No. I put a lot into this. He's not the only one putting something into it. And he [Shea] doesn't deserve all the spoils."

Coondog, who was not being filmed, said, "I'm glad I don't drink anymore. Two years ago I would have been totally stoned. We would have had some good stuff."

For Arnie, shtick is enough. Shtick is an end in itself. Bill, however, cannot live on shtick alone. Bill has to face realities that Coondog understands, as a fellow construction worker and media fixture, but that Arnie doesn't—such as the ramifications of local fame, and the daily indignity of a construction job, and the compounded indignity of the wide gap between the two. Arnie has a master's degree and a fulfilling career, and Bill drives a "roll-off" for a living, which is a truck with a long, flat bed. He shuttles between construction sites in South Jersey, loading Dumpsters full of scrap and hauling them to the landfill. "I'm a trash man. No, I'm not a garbage man. I'm just a guy who picks up cans. I never touch the stuff." And it's a not-infrequent occurrence that Bill, in his roll-off truck, hauling garbage-but-not-garbage, will come across one of his knucklehead friends or a random Wing Bowl fan, and this person will look at Bill stuffed into the cab of his roll-off and say something like:

El Wingador! What are you doing driving a truck? I thought you'd be rich by now!

And Bill will think: How? Seriously, *"How?* You tell me how to be rich, 'cause I don't know how to do it."

Maybe he needed to be more greedy?

"I would like to capitalize on it, I'm not gonna lie to you. I love chicken where maybe I can jump on one of these establishments locally and pro-mote 'em, you know what I mean? A KFC or a Popeye's, any of the two or more, it doesn't matter to me. Who better spokesmodel, you know? Or spokesman, you know? I could be the Jared of Subway, you know?"

KFC wasn't calling. Popeye's wasn't calling. His heartburn was worsen-ing, disrupting his sleep, socking him with hot sudden pain during the day. Debbie started to really worry.

Which is why, in 2003, as Bill contemplated his plans for Wing Bowl 12—the one he'd eventually lose to Sonya Thomas—Debbie told him to quit.

Eat? Retire? Whenever Bill popped into WIP to do a quick radio spot, he'd talk to Angelo Cataldi, and at least twice Bill told him he wasn't sure he could compete in Wing Bowl 12, on account of Debbie.

One day after Thanksgiving, 2003, Cataldi pulled Bill aside. What was the deal? Would Bill compete?

Bill said he wasn't sure.

That, it turned out, was the wrong answer.

Arnie Chapman and AICE competitors, planning their Fiesta Bowl hot-dog contest, poolside at the Tempe Fiesta Inn, 12:25 p.m., three hours to contest time:

DEBBIE: So tell us, what are the rules?

ARNIE: Oh! The rules are . . . give me a rule, Dave.

COONDOG: Okay, I'll tell you what the rules are. There's no dipping, dunking, or desecrating, okay? If you take the hot dog by mistake off the bun, as long as you don't eat it and put it back on the bun, you're cool.

ARNIE: Why would you do that?

DEBBIE: Yeah, why *would* you do that?

EDDIE THE GEEK: For example, you can lift it up and put your ketchup or mustard under.

COONDOG: Some of these guys might get a little tempted.

ARNIE: You know, I always suspect like a Communist conspiracy or something.

KID CARY DEGROSA: So, so, *water*—

DEBBIE: Yes, you'll have *bottled* water.

COONDOG: You'll have bottled water.

KID CARY: No ice?

DEBBIE: It'll be cold.

GEEK: So you can't dunk in the bottle.

DEBBIE: Right.

ARNIE: Right.

DEBBIE: Can you pour the water on top?

ARNIE [mock-dictatorially]: No. NO! Uh-uh.

KID CARY: You'll be ejected?

COONDOG: Listen, and we're gonna have a chipmunking rule, too. It's what, fifteen seconds?

ARNIE: No, no, ten seconds, dammit.

KID CARY: What's that mean?

GEEK: You can't pick a hot dog up with a second to go and still be eatin' five minutes later.

ARNIE: Don't put anything in your mouth you can't swallow in ten seconds.

KID CARY: What do you do, spit it out?

COONDOG: You pick it up and put it down.

ARNIE: The judges will make a decision on how much you spit out and what the value, the amount of that hot dog is.

·   ·   ·

"I was against outsiders coming in," says Eric Gregg, the longtime Wing Bowl judge, "and especially professionals. I don't mind you coming [from] outside the area, but don't say you have a *job* eating. I don't like that idea. I was against it, but Angelo said I got no choice. Do this. Make it competitive. Angelo said to me one time, 'I hope we get somebody [i.e., Wingador] defeated so we generate more interest. If he [Wingador] keeps winning, it's going to phase out.' And it probably could have. Nobody could beat this guy."

By late 2003, a few months before Wing Bowl 12, the event was getting stale. WIP had ratings to worry about. One day at the studio, Cataldi and Bill sat down to talk about Wing Bowl 12. Here's how it went down, according to Bill:

Cataldi told Bill that sponsorships were sagging because Bill was "being like Mike Tyson," says Bill, "knocking everybody out in the first round." Since Bill's wife was freaking out anyway, could Bill sit out Wing Bowl 12 and be a color commentator, and then return triumphantly at Wing Bowl 13?

Bill said he wasn't sure. He didn't want to lose out on the prize money.

That's when Cataldi got "bent out of shape," in Bill's words. "He said to me that if I do get in it, I was gonna lose. He got kind of offended." Cataldi promised he'd bring in national eaters to knock Bill off his perch.

Bill said he didn't care.

Cataldi told Bill he wouldn't finish higher than third.

Bill told him, "I don't care if you get a gorilla. I'm not going to lose."

And lo and behold, Bill finished third.

In calmer moments, Bill admits, "I don't know what happened," and he avoids using the word "fixed," but when you combine his certainty that he ate the most wings in Wing Bowl 12 with his belief that WIP brushed him aside for "political" reasons having to do with "the benjamins," his meaning is unmistakable.

So this year, for Wing Bowl 13, Bill put his massive foot down. He hired an agent and had the agent tell WIP that if WIP couldn't find money for El Wingador, El Wingador wouldn't be in Wing Bowl. An appearance fee would be fine. Nothing huge—ten grand or so. Even five grand would help.

Didn't seem like a lot to ask.

WIP said no.

And the reason they said no was the same reason that Arnie said he loved Wing Bowl: Wing Bowl wasn't about money. It was about fun. Marc Rayfield, WIP's general manager, frames the station's talks with Bill as an effort to protect the "integrity" of the event. Rayfield says that in contrast to the general trend in competitive eating—"events started getting crazier and crazier and people started to realize they could use it to build their own brands, meaning themselves"—he sees Wing Bowl as "being about fun first and about eating chicken wings second." Therefore, WIP won't pay anybody anything. "Nothing," says Rayfield. "Again, once you open that door, it's a door that you can't close . . ."

It's worth stating here that Wing Bowl makes in the high six figures for WIP, as Rayfield estimates. It "determines whether we get off to a good start to the year or a bad start," ratings-wise, and the ratings determine all the deejays' and managers' bonuses. Also, Wing Bowl drives ad sales through the year, because it's offered as a sweetener to non–Wing Bowl ad packages. It's worth restating here, too, that the company that owns WIP is Viacom, Inc., the $26-billion giant. Wing Bowl's apparent amateurism was just a gummy residue that obscured the polished megacorporation beneath.

You could drill down to the megacorporation if you asked the right questions. When I first asked Angelo Cataldi if he told Bill that he wouldn't finish higher than third in Wing Bowl 12, Cataldi leaned forward. "Let me roll this through for ya, Jason," he said, in a way that made me feel very young and very naïve, as if I had just asked him whether unicorns lived in caves or in enchanted forests. "All right," he said, "here's the way it works . . . the job that I had at that point, for the last three years, was to promote the possibility that he could be beaten. So every year, when he called in, I would say, 'You're goin' down this year, Simmons. You won't finish in the top five.' If I'm not mistaken, I said to him"—and Cataldi's voice gets cartoonishly gruff and evil—"'YOU WON'T EVEN BE IN THE FINALS. YOU AREN'T NOTHIN'. NOW YOU'RE DEALIN' WITH THE NATIONAL GUYS.' Now, if he wanted to take that seriously?" Cataldi's voice drips with disdain. "The fix was in," he says. "Yeah, how did I fix this, exactly? Jesus . . . The last damn thing in the world I need to do is fix the Wing Bowl. I will deal with whoever wins the damn thing."

Later I asked Cataldi specifically about Bill's declining-ad-revenue charge, and Cataldi sent me a carefully worded e-mail denying Bill's claims, attacking Bill as a poor loser, and arguing that eaters had always accused him of fixing Wing Bowl because "it is the nature of our event." Then he sent a similar e-mail to my magazine editor.

Then he talked to my editor on the phone.

Arnie, emceeing the collegiate portion (Pitt vs. Utah) of the First Inaugural Ball Park Tostitos Fiesta Bowl National Hot Dog Eating Championship* in Tempe, Arizona:

> ARNIE: All right now! Okay! I want to ask everybody in the audience for a second to be quiet. We are going to take an oath! All the eaters are going to take an oath that they will not violate picnic-style rules! You will not separate the hot dog from the bun!
>
> LARRY JOE (aka Frank, Ball Park spokesperson and cast member of *According to Jim*): No!
>
> ARNIE: No no! You will not pour water on your bun!
>
> FRANK [shaking head]: No!
>
> ARNIE: You will not mash, mush! You will not desecrate the American icon known as the hot dog! You will eat the hot dog the way God intended! Hot dog and bun! All eaters put your hand on the cookie and raise your left hand! I! Competitive eater! . . .
>
> EATERS: I! Competitive eater!
>
> ARNIE: . . . promise not to violate picnic-style rules!
>
> EATERS: . . . promise not to violate picnic-style rules . . .

"You have made a decision, correct?"

"Yes."

"All right," says Angelo Cataldi. "Well, dammit, I don't know what's taken

---

* And twenty yards from a U.S. Army recruiting trailer featuring a black Hummer blaring hip-hop and blazoned with painted yellow flames and a sign that says YO SOY EL ARMY next to a long table staffed by a dark-haired girl in a tied-off T-shirt and low-riding jeans whom a military guy confirms is *not* actually in the Army.

so long. But in eight minutes we will learn whether Bill Simmons will come back to the huge applause of his hopeful local audience ... My hand is shaking ..."

December 22, WIP studios. Since three weeks ago, when Bill told the deejays he wasn't sure he would compete, the other moving parts of Wing Bowl 13 have locked into place. Sonya Thomas has agreed to return, on the condition that WIP play the song "Maneater" upon her entrance. The IFOCE's New York contingent—Cookie Jarvis, Charles Hardy, Crazy Legs Conti, Tim Janus, Krazy Kevin, Don Lerman—have all qualified, as have several intriguing local eaters: Pizzazilla, a St. Joe's College student (one whole pizza in eight minutes); Totally Appauling (a raw cow brain in two minutes); Rich the Butcher (a pound of raw meat in one minute); and, most impressively, a man named Uncle Buc, who swallowed a 1.5-pound Yankee candle.

"But none of it works for me," Cataldi says, "without THE number-one guy ... Are we ready with an announcement, Bill?"

"Yeah, I am."

Bill, in the past few weeks, has been under incredible pressure, both public and private, to accept WIP's invitation. In private meetings, the station has refused Bill's demand for an appearance fee. It has even refused to plug Bill's sauce at Wing Bowl, owing to a conflict with an existing culinary sponsor. Instead, WIP has given Bill an open-ended invitation to come into the studio and plug his sauce—or his restaurant, should he open one. WIP's offer is not what Bill hoped for, but it's better than nothing. The public inducements have been even stronger. On air, Al Morganti accused Bill of not having enough "heart," jabbing a sharp thumb into Bill's rawest, sorest spot—basically calling him a bum—and Angelo Cataldi has been crowing that his new eaters are so good as to make El Wingador irrelevant. Cataldi has given a lot of airtime to one particular newcomer named Bob Shoudt, thirty-eight, a largish tech-support manager with a wide face and a soft voice. Shoudt, an IFOCE eater from Royersford, Pennsylvania, has several interesting, promotable hooks—his children help him train and know the lyrics to Booker's *Hungry & Focused* CD by heart; also, Shoudt is a vegetarian who has obtained a blanket dispensation from his vegetarian wife to eat meat in contests—but the hook Cataldi likes best is his nickname, "Humble

Bob," which reeks of the everyman. I was in the WIP studio the day Cataldi met Humble Bob for the first time. Cataldi shook his hand vigorously and said, "God, it's *such* an honor to meet you, I will build you into this monster, I will make you the biggest thing this city ever saw," after which Bob successfully completed his stunt (twenty Hatfield franks in three minutes and thirty seconds) and Cataldi declared Wing Bowl all but over—"get this man the color he wants in the Suzuki Verona"—because Humble Bob was "the new El Wingador." Cataldi added, "El Wingador should announce he's *not* comin' back."

Outside the swinging doors of the studio is the bustle of the WIP Christmas party. There's a table spread with strawberries and bagels and, of course, chicken wings. Advertisers from Canal Street Liquors, Beneficial Savings Bank, and Accurate-Lift Trucks munch bagels as coteries of exotic dancers from two different clubs weave among them . . .

"Well," Bill continues, "I just want to thank *all* the people, and I'm talking hundreds of people, that have come up to me and, ah, been my fans for the last years, years and years, and I won't"—and Bill pauses and squirms in his seat while Cataldi extends his arms forward like a televangelist seconds before he receives the Word and minutes before he opens the pledge lines—"I won't pass up the chance to go against these eaters," Bill says, finally. "I WILL be there."

"Ohhhhh! Oh! Wow! *Wow!* OH MY GOD! This is the best Christmas gift we could ever have here at WIP!"

The whole time, Felicia, Bill's daughter, has been sitting quietly in one corner of the sound studio, eating chicken wings.

Rhea Hughes notices and says, "Look how clean those are."

Cataldi says, "I looked carefully at the two wings she ate. I can only credit one."

The room explodes in laughter.

5

FOUR-X IS A LOVE LETTER

CHRISTMAS. WITH ALL the Wing Bowl madness, I've almost forgotten about Christmas. Three days later I drive to Bill's house for Christmas dinner. When I get there, Bill is out distributing presents to the kids of his less fortunate neighbors. Deb's mother and grandmother are watching *Godsend* on Bill's OnDemand system, so I plop onto a couch and accept Bill's mother Felicia's offer of coquito, a sort of Puerto Rican eggnog. It tastes like coconut. Bill arrives, a few minutes later, in a good mood, perhaps because he can smell the spread of Puerto Rican pork shoulder, ham, turkey legs, mashed potatoes, green beans, and soft warm rolls.

Bill eats at the kitchen table, with me and a small TV set tuned to the Raiders/Chiefs game, leaving the rest of his family in the dining room. Bill's present to Debbie this year was a small printer that connects to their digital camera, so when I start taking notes on the mounds of food on Bill's plate— a long, oval serving plate piled with pork, turkey, mashed potatoes—Bill photographs his plate and prints me an instant three-by-five. Good thing, because the food is already vanishing. "I'm eating faster than you, man," he teases. "What's goin' on?" Bill started eating at 4:30. By 4:44, everything but the turkey leg and rolls are devoured. By 4:49, he's done. "NEXT! Look a' that, man. Look a' that. You wanna take a picture of THAT?"

Bill gets up and goes to the dining room for seconds. "This is my last training meal," he says. "Might as well enjoy it." When Bill holds his dinner plate above the table, it's like a thunderhead blocking the sun. "I can't do it anymore after this," he says. "She'll divorce me," meaning Deb. Then he yells out to me in the other room: "OFF THE RECORD." Bill laughs. "Nah, that's a joke, you can use that. Just put a 'ha-ha' in there." He walks back into the kitchen and leans over the table like he's about to tell me a secret. Sotto voce, he says:

"We got a cheesecake, too."

By 5:05, the second plate is clean. In the interlude between dinner and dessert, Bill's family teases him about Wing Bowl. Bill's aunt Nidia says, "What's this—you're doing it again this year?" She hits him with a rolled-up magazine.

"I might as well beat her," Bill says.

"You're a glutton for punishment."

"That's the right word."

"So, what, you got five weeks left?" asks Mike, Deb's father, wearing a black sweatshirt that says SUPPORT OUR TROOPS.

"I could win that thing *tomorrow* if I had to."

"Oh yeah. You're gonna clean her clock this time. Send her back to Korea."

Back in the living room, someone has laid out the cheesecake. "Yo! Yo! You got the cheesecake out? You didn't tell me?" Bill procures a slice with cherries on top. "Oh, this is good," he says. "This is SO good. You sure you don't want a piece? Oh shit, man." He asks me a second time. Sure I don't want any? Am I sure? Really? Okay, I say, give me a piece. The three-by-five of his first helping sits on the kitchen table. Bill regards it with great focus. "Damn," he says, "doesn't that look good? Doesn't that look good? I would frame that fucker and put it on my wall." He picks up the photo and walks to the living room to show his family.

After dinner, the family shifts to the living room to exchange some late presents. Bill's mother hands him a box. Bill opens it. Inside is a burgundy flannel shirt, size Xtra-Xtra-Xtra-Large: 3XL. Bill doesn't even try it on. He has gone up a size. He is now Xtra-Xtra-Xtra-Xtra-Large: 4XL.

"It doesn't fit," he says. "I gained fifty pounds."

"Four-X," says Felicia, incredulous.

"What *is* four-X?" says Nidia, Bill's aunt.

"Four-X is a love letter," Bill laughs.

"Last time I heard, you were *three*-X," says Felicia, crisply. "Now you are four-X."

"I'm training now," says Bill, "so I gotta get all this gut back. It's terrible, isn't it?"

Felicia wraps up the shirt and shakes her head. "Ugh," she says, walking out of the room. "Yes."

Earlier, when I'd been checking out the presents under Bill's tree (video karaoke, a titanium nonstick skillet, a portable DVD player), Bill's mother Felicia had walked in, and I asked her how she felt about Bill doing Wing Bowl again this year. "I didn't even know he was going to go back till tonight," she said. "He said this is going to be his last, so I'll pull for him. But you never know."

Less than fifteen miles away, as we spoke, as we ate pork shoulder and unwrapped presents, Fino "Chili Dawg" Cachola was dying.

Joelle Cachola, pronounced CATCH-ola, has the body of a pixie—short dark hair, petite build—and the voice of a tough chick. As she sits on the navy couch in her family room, talking about her husband Fino, her eyes sometime glint with fluid, like she's going to cry. She doesn't, though. Joelle plays with the frayed ends of the hole in her jeans, and her son, Shane, plays with a teddy bear clad in a Yankees jersey. There are two Cachola children. Fino and Joelle rescued them from New Jersey's dysfunctional foster system. Shane is three, and in the process of being adopted as a Cachola. Devon is six, and officially adopted. They are the Shane and Devon to whom Fino "Chili Dawg" Cachola gave his shout-out on December 10—the day he qualified for Wing Bowl 13, and the day that Angelo Cataldi predicted he would lose, once again, on February 4.

In that sense, Cataldi was right about Fino: in Wing Bowl terms, he was a loser. He never finished higher than third. Year after year, Fino would start training in November. He'd order the T-shirts, he'd invite his buddies to tag along on his stunt, and on the day of Wing Bowl, he'd lose. Then, after the contest, he'd come home, stick his fingers down his throat, throw up, drive to the bar for a couple of beers with friends, and sleep the rest of the day. "It would hurt comin' out this way and that way," Joelle laughs. "Well, I don't know how these people who are professionals say they get enjoyment out of it, because you don't. He'd just be like, 'Oh, my stomach hurts,' and it would be hard as a rock." When it became clear Fino would never win, he took Joelle to Aruba anyway. Twice. "He just loved to go to Aruba and drink and not have to worry," says Joelle.

Joelle worried. Fino's health was already suboptimal. He was overweight, and suffered from sleep apnea; he wore a special mask at night, connected to an oxygen machine. Joelle wondered what Wing Bowl was doing to his system, and made him promise, after 2004's Wing Bowl 12, to lose weight. In November 2004, when Fino was thirty-six years old, he started coughing buckets of mucus. He ran a fever. He started hallucinating. Fino wanted to stay home, but Joelle and others persuaded him to check into a hospital, where doctors stuck Fino with an IV of antibiotics to kill what they thought was pneumonia. They also diagnosed him with high blood pressure, an enlarged heart, and borderline diabetes, which ran in his family. After a week in the hospital, Fino came home with a shiny new pack of afflictions.

Wing Bowl 13 was discussed.

"I told him no," says Joelle. "I said, 'You can't do this to your body. You *gotta.*' And he said, 'I'm not gonna, I'm not gonna.' And then the next thing you know, he was telling me, 'Put the radio on, I'm going to do my stunt.' I said, 'What are you doing?' He said, 'I'm going to eat grilled cheese.' I'm like, '*Feeeee*-nooo,' and then I figured, well, if he wants to do it, let him do it. He doesn't ask for much." Chili Dawg performed his Wing Bowl stunt on December 10, delighting Angelo Cataldi with the potential of "blood and snots."

A couple days after the stunt, Fino woke up with chest pain and drove himself to the hospital. Doctors gave him an EKG, said he was fine, and sent him home. He wasn't fine. "He was always blowin' up blood," says Joelle. "Blood, blood, blood, blood. I try not to question it now, because I can't do anything about it." Fino returned to work, but when he came home from his shift, he'd tumble right into bed, weirdly exhausted. On Christmas night, Fino's pain sharpened. He told Joelle, "My throat is just killin' me so bad." Joelle said, "What do you want me to do?" Fino said, "I don't know, but the pain was never like this." When Joelle woke up the next morning, Fino's sleep mask was in pieces at his side. Rigor mortis had already set in around the mouth.

Joelle is a dialysis technician. Fino worked the swing shift as a union electrician in South Jersey, wiring utility lights on Route 73. Joelle received a one-time death benefit of $10,000 from the union, plus Fino's pension, which was small since Fino was only thirty-six when he died. The couple had no life insurance. "Now my eyes are wide open," says Joelle. "Who thinks about life insurance when you're thirty-six?"

Blood, blood, blood, blood.

I am waiting for Joelle to get angry. *I'm* angry—but at whom? At Fino, for being so reckless with his health? At WIP, for egging him on? It's hard to be angry at Fino, because Wing Bowl made him so happy, and it's hard to be angry at WIP, because the radio station's employees were only doing their job, which was to market the station on the cheap, using only WIP's embarrassingly paltry "promotions budget," their own creativity, and their own local knowledge of Philly myth and lore—and WIP had done this so brilliantly that Wing Bowl had become the envy of every sports radio station in the country. When WIP people speak of Wing Bowl, they convey an obvious, and justifiable, pride.

So I wait for a cue from Joelle.

Joelle says the coroner told her "it could have been a heart attack" or an enlarged heart that killed Fino; her doctor friends said that Fino's pneumonia might really have been misdiagnosed congestive heart failure. Joelle declined an autopsy: "It wasn't going to bring him back."

I ask her: Does she think eating had anything do to with Fino's death?

Joelle pauses and sucks in a breath. "I think competitive eating's not healthy. It can't be. You're shocking your body so bad just consuming so much in that short period of time. There's no way it could be healthy."

Is she angry at WIP?

"See," she says, "he didn't do it for a living, where these other people do. He did it one time a year. And that made him happy. Like I said, that was his fifteen minutes of fame."

I wish I knew Joelle well enough to interpret the look on her face when she says this.

The next time I talk to Joelle, a year from now, she won't be so hard to read. She will have found her anger. She'll tell me about the memorial fund she set up in Fino's name to help pay for her kids' future college tuition. Cataldi will have plugged the fund on his website and on the air. But the people who'll actually donate to the fund are Fino's union brothers in Local 351—

not any of Cataldi's many thousands of well-heeled listeners, and not Cataldi himself ("the multimillionaire," Joelle will say, mordantly), and not any member of WIP's management. After Wing Bowl 13, Joelle won't hear from WIP again. "Nothing ever came of it," she'll say. "WIP ended up doing nothing."*

But that's all still to come.

As of today, it's too soon for Joelle to have been let down. Cataldi has contacted her. He wants to honor Fino during Wing Bowl 13. There will be a highlight reel of Fino's Wing Bowl appearances, and a moment of silence.

On my way out, she points me to a newspaper on the kitchen counter. It is the December 27 issue of the Cherry Hill *Courier Post*. It includes a ninety-nine-word item about Fino's passing on page 7B. The story does not mention Fino's wife, children, or occupation, but it does include a nice plug for Wing Bowl 13, "scheduled for Feb. 4 at the Wachovia Center."

"I think it's a tremendously positive event," says WIP general manager Marc Rayfield. "Few incidents have ever occurred at a Wing Bowl. There really are no losers, because everybody walks away with a smile on their face. Even the people who don't win. You know? I mean, to me, there's no downside to this kind of event. If there were more happy-type things like this where it really was based—it was more about fun than anything else, because that's really what it's about. It's about bringing guys together to do and talk about the things that they do and talk about when they're not with their wives and girlfriends. That's what Wing Bowl is."

"Guy wants me to back up to a fuckin' bar, pick up a can," said Wingador. "I pull away from it. I sunk three feet. I look like I'm in a hole or something." Bill's truck was stuck in the mud somewhere in Mount Laurel, New Jersey. I'd reached him on his cell. It was the middle of January. Wing Bowl was three weeks away, and he didn't want to talk about it. Felicia had been "starting to get a little bit of a mouth on her," he said, "and Debbie kind of blames

---

* Cataldi's partial response: "I would have loved to help the Cachola family more financially, but I cannot control where people choose to donate their money. Mrs. Cachola never heard any further from us because there was not much more we could have done for her. We are a radio show, not a social services agency."

me for the things she's around." Was he supposed to tell his daughter she couldn't go to Wing Bowl? Bill's evolving relationship with Wing Bowl had become like a child's evolving relationship with Christmas, looking forward to the big day less and less until last year he learned, to his horror, that there was no Santa Claus, just a ninety-nine-pound girl with star barrettes: Sonya, the Grinch Who Stole Wing Bowl.

Only one other Wing Bowl gurgitator was similarly unhappy, and that was Arnie "Chowhound" Chapman. By mid-January the video of Arnie's qualifying stunt had been removed from the station's partner website, arousing Arnie's suspicions that the Shea brothers had screwed him over yet again, perhaps by threatening to pull Sonya Thomas if Arnie were allowed to compete. He e-mailed Cataldi, asking for an explanation, and Al Morganti wrote him back:

> As for the subject of inclusion in the Wing Bowl, I am afraid that he [Cataldi] was forged [*sic*] an agreement of sorts with the IFOCE. . . . Unfortunately, there are times when business decisions have to be made in which all parties cannot be accommodated, and we appear to have reached such a point in regard to your participation in the event.

Arnie was filled, once again, with righteous anger. He circulated an e-mail arguing that anyone who failed to stand by him in his hour of need was no better than the Nazis: "Think about it; that's how 6 million Jews were killed when good people stood by and did or said nothing because they were not directly affected." I called Arnie a few days after getting his e-mail, and it seemed like his wife, Deb, had talked him off the warpath. He said, "Some of the feelings were connected just to me being a competitor and feeling like I was being denied the experience of Wing Bowl, and feeling the kind of injustice, you know, and then . . . actually like really feeling that I wanted to turn over tables in the middle of the contest, and boy, it's a good thing that I actually have assets and a good woman who told me to think about someone other than myself." Arnie wasn't angriest about getting kicked out; he had been sort of expecting it. What angered him the most was the tone of Morganti's e-mail. "He reduced my involuntary disqualification to, oh, just a simple mechanical business decision," Arnie said. All he wanted was a heartfelt apology—some blue-collar solidarity, man to man—but instead he got this bureaucratic kiss-off. "I mean, read the letter, man," Arnie said. "It's *so*... And this *contemptuousness* that he shows. This is the kind of guy who should be working for the sports radio station of Philadelphia, a working-class city? Contemptuous little bastard. I can't believe it."

Arnie wasn't ready to let it drop, obviously, and he kept trying to find a way into Wing Bowl. In mid-January, when Coondog O'Karma and I went to Japan for two weeks, Arnie e-mailed Coondog overseas, begging him to intervene with Cataldi on Arnie's behalf. I would dread the times when Coondog would check his e-mail in our twenty-four-hour Internet café because it always put him in a bad mood. "I'm sick of it," Coondog said one night. "Just sick of it. I said, 'Arnie, it's just a fuckin' goddamn radio contest. They don't give a FUCK.' You'd think he was crucified. I told him, 'Arnie, you're ruining your life.' It's all he thinks about. I KNOW it's all he thinks about." The e-mails from Arnie and his colleague Joe Menchetti, who had also been denied a chance to qualify for Wing Bowl, presumably for the same reason as Arnie, only strengthened Coondog's resolve to quit eating and move on to something else. Eating, he said, "lets you feel like a kid for a second. And I enjoy that. And now that there's leagues, and big egos, and guys stretching their wieners, it's no fun anymore... I'm thinking, fuck these guys, they can have it. I'm out."

By late January, Wing Bowl 13 looked like a blockbuster. Sonya was back. Wingador was back. Humble Bob, if he lived up to a tenth of Angelo Cataldi's hype, was poised to displace them both. The IFOCE had issued a press release titled "All Eyes Turn to Philly," and Philadelphia Newspapers Inc. created an online "Virtual Wing Bowl" video game* to drive Internet traffic to the *Inquirer* and the *Daily News. Jewish Week* magazine and the Game Show Network requested press credentials, and a trader from Deutsche Bank in New York wrote the station that he was bringing six of his clients. For the first time in Wing Bowl history, there would be an actual

---

* "Use your mouse to eat, chew, swallow, drink, and burp—and hopefully not vomit—your way to a high score!"

Wing Bowl ring, modeled after the Super Bowl ring: a diamond-studded gold number worth $5,000, crafted by one of Cataldi's most loyal advertisers. Molson had signed up as the official beer sponsor, along with Cars.com, Matt Blatt Suzuki, AdultWorld, Camden Harley, US Airways, Bob and Ron's Worldwide Stereo, the Schmitter sandwich, and the Resort Atlantic City Casino Hotel. The afterparty was set for Delilah's, Philly's high-class strip club. The number of Wingettes had pushed well past WIP's allotment of seventy-five, although Al Morganti demonstrated his compassion by admitting a handful of last-minute wannabes like Lisa, who explained that she had just given birth but still thought she had what it takes. Cataldi asked if she'd lost all her baby weight. Lisa said she weighed ninety-nine pounds, five pounds over.

"Can you lose it by Friday?" asked Morganti.

Big. It was going to be big. Then, on January 23, 2005, the Philadelphia Eagles beat the Atlanta Falcons to win the NFC championship, throwing the city of Philadelphia into a swooning frenzy. The Eagles, for the first time in twenty-four years, were going to the Super Bowl. On WIP, callers said that the game was more important than their firstborn child, and meant it. Banks reported a surge of interest in second mortgages and home-equity loans from male Eagles fans looking to finance trips to Jacksonville. Pennsylvania governor Ed Rendell rescheduled his budget address to accommodate a possible Eagles victory parade. Star wide receiver Terrell Owens had injured his leg against Dallas, and for a whole week the *Daily News* ran columns written from the perspective of T.O.'s fibula. Sometimes it was hard to tell where Wing Bowl fandom ended and Eagles fandom began. In the week before Wing Bowl, a guy called in to WIP—he gave his name as Greg—and said that his entire warehouse had just been laid off. "You gotta look at the upside," Greg said. "At least I have the Eagles to get me through my transition." Greg added immediately that "for the past twelve years, I've heard [Wing Bowl] on the radio and always wanted to be there but couldn't go." Now, happily, he could.

"Greg, would you like a sweatshirt?"

"I would like the largest of whatever you've got."

If the distinction was already blurred, WIP did its best to obliterate it altogether. WIP touted what they were now calling "Super Wing Bowl" as "the biggest Eagles pep rally ever." On the night of January 31, with Wing Bowl four days away, Cataldi filmed his weekly cable sports show at Chickie & Pete's bar in South Philly, and walking through the bar, talking to people, I couldn't disaggregate the Wing Bowl people and the Eagles people. The twin manias had merged. The bar was a glut of green. I said hi to Wing Bowl judge Eric Gregg, ensconced at a table, smoking a cigarette, and talked to a man who offered me a shot of vodka and gossiped about the Wing Bowl procession of a friend of a friend of a friend. "All I can tell you is there's gonna be blood." He paused. "From an animal." He paused again. "From a *dead* animal." Wingador was here, too, awash in drunken attention he didn't need. Though Bill was wearing a red TEAM WINGADOR shirt on the advice of his agent, "I wanted to wear my Eagles jersey," he said.

The buildup got so intense that WIP tried, in those last frantic days, to throttle it back. On air, Cataldi said, "We do not in any way advise throwing things," but it was like a gung-ho tank commander not in any way advising the painting of gung-ho slogans on tanks. WIP was scrambling to please both its listeners and its legal department, and it couldn't do both without tainting the precarious spontaneity that had gotten Wing Bowl this far. Live by the crowd, die by the crowd. Behind the scenes, WIP's Marc Rayfield was trying to be the responsible parent. He told me that for the first time the VIP passes had been printed in off-colors (teal, dirty yellow, deep red), and said, perhaps even believing it, that they would be difficult to counterfeit. Also for the first time, WIP sent all eaters a letter with an extensive list of rules regarding sponsorships (no cutting personal deals not approved by the station) and lewd acts (for which eaters would be not just ejected but sued for damages).

"A whole fuckin' list of rules they gave me," Wingador complained, but as Wing Bowl approached, his natural competitiveness crushed any remaining ambivalence. He went from being so bitter he couldn't think to being so anxious he couldn't sleep. On February 1, with three days left, Al Morganti issued the odds with Wingador live in the studio:

Cookie Jarvis and El Wingador at 2 to 1.

Sonya Thomas at even odds.

"Oh!" said Angelo. "El Wingador is not the favorite for the first time ever!"

Said Wingador, "It's okay . . . He just added fuel to my fire. I've been waitin' a year for this."

Weigh-in time. February 3, Wing Bowl Eve. Eleven hours to go. Chickie & Pete's bar is so packed in places that I can barely even move. The IFOCE eaters stick together near the bar's middle, and the rest cluster near the back bar. This is the first time they've all been together in the same room. An eater named Just Don, accompanied by two friends wearing black T-shirts that read JUST DON, says that his procession will involve "Andy Reid in tights, and *The Godfather*." Chunk, the Canadian eater, is here with his three Canuck friends, who sip Coronas and tell the story of how they got here, which is by car—they wanted to fly, but Chunk couldn't fit in one airplane seat and didn't want to pay for two. I spot past champion Tollman Joe wearing a white T-shirt as large as a bedsheet that is nevertheless stretched taut across his belly. He offers me a sip of his Absolut and cranberry. "Yeah, I had a stroke," he says. "Couldn't get around so well. Otherwise I'd be in there to try a comeback." I meet two men carrying a 610 WIP banner they claim contains the signatures of every Wing Bowl contestant in the past five years, and a forty-five-year-old Wingette wearing a homemade skirt embellished with 2,000 rhinestones and Eagles-green fabric she bought on eBay. WIP's Marc Rayfield elbows through the crowd in a topcoat and a grin. "This is blown out," he says. "I've never seen a crowd like this before at the weigh-in." He guesses there are 750 people here and says, "This is close to the legal limit. This is actually *past* the legal limit."

The only person not here is Wingador.

The weigh-in gets started without him. Chunk, the Canuck, is conned into taking off his clothes, in accordance with Wing Bowl tradition. Tim "Eater X" Janus outs himself as a Dallas fan, and is flooded with boos; Tim, shirtless, flexing his biceps, wearing a cornrow wig, has apparently decided to play the heel, and seems to be loving it—an extroverted side of Tim Janus I never knew existed. (Janus, after having been issued long odds, 20 to 1, sent me an e-mail complaining, correctly, that "there are so many worthless eaters ranked ahead of me," and that "Beast from the Northeast deserves to be ranked higher than Pizzazilla," but "whatever, I guess I'll just have to eat well.") Cookie Jarvis and Eric Booker, who qualified at a last-minute eat-off, weigh in at 475 pounds and 530 pounds, respectively.* Wingador is scheduled to go next, but Wingador is unreachable via cell. The deejays decide to go forward with the weighing of Sonya Thomas: 103 pounds, less than one-fifth the weight of Eric Booker. Still no Wingador. "His time is more important than yours," Cataldi says sarcastically, "so please wait. Thank you." Finally, there's a commotion in the crowd—Wingador!—and the Big Man pushes through to the scale, which pegs him at a magisterial 312 pounds.

Afterwards, I see him by the bathroom, banging his head against the wall; a little later I find him in a dark room away from the main action where, every few seconds, he swings his torso and neck 180 degrees, scanning the room with a distant look. "I'm anxious," he says, and turns. "I'm not nervous," he says, and turns again. "I'm fine." He mutters something that sounds like "Fffffuckerrrrrr."

The party is breaking up. Wingador climbs into his yellow Hummer limousine—supplied by O'Hara's bar in Gloucester, New Jersey, Bill's official sponsor—and heads home to get a few hours of sleep. At the Wachovia Center, fans are partying in the parking lot, tapping the kegs, starting small fires.

Ten hours to go and it's already begun.

---

* These numbers are a bit high. Booker had gained weight—and to look at him, 530 pounds seemed plausible—but in his defense, the scale was "not even a real scale," he says. "It was like a scale you weigh meat on."

6

SONYA, WHERE'S MY MASSAGE?

3:30 A.M.

WING BOWL MORNING is a white mess. It's snowing when I pull onto Wingador's street. I look to my right and hit the brakes when I see the ghosts. My window's partly fogged, so I duck my head to get a sightline through a cleaner part of the glass. Now I can see the ghosts more clearly. There are three of them, standing at the end of a driveway across from Wingador's. Their parkas are caked in white. They are holding beers. Drinking, at 3:30 a.m., in the snow. They stare at me as if I'm the strange one.

I park on the ghosts' side of the street and cross over to Wingador's front porch. Two of the Wing Bowl Nerds, who have slept over, let me inside. Deb is already awake—has been awake for hours. At 3:34, the house is quiet except for some muffled thuds from upstairs. Wingador. He'd set his alarm for three. "I just lie there for a while," he told me yesterday. At 3:40, the first two Friends of Wingador (FOW) show up, holding coffees from the twenty-four-hour Wawa a few blocks away. At 3:45 Deb pulls a package of Hormel bacon from the fridge, slices the whole thing in half, and starts laying the bacon strips on a tray atop the stove. She sprinkles the bacon with what looks like half of a chopped onion. She twists on the heat.

Two more FOWs arrive. Bill plods down the stairs in his sleep clothes, a white tank top and Tarheel-blue shorts. "What's up, man?" he says to the

FOWs leaning against the wall, cradling coffees. "Good morning. Good morning. Good morning." His skin looks more leathery than usual. There are large half-moons under his eyes, and his mullet is scuzzy. He rubs his right arm. "I think I slept on my wrist," he says. Bill spots the two Nerds and asks how much they slept.

"A half hour," say the Nerds, in chorus.

"What are you, a fucking vampire?"

Bill turns on his giant HDTV and flips it, inexplicably, to the "old-school rap" music channel, treating us to "Double Trouble at the Amphitheater," a classic cut from the *Wild Style* soundtrack. Then he hands the remote to an FOW. "If you put country on," Bill tells him, "we're fightin'."

By now the FOWs are coming faster than I can keep track. One is John Petroski, Bill's old coach in Babe Ruth League baseball. "Great pitcher, very strong, great hitter," says Petroski, a grandfatherly figure wearing a Team Wingador ballcap. "He's always been a big boy. Damn near six foot when he was twelve. Nice guy, too. Good thing they made the big guys nice guys." Petroski laughs. "Billy says this is his last year. But he's been saying that for a while." Then, possibly out of embarrassment at telling me something slightly critical, Petroski adds, "My wife passed away recently. He spent time with her, brought her books and stuff. My wife loved him."

Bill heads back upstairs to take a shower while the onion smell fills the first floor. Bill's daughters, Felicia and Ashley, both wearing Eagles jerseys, bounce into the living room and sit down next to Coach Petroski, who asks them what Daddy told them about how to behave today.

"He says if he loses, don't cwy," says Felicia.

Deb busts out a cardboard box full of Team Wingador gear, offering the swag to the assembled FOWs. "I don't know you," she says to one guy in a Harley cap. "I've never met you." The guy shrugs. Debbie laughs, lets it ride. Even Felicia and Ashley are unfazed by a dozen large and semi-strange people tramping through their living room at 4:00 a.m. They're used to it. Both girls are gamely rehearsing their cheers. For biological daughter Felicia: "Go Daddy!" For stepdaughter Ashley: "Go Billy!"

At 4:23, Bill descends, mullet coiffed, wearing a red and black long-sleeved jersey with obscure, vaguely Asian markings. If not for his size, he'd look like a comic-book ninja. Bill's first stop is the kitchen, where he glances at the sizzling bacon. He knows he's not allowed to partake. This is a Simmons family ritual. Debbie is the matador, and the bacon is her red cape. The smell alone gets Bill "hungrier than a mud bear" and ready to plow through wings. He points to a two-foot-long Wawa hoagie box on the kitchen table. "I ate this yesterday in ten minutes," he says. "You think I'm ready?" Bill turns to the sill above the sink, grabbing a pill bottle. "Nexium," he says, popping his heartburn medication. "My vitamins," he says, popping several. "That'll get the motor runnin', right?" He swigs some water, then says, "I gotta go relax. I'll be back in a couple minutes." Exit Wingador.

Ten minutes later, at 4:33, Bill comes down the stairs one last time. "I didn't wanna get out of bed," he says. "I could just stay here and call in my score." He laughs, then says, "Let's go." The house empties. Wingador and his entourage pile into the yellow Hummer limo. I get into my sedan with B.J., one of the Wing Bowl Nerds, and we join a seven-vehicle caravan following the Hummer.

And that's when things start to fall apart.

5:00 A.M.

Toll plaza, Walt Whitman Bridge. I hand three dollars to the toll taker, and as I drive away, he tells me, "Shoulda left earlier."

Even the toll guy knows I'm screwed.

I sluice along I-76, exit at the stadium, and pull into a long lane of snarled traffic. The snow has turned to rain. Nothing's moving. The road is all flashing yellow lights and orange-vested cops directing the traffic, which moves a few yards with every green light. The Wachovia Center is only a few hundred yards away, but we're running out of time. Wing Bowl starts in less than an hour. I turn on the radio to WIP, and immediately hear a befuddled but stern Big Daddy Graham, the overnight deejay, telling us to go home:

"I never thought I would make this announcement at 5:11 in the morning, but I got it straight from the top. So listen to me and listen to me good. *If you are not. Down here. Already. We are asking you. Not to come.* Every single lot is full. . . ."

I look out my driver-side window at the guy next to me in a dark SUV.

He shrugs. I shrug in solidarity. Mine is perhaps a false solidarity, because I have a pass. I don't know if SUV Guy has a pass. My pass says MEDIA and is laminated in purple, so if I can find a parking spot, I might still get in. Where do I park? I've got another fifteen minutes of gridlock ahead of me, at least, before I get to the parking lots, which Big Daddy says are full. If it's bad here, I wonder, what does it look like at the front gate? The next day's *Daily News* would have the answer:

> . . . wing-crazed crowds surged toward the building like a tsunami and cops struggled to hold them back. A female officer was hit in the head by a thrown bottle and removed to a hospital. There were no arrests, police said.

B.J. takes out his cell phone and calls one of his cameramen inside, who tells B.J. that Al Morganti himself—Wing Bowl's creator—had to park two miles away.

If Morganti can't get a spot, neither can I. Parking is not going to happen. I slip into the turn lane and cut across several lanes onto Pattison, heading west away from the arena; I gun it until I hit 20th, about three quarters of a mile away from the Wachovia. I park in front of a driveway on a cozy street of new brick town homes. B.J. and I get out and check our watches. Six a.m. I'm missing Wing Bowl.

6:00 A.M.

"GOOD MORNING EVERYBODAYYYYY! WELCOME TO WING BOWL THIRTEEN!"

Wing Bowl, as best I can reconstruct the parts I'm missing—thanks to audio tapes of the WIP broadcast and the Nerds' forty hours of videotape— begins with Cataldi's buoyant greeting, with Cataldi roaring at the crowd and the crowd roaring back. "Oh my God," Cataldi says. "Wow. See what you started, Al? I hope you're happy, Al." Cataldi's voice is the voice of your first-grade teacher just before she lets you out of class on a sunny day. *Behave, children, don't blow it.* "First of all," says Cataldi, "before we go any further with this, we have got to *please* ask, *please* ask the people inside the building"—the people are whistling en masse, a high quiet whistling—"the doors have been shut, they will not be reopened for more to come in, there is no room, we have reached the fire department capacity . . ."

The people cheer.

Cataldi briefly acknowledges the "problems outside." Morganti, more direct, tries to head off problems inside. "I wanna plead with the people in the building here," Morganti says. "Please don't make this the last Wing Bowl."

With that, WIP starts checking off items on their production script: the singing of the Springsteenesque Wing Bowl anthem *(we got some boys that can take the heat / it's more than just a gastronomical feaaaaattt)*, the hoisting of the live chicken by a thong-clad Big Daddy Graham, and the introduction of the IFOCE's George Shea, who will be adding his color commentary to the mix. "Angelo, a great day here," says Shea, "a moment in history." Shea riffs on Sonya, claiming that "she's doing Zen meditation right now, trying to focus." Sonya, as Wing Bowl royalty, has been given her own separate locker room this year. She is not required to mingle with the other eaters and their entourages, who have been relegated to the dull cinder block of the main locker room, which is hardly big enough to hold a football team, much less twenty-seven eaters and their fleshy compadres. It's a cluster of bumping shoulders and trash talk and video cameras. Sonya, for some reason, wants no part of this. She keeps her door shut, only popping her head out for a brief interview with the Game Show Network:

> GSN: Sonya, we need to know, what is the secret, what is your secret? You've been asked 153 times, what is the secret?
> SONYA: Secret is, I [am] always thinking about myself. I'm gonna win. I cannot think of lose. That is my secret. Bottom line, you're focused. You're ready.
> GSN: You're ready?
> SONYA: Yes, I'm ready. [Smiling.] I'm ready to kill the man.

Wingador has his own room, too, containing his whole family—Deb, the kids, his friends, Coach Petroski, and now Jere Longman of the *New York Times*, asking Bill the same questions he gets asked every year:

NYT: Are you confident you're gonna win this thing?

WINGADOR: I'm always confident. I don't think I've ever lost.

NYT: How many do you think you can eat today?

WINGADOR: Depends on the wings, the texture.

NYT: . . . What are you gonna do to her?

WINGADOR: Beat her. By a lot.

6:04 A.M.

B.J. and I walk across the parking lot north of the Wachovia. At about fifty yards, we start crunching on tailgate debris, a brown carpet of aluminum cans giving off a sour smell—beer mixed with other unpleasant fluids deposited by the all-night tailgaters, who've arranged their cans in neat circles around the bases of the Wachovia parking lot's shrubs. To our right, by the closed main gate, are a hundred or so diehards who have been shut out but still refuse to leave the premises. A few raise their fists and shout something I can't make out. I feel lucky to have a pass.

The main action is to our left. Several hundred Wing Bowl hopefuls are streaming toward a glass double door marked VIP. B.J. and I insert ourselves into the flow, which involves stepping into the accumulated inches of snow and hopping a four-foot-tall iron fence lined with shrubs. Almost immediately we're stopped up again, a new gridlock—400 people, maybe more, crammed into a throng outside the VIP door. I can't see beyond the crowd. I assume these are all disaffected passless morons trying to scam their way in, but then I see a coatless girl in a tight white top and white short shorts. "I'm a Wingette!" she says, holding up a yellow pass. "I'm a Wingette!"

These people have passes, too.

Now I'm close to panic. Somewhere inside, official Wing Bowl jeweler Steven Singer is pinning the Wingettes with his heart-shaped pendant, and Angelo Cataldi's wife, Gail, is checking that the Wingettes are all wearing panties, and I'm missing it all. I'd cry if there was a chance I wouldn't get stomped.

I hear a subtle *thunk*.

The *thunk* is what I imagine a magnetic door would sound like if it were being locked.

Four hundred necks angle toward the magnetic door, looking for confirmation.

Yes, the crowd senses—yes, that *was* the sound of the magnetic door being locked.

People start whispering. B.J. hears a rumor of a media-only access door on the crowd's far side. We'd have to slice through fifty bodies, tightly packed; we'd have to wade into the mob. I vote No. No, I do not want to be in the middle of those bodies when a drunk decides to shove his way to the door—

A flash of peripheral motion.

Beer can?

The crowd audibly sucks in a breath, the sound of instinctual girding for bad things to come. The beer can is prelude to a riot, of which irony and karmic cruelty would certainly require a human sacrifice, a crushing underfoot. And why not me? Dead in a Wing Bowl stampede . . .

My vote on the media-door gambit has been swung. B.J. and I start plowing through the bodies. After a minute or two, we break free only to find that the media door, though real, is clogged, too. The fifty or sixty people waiting in line—though *line* is too formal a word for this splay of cold bodies in parkas—are even angrier than the people we'd left behind. "Hey," says the guard to a fan trying to elbow his way through, "didn't I tell you before? How fuckin' hard-headed are you gonna be?"

The media-door supplicants aren't all pretenders. Some are even participants, like Mr. IFOCE himself, George Shea, his neatly slicked hair and sharp suit putting the Philly mooks to shame. Butter champ Don Lerman is here, too. I'm standing right next to him. I know it's Don Lerman because it says so on his wool hat.

Somehow, we push through the first door, and I feel that same pulse of glee I get at rock shows, anticipating something loud and joyful in those final minutes before the band comes out and straps on guitars—and then I see the second, inner door. And the second, inner line. For the first time I can hear it, we all can hear it, the thrum of 20,000 drunk Philadelphians. It sounds deep and muffled, like we're still very far away. We're stopped again, behind another door, with another security guy and another set of cold guys in parkas I want to make common cause with; I want to link arms and shove the security guy into the floor and step on his chest. And then, before I know it, I'm chest-to-chest with the security guy, and I flash my purple media pass, and I'm in. Yes, amazing: I'm in.

I look around to get my bearings. I am in the Wachovia's concrete bowels. Behind me, a long, gray maintenance corridor; ahead, a mass of activity. I walk toward a rugby scrum of cleavage and smiling people in complicated costumes. After spending an hour in the cold with guys in dark parkas, I'm suddenly surrounded by bare flesh and laughter, noise, motion, color—especially color: baby blues and oranges, greens, cotton tank tops and silk camisoles spilling breasts like Thanksgiving cornucopias. The Wingettes.* Some have the fake racks and pinched eyes of downscale exotic dancers, which they are. One Wingette, a tiny blonde, wears an Eagles jersey cut into a halter top so paltry that she's had to go to Plan B, putting pasties over her nipples.† Attractiveness is beside the point. The point is the display: panties and skirts, and messages like CATHOLIC GIRL written on tank tops and other more tantalizing locations.

I start to see people I recognize. There's Crazy Legs Conti, the IFOCE's token eccentric white guy, leaning against the wall with his dreadlocks peeking from a giant blue Dr. Seuss hat; two or three other people stand next to him, similarly dressed. There's Tim "Eater X" Janus, wearing the canonical navy blue IFOCE T-shirt, standing next to his friend Jason, who sports dark sunglasses and the kind of jacket that gets worn at collegiate "pimp and ho" parties. In a corner near the floor entrance I spot a few friends from last night's weigh-in: the two guys with the many-signatured WIP banner, and the Oldest Wingette, her rhinestone miniskirt ready for its moment in the light. I wave. There is a gaggle of girls in orange shirts and red punk-rock wigs. The shirts say, TEAM SMOKED JOINT: PORK THAT'S PULLED, NOT JERKED. The eaters and their entourages are distinguishable by

---

* Shaving Katie is nowhere to be found. Later, I learn from a WIP source that even some of the Wingettes "think Katie's pretty out there."

† Later, during the Wingette beauty pageant in the 9:00 a.m. hour, a TV camera shot this woman from a low angle, and you could see, on the Jumbotron, the horizontal plastic-surgery scars under both of her breasts. She was named Wingette of the Year.

their T-shirts, which plug whatever bar or restaurant is paying the tab for their afterparty. If strip clubs had their own softball league, this is what the awards banquet would look like.

And this, all this, is only what's happening *backstage.*

The main arena is just up ahead. There's a light, and a sound, the sound of the crowd. I walk toward it. The light and sound converge at the end of the corridor, at the floor-level gateway where each Wing Bowl contestant and his entourage will enter and exit the arena. The foul beast's cloaca. And beyond it, the foul beast itself. Thirty, maybe forty people line the gateway. I step through and see, for the first time, the inside of the Wachovia. It's full. Every seat. Even the bad seats near the top.

And I experience the inverse of what it's like to see a large city from an airplane: the feeling of walking smack into something impossibly big, being embraced by it, becoming instantly a part of it. The crowd is capacity-plus. Let's say 22,000 people. I have to recalibrate my senses again. I look up and realize that I am behind the twelve-foot-high stage from which the *Morning Show* deejays are broadcasting, live, albeit with a standard fourteen-second delay in case the crowd starts chanting something obscene. I'm staring straight at Angelo Cataldi's back. I look back toward the orifice from whence I came and see that the eaters and their entourages have begun massing at the orifice in tight, color-coordinated ranks, holding banners, like extras in a Kurosawa war film. Some have floats, which are quite massive and unsturdy-looking. I am standing on the oval track they'll be riding on, separated from the thousands in the stands by a white floorboard and sheets of Plexiglas. I flatten myself against the Plexiglas so as not to get in the way of the coming gladiatorial procession of eaters.

WIP does a play-by-play of each eater's procession, commenting on its cleverness and humor, or lack thereof. For instance: "Eater X is coming in and it's a really pathetic, pathetic entrance," says Rhea Hughes. As Tim walks around the arena, slowly, he holds up a white piece of posterboard that he's decorated with a crude Sharpie drawing of a naked woman. He waves it and taunts the crowd, affecting an evil grin.

"Rhea, the fans *hate* Eater X," says Cataldi.

This is what the radio listeners are hearing, as I find out only later when I listen to the tapes. Theoretically, I should be able to hear it too, because the radio broadcast is being piped through the Wachovia's sound system. But it's muddy. I can't make it out.

Without the audio soundtrack, I feel a little lost. From my vantage point I can see the eaters when they emerge and when they go back inside, but not in between. The floor is chaotic, the crowd is loud, so I latch on to people I might find common cause with, like fellow reporters. There's a "media pen" in front of the stage, but I don't want my movement restricted, and neither, apparently, do a few others. I see a blonde Channel 3 reporter leaning against the Plexiglas. She is frowning.

"You look kind of afraid," I say.

"Nah," she says, in a high-pitched, drawn-out tone of affected casualness, wearing her casualness like a shield. "Just hangin' out."

Now the Wing Bowl villains make their way onto the stadium floor. Chunk, the eater from Canada, is one such villain. Four of his buddies carry a large white sheet attached to four poles. The buddies hold the sheet horizontally above their heads, so that people in the crowd can see the message written on top: CFL FOOTBALL IS REAL FOOTBALL. The Canucks start walking. They get maybe ten yards before it starts raining inside the Wachovia. It rains small items at first, splashes of liquid, and then, as the Canucks get farther along, the projectiles grow in size, become a cresting wave of crushed cups and beer cans. Five minutes later the Canadians lower their sheet and dump its contents onto the ground, right at my feet: a soft pretzel, a can of Keystone Light, three 24-ounce Pepsi cups, a box of fries, an Aquafina, a crushed Miller Lite.

After Chunk clears the arena, followed by the procession of an eater named Wing Kong, there's an odd and awkward interlude. "Ah, ladies and gentlemen," says Angelo Cataldi, "if I could have your attention please. Could I have your attention please. Ah, yes, ah, a very important announcement to make to everybody here. Ah, for the last seven years, we have had one of our great contestants, [who] has been a part of Wing Bowl, and I'm very very sad to say that he passed away in the last month. And I believe his family is here."

Joelle Cachola, Chili Dawg's widow, walks onto the stage with her two sons. The three of them are wearing the orange shirts that Chili Dawg had planned to wear today, had he lived. "Fino Cach*ara* is his name," says Angelo, misprouncing Fino's name. "And ladies and gentlemen, if we could please observe a moment of silence, in the memory of Chili Dawg."

To the crowd's credit, people start violently shushing at Cataldi's signal. Silence is granted. The microphones feed back. Joelle and her kids stare up at the Jumbotron, which shows a picture of Chili Dawg. Joelle is immobile.

"Thank you very much," says Cataldi. "WIP sports time, seven o'clock."

It had lasted all of eight seconds.

I feel, I'm ashamed to say, relieved that it is over.

Onward:

The beer concessions open, pulling people from the stands. WIP has counted on this. WIP has scheduled its most villainous eater, a man named Uncle Buc, for just this moment, thinking that fewer people in the stands might lead to fewer thrown objects. Uncle Buc's float is Patriots-themed. *Pro*-Patriots. A security guard tells me, "Better get out of my way. You're liable to get hit. As soon as this guy comes out, the shit's gonna start flying." A WIP intern says, "Morganti was worried about Uncle Buc. And he don't worry about *shit*."

The Channel 3 reporter crams herself into a nook in the bleachers.

Buc emerges carrying a giant cardboard Patriots logo. On top, he has written his prediction for the score of Sunday's game: Patriots 30, Eagles 0. Buc, and his entourage, run. Again, the beer cans and crushed cups rain down; again, the phenomenon of the cresting wave. An eighth of the way around, Buc scuttles through a side exit and tries to take his sign with him. The fans won't let him. They grab the sign and tear it, as the crowd cheers, to shreds.

8:00 P.M. LAST NIGHT

What's fueling this?

I can only explain by jumping back about eleven hours, back to last night. Back to when the snow started falling and the first of the tailgaters rolled into the Wachovia Center's parking lot. The atmosphere was Mardis Gras in

Alaska—lots of wool hats, beer bongs, keg stands. There were portable boomboxes playing the kind of hip-hop songs you hear at suburban middle-school dances, and men and women grinding to those same songs. There was a small, fiery explosion, origin unknown. A man directing traffic said, "It's getting *crunk* in Philly." Three girls climbed to the roof of a U-Haul trailer and started dancing, but a volley of beer cups slung upward—perhaps out of pique that the girls had neglected to remove their shirts—forced the girls to dismount. (Months later I heard a thirdhand rumor of a parking-lot gangbang.) One guy, slurring his words, sang, "I lovvvvve Asiannnn gur-rrrls," presumably in homage to Sonya Thomas, and his friend replied, "El Wingador needza fuckin'—*effing*—take his GOD DAMN CROWN BACK! El Wingador! El Wingador! El Wingador!"

The tailgaters were drinking themselves into a nationalist frenzy. A phrase they kept repeating was, "Only in Philly." As in: "Three words. Only. In. Philly. Woooooo! Only in Philly! Only in Philly! Only in Philly!"

Another thing they kept repeating was "gook," in connection with Sonya.

"Everybody says Wing Bowl's all about the Eagles," according to one youngish man in a wool hat, "but technically it's all about stamina and nationalism . . . you know, nationalism, man. It's all about our country. The United States of Philadelphia. Our country, man. Our country. Eagles. Philadelphia Eagles, man. Our country."

7:22 A.M.

Think about this. Twenty-two thousand drunk men and women in the stands; beer consumed in industrial quantities since 8:00 p.m. last night; beer being consumed still, inside the Wachovia, this very minute; and no one—not the arena, not WIP, not the drunk people themselves—the least bit restrained or embarrassed even though, and perhaps because, the lights are on at full blast. As bright as a hospital corridor. You can see everything. The big and the small. You can see, clearer than you've ever seen it, the long, thin phrase blazoned across the balcony like God's final message to his creation in that Douglas Adams book: WELCOME TO COMCAST COUNTRY. You can distinguish every face in the crowd, even those at the far end, a basketball court away. The light makes it possible for you to have a very good time without necessarily watching the processions or the eating contest at all. The event becomes multi-threaded, more like a street carnival than a Broadway play. You can pick and choose what to watch.

And mostly, the crowd is choosing to watch itself.

The most obvious way is via the Jumbotron, which displays a running reel of crowd images. It seems like the roving Jumbotron cameraman's MO is to look for the drunkest people in the direst of straits. At one point the Jumbotron focuses on a college-aged man whose neck is bobbing forward, limply, like the doomed colonist woman in *Aliens*. I can pinpoint the exact second when he passes out. Other crowd events aren't televised, could never be televised.* There are brawls. In an arena where everybody is wearing Eagles green, and everybody is on the same team, there are brawls. One breaks out in the fan section almost directly behind me. There's shouting and a locking of arms; five or six guys lose their balance and fall into each other, and security here on the floor gets agitated, and it's broken up.

The most popular thing to watch, though, is the breast-flashing. There's a slow build of sound. The sound, an amplified murmuring, comes from all over. I can't pinpoint the source. Suddenly the noise swells and bursts into high-pitched cheering and clapping. Up in the stands, I spot its afterglow: smiles, guys still looking at the girl, her shirt now returned to its proper place.

Five seconds later it happens again.

Now no one is concentrating on the WIP deejays or the entourages. Everyone is waiting. Which girl will be next? A stripper or the girl next door?

Forty-four thousand eyes scan 22,000 bodies.

Then: another flasher, another roar. And then a fourth. Four flashers in a minute's time. And then, just as suddenly as it came, the spontaneous flasher eruption dies down, and people start watching Wing Bowl again.

---

* The Jumbotron used to display breast-flashers in all their glory, but stopped, due to complaints from sponsors.

7:30 A.M.

"I came all the way from Virginia, man," says the man in Wingador's locker room, now leaning over to whisper in Wingador's ear. "Do it," the man says. "I can't stand that fuckin' Sonya Thomas."

"All right, man," says Wingador. "I'll get it."

"Good luck, man. Sorry to bother ya."

Wingador waves his hand. "Not bothering me," he says, a little too cheerily. He is wearing billowing white shorts so large they look like long pants. The pants are white and satiny. Wingador leans back against the wall, under a framed photo of an old Flyers star, and knots his hands together. He rubs the pants and yawns. He works his jaw back and forth to keep it loose, then rubs his head and leans forward, his knees arranged Indian-style. He closes his eyes as if to block all sounds. Wingador looks like a man doing an impression of the most relaxed person on earth. Meanwhile, his daughters amuse themselves by zipping around the locker room with a tiara, trading it back and forth, taking turns at playing princess. Debbie chews gum and watches the Wing Bowl entourages on closed-circuit TV. She looks worried.

Until now, most of the entourages have been, if extreme and frightening, pretty hilarious, too. Rich the Butcher, aproned and mustachioed, carried a meat cleaver in one hand and a dead pig over his shoulder. The pig was not some fake plastic pig. The pig was a real dead pig. It was about to get deader, because the pig was wearing a Patriots jersey. Rich gave the pig what it deserved. The Bermanator? He circumambulated in a chicken suit. The Wolfman's rig steamed with dry ice. Sloth, enshrined in Wing Bowl history for his famous act of projectile vomiting at Wing Bowl 9, circled the floor while his famous puke tape was played, and replayed, on the Jumbotron. "We're all damn proud to be associated," said Cataldi. And there was Humble Bob, Wingador's putative nemesis. Humble Bob emerged with his broad arms clutching his wife and his mother, mom with a bewildered smile and wife tucking her head under Bob's shoulder, for protection. "He's new to the circuit," commented George Shea, adding, "but you know he loves the wing. And I don't know if you know this, but wing sauce, like many drugs, actually crosses the blood-brain barrier."

But now Debbie is seeing, on the closed-circuit monitor, the Chunk procession. She sees the Canucks get slaughtered with beer cans. She sees Uncle Buc endure the same. "[Bill's] gonna be a target," she says.

Just before 8:00 a.m., Wingador makes his final preparations. He puts on a white toga and a crown, and walks out of the locker room to the staging area, where his entourage and his agent are waiting with a ten-foot-tall, $2,000 throne marqueed with the EL WINGADOR name. Bill climbs into the throne, flanked by Debbie and his two daughters, as reporters yell questions:

"Hey Wingador! We hear you got engaged!"

"I've been married for seven years."

"All right," says the agent, "the entourage is gonna go out before Billy. Listen up! . . . Wait, I want two people in red shirts *behind* the two guys pushing."

WIP has cued music from the *Rocky* soundtrack.

"I don't even want to say the next contestant," says Al Morganti, as Wingador emerges, "because he's so much more than a contestant. He's become the soul of the Wing Bowl. He's the hope of Philadelphia. He's the reason these seats are filled along with us. He's the guy that made this an enormous event. And he's here as a *challenger*. Legendary, legendary wing-eating champion, all I can say is, Ellll Wingador!"

The fans give Wingador a standing ovation. Felicia and Ashley wave glittering wands and smile. A chant develops: "Wing-a-dor! Wing-a-dor! Wing-a-dor!"

"Oh yeah!" says Cataldi. "Wow! What a reaction!"

WIP's on-the-ground reporter sticks a mic in Wingador's face. "The fans love you!" the WIP reporter says. "You're gonna bring the title back to Philadelphia!"

Wingador is overwhelmed and barely coherent. "I'm here for them just as much as I am here for me, and for them," he says, nonsensically. "So I'm here to win."

"Give everybody an Eagles cheer from the champ?"

"No problem. E! G! Eh . . ."

Wingador has forgotten the letters.

He skips to the end. "Eagles!"

"Angelo, he's ready for number five!"

Now it's Sonya's turn. Sonya, as defending champ, goes last. In the staging area, she's carried aloft, Cleopatra-style, on a wooden platform adorned with large, stringy materials resembling spiderwebs. She stands on the platform, waving an Eagles flag back and forth in jerky motions.

"Okay, baby!" claps a male friend. "Okay, baby! Okay, baby!"

Sonya enters the Wachovia to an immediate chorus of boos. She is the main villain this year. One of the eaters, Hank the Tank, had already circled the arena holding a crude sign that read SONYA, WHERE'S MY MASSAGE! Now fans brandish signs with similar sentiments. SHOW YOUR WONTON. SUCK MY EGGROLL. BLACK WIDOW, SUCK MY WING. BLACK WIDOW, SWALLOW MY BLUE CHEESE. The rain of garbage begins immediately. "Please," says Cataldi, halfheartedly, "no debris for our champion. She is a magnificent eater . . . Oh man. Now we gotta protect her."

The barrage of debris thrown at Sonya is even heavier than for Chunk and Uncle Buc. Whole cans of beer, whole cups of soda, in that same cresting wave. She seems surprised that the fans have tagged her as the villain, but continues to smile and wave her little flag. When she's only a quarter of the way around the arena, someone throws what looks like a roll of toilet paper, and she has to duck and lean forward to avoid getting hit. WIP's Dave Helfrich takes off in a frantic run, trying to catch up with Sonya's float, to get her out of the line of fire.

"Please," says Cataldi, "let her off the—the—the—the thing. Let her off and allow her to go by. They are *killin'* her over there."

The national anthem is sung.

Now one last piece of business before the actual eating: the entrance of Miss WIP, borne into the Wachovia on a twenty-foot-tall replica of the Lombardi Trophy. Miss WIP has a sacred duty. She holds a mallet, and it is poised above a football with a Patriots logo. When she brings the mallet down to the football, the first fourteen-minute period of Wing Bowl will begin.

Chief judge Eric Gregg, dressed in brown leather pants, a leather jacket, and a brown cowboy hat, addresses the twenty-nine eaters, who are lined up at three tiers of tables. "To all you wing eaters," says Gregg, rhyming like a fat Johnny Cochran, "the deal is not how fast you eat. It's how much *meat* you eat. If you don't eat, you get beat. Simple as that. We're gonna be counting the wings thoroughly. Gonna be tougher than ever. So make sure you clean 'em up, because if you don't clean 'em up you don't get credit for it. Good luck everybody."

Miss WIP lowers her mallet, and Wing Bowl begins.

8:11 A.M.

After all this time waiting—360 days since Wing Bowl 12, two months since the start of Wing Bowl 13's stunts, three days since the issuing of the odds, twelve hours since the weigh-in, two hours since Big Daddy Graham's kick-off, ten minutes since the final two processions—we're finally, finally here at the actual eating portion of Wing Bowl, and suddenly the place just... deflates. No spark of chaos in the crowd any longer—no tit-flashing, no brawls. Everyone is sitting down, leaning back, bloated, murmuring. A sour-faced girl with a Wachovia badge spots me wandering outside of the desig-nated "news pen" and scolds me, ushering me into the one place I've been trying to avoid. All I can do now is watch the stage, which is a mess. Includ-ing the twenty-nine eaters, the four judges, various WIP production staff, and the eighty-some Wingettes, the stage holds more than 120 people, all in different uniforms. It's impossible to make out what the hell is going on. I can't even see Bill. He's up on the top tier, and I'm down on the ground. I have to leave the pen. I lie to the sour-faced girl, telling her I have to go to the bathroom. She lets me out of the pen and I try to get a better view from my old spot near the gateway.

Okay: Bill looks good. He's eating like he always does, rhythmically, with ferocious stripping power. He may even be faster than Sonya, who sits at the opposite end of the long topmost table, wearing a blue IFOCE T-shirt. Sonya's hand movements are jerkier, but her real strength seems to be her cheek capacity. She's like a miniature Badlands Booker, puffing her cheeks full of wing meat. All of the eaters have a white paper plate of twenty wings and a separate plate for the discarded bones, and when she finishes a plate, it's clean—zero meat, just little red trails, like a child's fingerpainting. Yet on the first plate of twenty, Wingador gets full credit, and Sonya is only credited for eighteen. She failed to clean two, according to the judges. Al Morganti says of Bill's wings, as Bill finishes his third plate, "This time there can be no question about what he ate. I mean, these things are clean. . . . He got all twenty on that one, too." Tim Janus eats fast and with focus, as does Badlands Booker, his cheeks twin red roses of sauce. The Wachovia's airhorn blows, signaling the end of the first period.

The eaters wipe their mouths as the Great Mize steps onto the stage. WIP cues the theme from *Rocky*. Mize has a beer in each hand. He starts thwacking the beers on his forehead, one hand after the other, until after twelve or thirteen thwacks, they puncture and spray beer. For his finale, he repeats the trick using not his forehead but the ass of a particularly adventurous Wingette.

As the judges continue to tabulate the wings, Eric Gregg reviews the first round. "Everybody was cleaning the bones good," says Gregg. "I was very impressed with everybody, especially Wingador. He was really comin' back to his old form . . . they're actually eating the meat this year, yes."

Bill is smiling. He says to his Wingette, "Sonya ate four plates to my two. But he [the judge] said the wings weren't that clean, so everything I got I got counted for."

"But you were way ahead of her," says the Wingette.

"Eh," says Bill. "Who knows."

Sonya's judge walks over to Bill and says that Sonya's up by two wings. "Billy," says the judge, "she's not cleanin' everything. She's not cleaning everything."

"Then why are they countin' them?" Bill asks.

The judge turns away.

"Aw, fuck," says Bill.

Bob Blutinger, the "director of operations," announces the totals:

10. The Bermanator, 62 wings.
9. Sledgehammer, 64 wings.
8. Cookie Jarvis, 64 wings.
7. Damaging Doug, 68 wings.
6. Uncle Buc, 68 wings. (Cataldi: "Uncle Buc! No way! That would be a tragedy!")

5. Sonya Thomas, 71 wings.

4. Mo Green, 72 wings.

3. Charles Hardy, 73 wings.

2. El Wingador, 76 wings.

1. Eric "Badlands" Booker, 80 wings.

I watch Tim "Eater X" Janus, who has been eliminated, put his hands on his hips and mouth the words, "You're kidding me." He walks up to Blutinger and asks him something, and Blutinger walks away. I know exactly what he is thinking, because it's the same thing I'm thinking. Four IFOCE eaters—Tim, Krazy Kevin, Don Lerman, and Crazy Legs Conti—have been eliminated, and a bunch of local guys with zero wing experience (Uncle Buc at 50 to 1, Mo Green at 35 to 1) have advanced instead.

Tim calls me on my cell.

"Wing Bowl is a fucking joke," he says. "It's rigged. And there's not a guy here"—meaning the other IFOCE eaters—"who doesn't think the same thing."

The final ten eaters have been removed to the top table, along with ten Wingettes, for the second fourteen-minute period. "Now this is it," says Eric Gregg. "This is it now, so you really have to get serious. You can't blame anybody but yourself. This is the finals, and you have to eat 'em. If you don't eat 'em, you get beat. I don't wanna hear that you didn't get credit for it. If you don't eat it, you ain't gonna get it. Good luck everybody."

Cataldi counts down, and they're off again.

"Sonya is finally at ease," says Shea. "She has settled in. But so is El Wingador . . . I think Booker's got strength down there . . ."

Booker is in the lead by three or four wings.

"Sledgehammer may blow at any minute," says Rhea.

"Oh," says Cataldi, "Sledgehammer looks distressed . . . if somebody kaplooeys in the middle of the round, you have to eat while an odor permeates the room!"

As it turns out, Booker is the one to blow, according to WIP. The airhorn signals the end of the round, and there is commotion around Booker. Booker—his hands a greasy mess of meat, his cheeks red and saucy—still has those copious cheeks full of food.

"Booker, I'm workin' witcha," Eric Gregg tells him. "I'm gonna give ya—I'm gonna give ya ten seconds, Book. If you can't get it down, you're done."

"He may have overfilled his mouth," says Shea.

"Alright, yes," says Cataldi.

Gregg counts slowly to ten as Booker chews and tries to swallow. "This is a dramatic moment," says Cataldi. "Our leader could be eliminated . . . what is the ruling? What happened?"

"Eric," says Rhea, "is he out?"

There's a pause.

"Eric has disqualified him."

Booker opens his mouth to show that there's no more food, but it's too late. He shakes his head as Rhea explains, "Ange, I will tell you, he did throw up and pushed it back in his mouth. It didn't come out . . . Eric [Gregg] gave him every chance to stay in it."

"Alright, so Eric 'Badlands' Booker has been disqualified for vomiting and then not swallowing it," says Cataldi.

"That's a badge of honor," says Shea, "and you know it really comes down to the semantics of what you say vomiting [is]."

The second-round totals are announced:

  5. Uncle Buc, 101 wings.
  4. Charles Hardy, 114 wings.
  3. Cookie Jarvis, 131 wings.
  2. El Wingador, 132 wings.
  1. Sonya Thomas, 134 wings.

"Wow," says Cataldi.

"We got a hell of a race," says Eric Gregg.

"Here we go again! Three competitors, three wings apart."

The final two-minute round is the most hyped yet. It's all angled camera lenses and tense shots on the Jumbotron, which alternates shots of Sonya and Bill. When Sonya's face is shown, the crowd boos; when Wingador's face is shown, the crowd cheers.

"El Wingador's back is against the wall!" says Shea.

"This is the real test right here!" says Cataldi.

"Cookie got a bad swallow there and it knocked him back on his heels . . ."

"Twenty seconds! Twenty seconds!"

"Fifteen seconds!"

The crowd counts down from ten.

"Wing Bowl Thirteen is over!" says Cataldi.

"WIT. NESS. HISTORRRRYYYY!" screams Shea.

"IT'S OVERRRR!!!" screams Cataldi.

"This could not be any closer."

"This is as close as it could be."

The four Wing Bowl judges convene in a huddle. "I've never seen this before," says Cataldi.

Eric Gregg emerges from the huddle and brings the official totals to Cataldi.

"Ladies and gentlemen," says Cataldi, "I believe we are about to crown the next Wing Bowl champion."

Bill asks his Wingette, "Did I win?"

"I think it's tied," she says.

A judge announces the totals. "It's a two-way tie between El Wingador and Sonya, 147 each!"

"One-forty-seven!" says Cataldi. "We go to overtime for the second straight year!"

"Dear God in heaven," says Shea, "witness this for us!

"I can't *believe* this has happened again!"

Ed Jarvis, defeated, comes up to Bill and says, "Do this. Do this. Don't let happen what happened last year. Got it?"

Cataldi says, "All right, Al. Al, get a word with Sonya. Sonya's shakin' her head. I don't think Sonya Thomas is happy right now . . ."

Al says to Sonya, "Not happy with this?"

"No, yeah, I'm not happy . . ." The rest of her answer is drowned out in boos.

"Uh-oh. This has gotten ugly. George, what's the story?"

"She is a porcelain God. She has come down to this earth to practice her craft. She makes no bones about it. She doesn't care about the boos."

Then: the final two-minute round. It will begin when Eric Gregg pounds the table with his hand. "Sonya," says Al Morganti, "do you understand? Sonya, when his hand hits the table, you start."

This is it. The final finale.

Gregg hits the table.

Bill and Sonya go for the drumsticks first. Same speed. Same strategy. It's close. After eight drums they take a drink. Synchronized. Move to the paddles with less than a minute left.

Forty-four thousand eyes on the Jumbotron.

Shea says, "Here at the sanctum sanctorum of competitive eating . . . the pace obviously going above and beyond . . ."

"It is torrid," says Cataldi, "how do you even describe this . . ."

"Oh my God . . ."

"They are being crushed by the cheers . . ."

"They're cheering for Bill Simmons!" shouts Cataldi. "The crowd is trying to lift Simmons up! . . . The crowd is on his side!"

"There are no white flags in Philly," says Shea, "and Bill 'El Wingador' Simmons . . ."

"ONE MINUTE! ONE MINUTE TO GO," interrupts Cataldi. "TWENTY-THOUSAND-DOLLAR CAR AT STAKE, THE GREATEST FINISH IN THE HISTORY OF WING BOWL, WHICH ONE OF THESE TWO . . ."

Says Shea, "Look at her go . . . this is approaching artwork, artwork . . ."

"Oh my God, look at them," says Cataldi, "it's like a rabid dog on a T-bone . . ."

"Sonya Thomas, effervescing an unforgiving angel . . ."

"Four seconds! Three! Two! One!"

Bell. Screaming.

"Wow. Wow. Holy mackerel," says Cataldi. "Hooo-leee mackerel."

Bill looks over at Sonya, and down at his plate, and he flicks his right hand at the table out of what appears to be disgust. He didn't want it to even be close, but it is close. Bill turns around and walks back into the throng of onstage bodies. WIP has cut to a commercial; no words are going out live to the thousands. The crowd is still cheering. Then, a murmur onstage, unconfirmed: Bill has won. Somebody tells him, "You won." Bill turns to the crowd and mouths, "I won," and raises his fist, and the crowd rises up and cheers him. Nothing's official yet—but now Cataldi comes back on the air:

"It is nine-twenty-six at the Wachovia Center," says Cataldi, "and the tabulations have been completed in our closest Wing Bowl ever and we do have a winner. I now turn it to our commissioner, Eric Gregg, for the final announcement."

"It's the toughest one I ever had to call," says Gregg. "I take my hat off to all the contestants, but the final goes . . ."

Bill stands onstage facing the audience, holding a white towel. He presses the towel into his face with both hands. Hard. He can't bear to look . . .

". . . El Wingador won by one! He's back as champion!"

The crowd erupts. Bill raises both hands as confetti streams from the ceiling. Bill 162, Sonya 161. Sonya, frowning, claps and walks over to Bill, who gives her a big hug. She walks off the stage and doesn't look back.

"I think it was my best ever," Bill tells Cataldi. "I put a lot of emotion into this. I wanna thank all my fans. Now we gotta bring home the Super Bowl!"

Bill walks over to the Suzuki Verona that is his prize, sits on top, and gives an interview to a scrum of media. His daughters flank him on both sides, looking adorable for the cameras. Then he walks back to his locker room, where friends and family are waiting to congratulate him. Wingador flits from person to person like a deer who's just narrowly escaped some trucker's headlights. I overhear Debbie explaining Bill's future plans to the old reporter in the leather jacket, the one who wants to ghost-write Bill's book, *Chicken Wings for the Soul.* "He'll still be involved," Debbie says of Bill. But not as a competitor. "He doesn't have anything to prove." She sounds relieved.

I shake Bill's hand and notice that he has already put on his Wing Bowl ring. I tell him I'm surprised they gave it to him so quickly after the contest.

"They didn't *give* it to me," Bill says. "I earned it."

Five days after Wing Bowl, the *Daily News* reported an interesting tidbit. A Hollywood producer named Mike Tollin was thinking about buying the film rights to Wing Bowl. Tollin, a Philly native, makes sports movies: *Summer Catch* with Freddie Prinze Jr., *Radio* with Cuba Gooding Jr., *Coach Carter* with Samuel L. Jackson. Eventually, when I spoke with Tollin—he came to Philly to take meetings at the Ritz-Carlton hotel—he told me that "structurally and tonally," the story of Wing Bowl was similar to his other successful sports movies. "It's almost like a next-generation *Rocky*," Tollin said.

Wingador would be Rocky.

Wingador would get his heroic sports story after all.

Wingador didn't know this yet.

So: Now Bill had five titles, a nice round number. Now he could start a restaurant or write *Chicken Wings for the Soul.* Lose fifty pounds. Be boring, if he could stand it, or if Debbie could. Nothing stopping him. What would he do with himself?

The night of Wing Bowl, Bill called and left a message on my cell. He laid it on the line, one more time, for the record.

"My eating career," said Wingador, punching the syllables to make sure I got it, "is *ohhhverrr*."

But it wasn't over for me.

In the hours and days after Wing Bowl, I made a decision. I decided to investigate whether Bill really *did* earn his fifth Wing Bowl title. Was Wing Bowl fixed? I tried to find out. I really, earnestly did. I looked for my own personal Deep Esophagus. I solicited the opinions of people in bars. I talked to a sloshed woman at Wingador's afterparty who was certain it had been fixed last year but not this year, and then I talked to her sober friend, who pointed out that if it was fixed last year, it was fixed this year, too. He said, "Yeah, it's fixed. It's Angelo's game, and Angelo is an egotistical asshole." Once the wife of an *Inquirer* reporter told me that a bouncer at Chickie & Pete's had revealed to her the details of the fix: WIP had paid Wingador $20,000 to throw Wing Bowl 12. I nodded and thanked her for her candor, but I didn't believe the story. One, you couldn't persuade Bill to throw a neighborhood softball game for $20,000, and, two, WIP would move mountains to avoid paying an eater even twenty dollars, much less twenty large. Still, I was happy to know that conspiracy tales were proliferating. I was developing an appreciation for folk wisdom, that psychic epidermis of the people. And folk wisdom was calling bullshit on Wing Bowl, and getting over it, and loving Wing Bowl anyway.

I talked to the victims, too. The eaters. At an oyster contest in March, I asked Sonya how she felt about Wing Bowl. I started off by apologizing for my city, meaning the racist signs and the volley of beer cans, but she said she didn't care about that. What bothered her was the judging. "The best way is for them to be weighed," she said. "Then you cannot LIE." Since WIP wouldn't weigh them, she said, she might not return. "They don't want me to win, or something," Sonya said. "Even though I eat, [they] don't count it! I lose my pride. No." I talked to Eric Booker, who said he was upset—he denied vomiting—but who also said he'd be back next year anyway. Tim "Eater X" Janus felt that Booker's stoicism was a model of athletic dignity. Tim sent me an alternately passionate and carefully argued 960-word e-mail missive:

> . . . If vomit had been in Booker's mouth, and it wasn't, it couldn't have been seen, which means it didn't competitively exist . . . The whole thing was a sham. Booker got fucked. Sonya got fucked. Wingador's a dick for taking that title . . .

Was there a way to settle these questions definitively? Did Booker vomit? Did Sonya get robbed? I thought there might be. I prevailed upon the Wing Bowl Nerds and their forty hours of digital tape. One evening, I had them play me their Booker/Sonya/Wingador material. The Booker tapes were inconclusive; we could neither confirm nor rule out the presence of vomit. The Sonya/Wingador tapes were more interesting. During the two-minute eat-off, the Nerds had a cameraman focusing on Wingador and a cameraman focusing on Sonya. I watched each tape and counted the wings. Bill very clearly ate fifteen in two minutes—drumsticks first, then paddles. Sonya did the same—drumsticks, then paddles. She cleaned fourteen, easy. Then, on the fifteenth—a paddle—she had trouble stripping the meat from the second splintered half, then took one last valiant bite and threw it onto her "finished" plate just as the airhorn blew. Then she picked up her sixteenth wing, ate it quickly, and threw that down as well, as the judge put up both his hands to say stop.

Sonya, 16. Bill, 15.

Sonya, I concluded, must have been docked two wings.

Now I watched the tapes again, more closely. I ruled out Sonya's sixteenth wing, assuming it was discounted because she'd run out of time. That left me with the crucial fifteenth wing. I needed to figure out whether that wing had been cleaned. I needed a better look. More clarity, a slower speed. The Nerds, on their digital editing rig, enlarged the clip by 350 percent and slowed it down. They let it run. I couldn't tell. They ran it again. Still couldn't tell. Play, rewind. Play, rewind. I felt like a JFK wingnut looping the Zapruder tape in his darkened apartment. As the Nerds ran and reran the clip, we all laughed. It was so ridiculous. Still, I swear: I really wanted to know the truth. And when the tape revealed nothing definitive, I felt disappointed.

Only one stone remained unturned.

A few weeks after Wing Bowl, when everything had cooled down, I went to visit longtime Wing Bowl judge and wing tabulator Bob Blutinger at his Mays Landing, New Jersey, condo. We sat on his wraparound couch and watched SportsCenter on his new forty-two-inch flat-screen HDTV. Blutinger looks exactly like his name sounds: walrusy and paunchy, with big round glasses. He spent four years as a referee for the Harlem Globetrotters, from 1978 to 1982. He was in the audience at Wing Bowl 1, competed in Wing Bowls 2 and 3, and officiated from Wing Bowl 4 onward. Leaning back into the couch cushion, he alternated stories of Wing Bowl greats like Damaging Doug with stories of Globetrotter greats like Geese Osby. There is probably no one, anywhere, with more expertise in officiating at sham athletic events than Bob Blutinger.

"I absolutely have no knowledge of anything about a fix," Blutinger said.

"Yeah," I asked, "but do you *think* it was fixed?"

Blutinger huffed. "No comment," he said. "No . . ."

He paused, exhaled, started again. "I don't think it was fixed," he said. "I can't *imagine* it being fixed. Because there's too many variables. I mean, I just can't imagine it. But then again I can't tell you for one-hundred-percent sure because it wasn't my ballgame."

Even a Wing Bowl official couldn't, or wouldn't, tell me categorically that the event was not fixed. And that, of course, was the whole point, of course, *of course*, I thought, *you moron*, and I sank into Blutinger's couch cushions and thought about the brilliance of Wing Bowl. WIP could pretend Wing Bowl was an eating contest, and the participants could pretend they only cared about having a little fun, and everyone could ignore the darker confluence of death-wish appetites and corporate intrigue that made the whole thing so rippingly awesome and darkly consequential.

"Hey," said Blutinger, as I was leaving his condo, "whatever they tell me to do, I'll do. You know, I'm there for the fun of it."

The fun of it.

God, I was sick of hearing that—and sick of hearing what he said next, too.

Wing Bowl, he said, was his fifteen minutes of fame.

I wasn't going to get a satisfying answer on the judging controversy, but I realized, leaving Blutinger's place, that it didn't matter. Blutinger had left me with a piece of the real mystery of Wing Bowl: Why can't people talk about what it means without resorting to this paltry cliché of the fifteen minutes of fame? I'd heard that so often, from so many eaters—Heavy Kevie, Chili Dawg's wife Joelle, Tollman Joe, "Big Rig" Vogeding—and always jokingly, abashed, always belittling it, always with a shrug. Every time. Yes, Wing Bowl is fun, as one longtime WIP employee told me over beers, "but is it so much fun that you'd even DIE for it?"

We were talking about Chili Dawg. The WIP guy leaned into the bar and looked straight ahead.

"It's ridiculous," he said.

So why do they do it? I asked.

The fifteen minutes of fame, he said.

I'm sorry?

A man dying young, leaving his children fatherless and his wife a widow; a garbageman trying to redeem a life of bad decisions; a Long Island social worker making ill-conceived Nazi analogies and having to be talked down from full-scale rhetorical war by his loving wife and practical fears of possibly losing his home in a lawsuit brought by an international megacorporation— these things are manifestations of people's desire for fifteen minutes of fame?

When it comes to Wing Bowl, Andy Warhol's fifteen-minutes line packs as much descriptive truth as a drawing of a peacock made with an Etch-a-Sketch, but if you're Joelle or Bob Blutinger, you use the line anyway because there's no other obvious way to explain, in a way that won't expose you to ridicule, about how a chicken-wing contest can become a focus of your life.

So you fall back on the road-tested explanation. And if you're me, you spend hours investigating whether Wing Bowl is fixed, because it's easier than talking about what it means. I'm not sure I know the answer—the best one I ever found was very short, just a few sharp-edged words in the *Inquirer* that began, "Sometimes, you feel like life is nothing, with no purpose," and continued, "But after eating contests, there is no stress, and no depression"; odd that with all this testosterone and bravado and trash talk, the only one who could talk about Wing Bowl with any balls was Sonya Thomas*—but I do know that we need a better language before we can begin to figure it out. Wing Bowl is a Freudian id-release on the scale of a city, it's a barrel of laughs, it's a death cult, it's a protean myth, it's deeply mysterious: *what a crazy species*, as psychologist Paul Rozin told me (and who, by the way, did not get to attend Wing Bowl 13 because he got stuck in the traffic and had to turn around)—I'm saying that this is a vocabulary problem. The impact of these spectacles, as they're actually lived, is outpacing the culture's ability to talk about what the spectacles mean. There is dignity in language, and without access to a less impoverished language, Joelle and El Wingador and Tollman Joe and Big Rig and the rest have no dignity. They've only got this idea of the Warholian fifteen minutes, which has become archaic and inappropriate. That leaves them at the mercy of corporate media entities like WIP/Viacom and the IFOCE, whose primary function and competence and experience is in using language to control meaning.

And that's why I respect Bill Simmons, for refusing, when it counted, to see Wing Bowl as WIP's management did—as "being about fun first." And that's why I also respect Arnie and Coondog, even if Coondog is a little raw and Arnie is a little crazy. Those two, with their jeremiads and fevered letters, their quixotic insistence on autonomy and self-determination, are trying to enrich the literature of the twenty-first-century media spectacle. Today, Arnie and Coondog suffer the ostracization common to all pioneers. Will they always look so silly? Our kids are being born into the weird world. Wait twenty years, and watch them live a new language into being.

---

* Sonya continued, "The only bad thing is, your jaw gets tired."

part three

WHO IS THIS
MYSTERIOUS EATER X?

Tim "Eater X" Janus on his way to a shoofly pie victory in Lancaster, Pennsylvania. (Rockvale Outlets)

1

SLAUGHTERHOUSE-FORTY

IM "EATER X" JANUS works as a day trader on the fortieth floor of a building two blocks from the New York Stock Exchange. The building's lobby is all brass and shiny surfaces and security-guarded, but up on the fortieth floor it's a different ecosystem, forgotten, with a husk of an old PC sitting on the floor next to the elevators, neglected, like some redneck's lawn's rusted T-Bird. "This is pretty great, huh?" Tim says. "It looks like a Communist building. Really. It's like a slaughterhouse."

The first thing you notice up there is the light, which is bluish like the light that comes from a TV in a dark room. The room is slightly smaller than a basketball court, with low ceilings. A series of flat computer screens are propped up on maybe a dozen tables spread throughout the floor at right angles but in no particular geometric pattern. It less resembles Charlie Sheen's boiler room in *Wall Street* than it does a very large college dorm room, complete with a Bruce Lee poster on the wall. Large windows on all sides are completely darkened by venetian blinds, giving the whole place a subterranean feel, even though we're forty stories up. If the blinds were open, we could see clear to the Statue of Liberty in the Upper New York Bay. Tim says that if the blinds were ever open and he looked out the window and saw the Statue of Liberty bombed in a terrorist attack, he would immediately short-sell the Spyders, the index stocks of the S&P 500. "I mean," Tim says, "I would donate money—if I did that, it would be blood money—it's disgusting, but still, I would short it. Make sure that sounds decent."

Tim isn't a bad trader but he isn't a good one, either, partly because this sort of opportunism makes him uncomfortable and unruthless, a wussified

Gordon Gekko. In college at Southern Methodist University in Texas, Tim had an honors scholarship to study political science and public policy, but he hated his classmates—he dreams of someday earning enough money to endow a campus building and call it the SMU Assholes' Recreation Center—and was too smart for his own good, skating by in class without doing much work. After graduating, Tim moved back to Connecticut, got a job tending bar, "got really comfortable there," and didn't leave until two years later, when he decided that "I had to do something different." Tim had a friend in New York who was a day trader. The friend "really enjoyed it." So Tim moved to the city in August 2001 and became a day trader. He's been day-trading ever since. (Recently he took a second job answering phones and waiting tables at an artisanal pizza place on Second Avenue, because he says that "one of my goals for the future is to own a pizzeria," but this is never mentioned at contests, for promotional reasons; blue-collar gurgitators are a dime a dozen, but white-collar gurgitators are far rarer, especially ones with Tim's all-American looks, and hence are valuable media commodities.)

We walk toward Tim's workstation, which is anchored to a table about ten yards long. He says hi to no one. He's wearing jeans and a T-shirt and a ballcap and a week-old beard. It's late in the trading day, about 2:00 p.m., and many of the other traders have left, so the only sounds come from the ubiquitous wall-mounted TV monitors tuned to CNBC. Tim sits down in front of two black, eighteen-inch flat-screen monitors flashing stock graphs. "This is what I do," he says, pointing to the screens. "Actually, *this* is what I do." On a separate computer to his left, he loads a web browser, types in espn.com, checks the stories, then checks his Hotmail account. Tim is a day trader who spends most of his day avoiding making trades. He diddles around with the Internet, calls his friends, reads books. Plunked alongside his bottle of Sierra Mist Free is a paperback copy of *Silas Marner*. He often carries a paperback copy of a Great Book to eating contests; I've seen him with *The Prince and the Pauper* (Krystal burgers) and *The Picture of Dorian Gray* (tiramisu). He tells me that *Dorian Gray*, which he's been reading lately, got him thinking about "how stained my own soul is," and now his task is to "find responsible hedonism." I have no idea what the fuck he's talking about.

Tim is a hard guy to figure out. He doesn't present as a self-conscious character like Coondog O'Karma or El Wingador. Maybe he is too young to have settled on a single character. Once, at a bar in Manhattan, he tried to pick up a girl by pretending to be a NASCAR driver from Charlotte; afterward he wrote a searching blog post about the experience. He seems to have two modes: introvert and exhibitionist. Sometimes when I called his cell I'd get both in quick succession. His voice mail would click on, and I'd hear a fierce message delivered in the sneering tone of a professional wrestler. *Hi,* the message would say, *it's Mister Janus. If you don't know me well enough to know that I want to be called Mister Janus, then you don't know me well enough to call me Tim. It's Mister Janus to you. Show some respect.* And then he'd pick up, sounding tired and down, and update me on his training. When I first met him, he said his ambition was to be a footnote in any history of competitive eating, but now Tim was a bigger deal. As of March 2005, he was the ninth-ranked eater in the world according to the Federation, which had big plans for Eater X. "This rookie clearly represents the future of competitive eating in style, composure, and ability," according to Tim's Federation "bib sheet," and George Shea told me, "He's a handsome kid, he's in terrific shape, and there's an element of mystery for a lot of women who have not fully embraced our sport." Now that Tim's standing had grown, and he knew he would be a prominent character in my book, he said he was excited to read it because he enjoyed seeing himself from different perspectives. It sounded like Tim had decided to triangulate an identity from books and magazine stories and guest appearances on *Good Morning America*, which was theoretically possible because by now other journalists had become interested in Tim. A crew from MTV's *True Life* series, intrigued by his appearance and the fact that he's a day trader, had started following him around with a digital camera, asking questions—"Tim, do you want to say where you are right now? Hunger level, confidence level?"—for a one-hour documentary on pro eating. Tim initially disliked being filmed, but came to enjoy it because it "gave me a purpose to my day." Tim was outsourcing the process of self-discovery to other people.

Here in the day-trading boiler room, Tim returns to his web browser and cycles quickly through the eating gossip sites, looking for news of himself and his eating buddies. Elsewhere, five or six dark forms stir occasionally behind their own desks. They don't make much noise except for occasional contextless outbursts:

"Two-fifty! Two-fifty! My man."

"Sixty bright men are going *down*, motherfucker. Motherfucker!"

Tim picks up his cell phone and calls a friend. He asks the friend for a certain web address, nods, and hangs up. He types compfused.com into his browser—compfused is a time-wasting website for the working bored—and loads a video called "Ice Skater Dropped." We watch it together: a pair of figure skaters, man and woman, are performing a lift when the woman slips from the man's upraised hands, plummets to the ice, and absorbs the blow with her face. Tim calls his friend back and says, "It's not as interesting as I thought it would be," and then he turns his attention, for the first time, to his stocks.

Tim's firm gives him a pot of money he can use to buy and sell stocks. He keeps all of his profits and pays the firm a half cent for every share he buys or sells, so it's possible for him to go to work and actually lose money. Right now he has a tenth of his pot actually invested, or "riding," in the market—about forty-eight grand. At 2:31 p.m. he decides to buy Spyders at about $120 per share. "I only bought four hundred," he says. "I'm a pussy." He points to a line that reads BRO, the ticker symbol of Brown & Brown, Inc., an insurance broker. "I used to trade this one a lot," he says. "It's called Brown & Brown, which reminded me of this song by Ratt in the eighties, 'Round and Round.' So I would just sit there makin' money and sing *Brown and Brown, what comes around goes around.* It was a great stock. I could sell nine hundred shares and then . . . I was up $400 in, like, three minutes. It was fun. But the whole thing's turned to shit now."

Lately Tim is not doing well. Today he is seventy-one dollars in the red. "It sucks, man," he says. "You just kind of spiral down. It affects your confidence, it affects your life . . . it colors every other part of your life . . . this is an awful way to live." It was maddening, the randomness of the market. He felt he couldn't tell the difference between trades that made money and trades that didn't, so he couldn't improve. He was stuck in this dorm-room slaughterhouse of bluish light as his confidence drained and his salary rode every day until eventually he spent most of his working time looking at his websites and not making trades, fantasizing about a better career, like perhaps a career as a Secret Service agent, which had always appealed to him because it wasn't some "bullshit job" like working for a corporation and it wasn't being a "bully" like a cop, but it was still law enforcement, and hence noble, and he would be a part of a very clear hierarchy that made sense.

"You should be learning lessons that you look back on," Tim said. "Your lessons shouldn't be that you have to be stupid or stubborn. Your lessons should be that you have to have a system that you develop." In trading, he said, "You can't develop a system. My system is, like, crossing my fingers."

It was easy to see, after watching Tim struggle with stocks, why he so appreciated competitive eating. It didn't feel like some abstract amorphous black box with few rules and enormous consequences for screwing up. Eating was so literally *material.* Instead of computer screens and trend lines, it was calories and scales and barbells and belches and big, messy dumps. Honest bodily feedback. A virtuous cycle, not a vicious one. As an eater, he was learning lessons he could look back on, and the lessons would be the right ones.

The amazing thing about Tim Janus? He came to feel that competitive eating would not only make his life better. It would make him—and his belief only grew stronger as he surged upward in the rankings—a better person.

2

THE TEETH OF JIM MULLEN

To UNDERSTAND WHY Tim Janus is a genuinely new and perhaps even revolutionary figure in competitive eating, you need to understand George Shea, and to understand George Shea you need to understand the teeth of Jim Mullen.

Jim Mullen* is the original hot-dog champion. In 1916—the year that Nathan Handwerker, a poor Polish immigrant, opened his first hot-dog stand on Coney Island—Mullen, an Irish immigrant, and three of his friends, also immigrants, found themselves at Coney Island on the Fourth of July. Naturally, they started arguing about who was the most American, settling the argument by speed-eating Nathan's franks. Mullen, having eaten 13 in 12 minutes, came out on top, and in years hence, "reigned intermittently," in the words of the *Post*'s Gersh Kuntzman. "The contest has been held each year since then," according to the IFOCE, "except in 1941, when it was canceled as a protest to the war in Europe, and in 1971, when it was canceled as a protest to civil unrest and the reign of free love." The glory years of the contest, despite generating such champions as Stan Libnitz, who was tight with boxer Joe Louis, and Gerta Hasselhoff, who "trained on bratwurst," may never have produced a personage as "titanic" as Jim Mullen, seeing as Mullen, though only a thirteen-dog man, was eating in what Shea has referred to as "the so-called 'Dead-Dog Era.'" Kuntzman, in recounting some of the foregoing in a 2005 *Post* article, prefaced it with the phrase "legend has it." Because of course there is no actual historical record of a Jim Mullen eating hot dogs in 1916, or any record of Mullen "reigning intermittently" in years

---

* Sometimes spelled "Mullin."

hence; and there's also no record of a Stan Libnitz being tight with Joe Louis or a Gerta Hasselhoff "training on bratwurst," and no record of a contest being canceled in 1941 due to the war, or in 1971 due to free love, and so on. There is only George Shea's imagination, to which most of these stories accrue, and which I had the pleasure, in 2005, of watching get put through its paces.

It was the Fourth of July, the day of the Nathan's finals. The big day. I got up early and took the F train to Coney. When I got there, Shea was on stage, doing a dry run of his material for that afternoon's big show. It was the first time I'd ever seen him without his blazer and tie. He wore khakis and a navy T-shirt that puffed out a little at the bottom thanks to some modest belly fat the blazer usually covered. His straw boater was doffed. He squinted in the rising sun and ran his lines, looking down occasionally at a sheet of paper. The crowd gathered around the stage was small but not negligible, maybe twenty or thirty people, so Shea's practice session still felt like a performance—but a loose one, playful, heavily improvised. It was possible to hear his thought process because he edited himself as he went, discarding various lines for being overly technical (a line about the IFOCE's female eaters and their "X chromosome" was tossed as "too scientific") or insufficiently G-rated (Sonya, he riffed, is "that cold chill that you get in the middle of the night when you don't recognize your partner in the bed," which he changed to the less-sexy "you don't recognize *yourself in the mirror* . . ."). Shea stepped through each eater's introduction, taking special pleasure in that of Don "Moses" Lerman: "He is son of Daniel, son of David, son of Saul, son of Michael, son of Menachal, the son of Josephia, son of Ezekiel, son of Zebediah, son of Gandhi, son of Boothrah, *son of a bunch of biblical names*, biblical biblical biblical biblical— Son! Of! Moseeeeeeeeeeeezzz!!!"

Shea also enjoyed practicing his set piece about the teeth of Jim Mullen. The story went like this: Shea had located, after lo these many years, the teeth of Jim Mullen. The ur-gurgitator's choppers. They'd been dug up on a construction site in Coney, and Shea planned to incorporate the teeth into the Nathan's ceremonies later that afternoon, parading them onstage as a sacred relic from eating's past. "I'm holding the teeth," Shea was saying, pretending to hold the teeth. "Once they were dropped on the cement but they cracked and we lost the teeth ... and here, here are the teeth of Jim Mullen, oh, welcome, welcome! ... and here's Don 'Moses' Lerman, Don, Don, I am not a religious man, I am not a religious man, Don ... but when I see these teeth, when I saw those teeth enter the arena, I actually got a deep and powerful sense of spirituality. . . ."

The teeth of Jim Mullen, now interred in pickle juice; the teeth of Jim Mullen, on which people used to swear "when they wanted to make a vow," as Shea had told Gersh. The story, and its delivery, were quintessentially George Shea: some ironic blasphemy, some invented history, some classic American archetypes spun against a classic American backdrop, "amid ghosts of Coney Island, ghosts of championships past."

But by the time Shea got to the ghosts of Coney Island, he had transitioned. He wasn't talking anymore about Jim Mullen, American eating's progenitor of legend. He was talking about the real progenitor. He was talking, in a voice genuinely reverent and deadpan-free, about "a great man and a great PR man who was the steward of this contest from 1972 until 1991* when he passed away from cancer. Just a moment of silence, please, for Max Rosey ..."

Rosey. A Jew from Alabama who fell in love with New York. Grew up in the Depression as Max Rosenberg. Quick-witted, workaholic. Let's say that he probably knew Damon Runyon personally. Maxie—they called him Maxie— wore, like his press-agent colleagues, a striped suit and tie. He looked like "either a press agent or a gangster," according to Hal Buell, a longtime Associated Press photo editor, who was just one of the hundreds of media professionals across Manhattan known by Maxie, and who found it useful to know him back. "He was on the conservative side of a crazy line," says Buell. "He wasn't a cuckoo. He was a smart guy. He'd come up with ideas that were usable." He asked for things from strangers, from out of the blue, and got them:

I need you and you.

This he says to Jerry Cammarata, age twenty, in an Italian restaurant in Brooklyn called Gargiulo's. Jerry's holding drumsticks. He's playing a wedding gig in this restaurant. *I need you*—the man's pointing to Jerry—*and*

---

* In fact, Rosey died in 1990.

you—now he's pointing to Jerry's accordionist.* Jerry thinks: *Nutball.* The man leaves. Later that night Jerry flips on his TV and sees what he missed out on: a wedding staged by the nutball man in front of the Cyclone roller coaster, and the TV says that the man is Max Rosey, and Max Rosey is a big-time press agent for the Coney Island Chamber of Commerce and Astroland and the Cyclone roller coaster—and Jerry feels like a moron, so he calls Max the next day and says *sorry. I was wrong. I apologize.*

And after that, Cammarata becomes an acolyte of Max. He starts hanging around, and Max teaches him what it means to be a press agent in fifties New York. How you don't need to make an appointment to pitch a story to a city editor. You just walk right into the newsroom. Maxie can stroll, for instance, right into the AP building at Rockefeller Center—taking the elevator to the fourth floor of the massive newsroom and walking to the photo department, where twenty-five-year-old Hal Buell, who will later become the AP's worldwide photo chief, is a mere assistant city editor, writing captions on hot pictures fresh from the darkroom. Buell sees Maxie mesh with the tone of the place, with its million inputs and outputs, a nexus of things coming in via wire and going out via motorcycle messenger to the train station, film and mail and coffee being input into the mouths of the shirt-sleeved men in carb comas from the saloons and delis lining 51st and 52nd Streets, the wire machines on each end of the desk spitting out copy for the supervisor reading it out loud to keep the guys informed. *How we doin' on the ballgame. We got second-base action. We got the presidential press conference. We got Carter falling down.* Cream-colored walls, smoke, smells of newsprint, London's coming in on one wire, Tokyo on another, Buenos Aires, a building's crumbled to the ground in SoHo, the GW Bridge's stacked with traffic, *and in walks Maxie with some dipsy-doodle idea.*

His dipsy-doodle ideas were prolific and versatile. He enticed news professionals to photograph silly things, like marathon singing contests and

---

* George Shea once did the same thing to me. I was covering a contest, and Shea was one eater short. He needed someone from the crowd. At that point, he didn't know who I was, so he fixated on me and said, in a flat, direct tone, "You. C'mere." It didn't feel as if he was giving an order, though. Something in his tone of voice made me feel as if I had been *plucked*, and now I was going to be let in on something really cool. It was friendly and aggressive and conspiratorial at the same time. "C'mere. . . ."

water-skiing elephants in the Hudson River (a stunt on behalf of Palisades Amusement Park), and he promoted serious things, like politicians and Hess's Department Store, and he also promoted people who were dead serious about their silliness, such as the Amazing Kreskin, the famous mentalist and *Tonight Show* fixture. If there is a common thread to Rosey's PR work, it's his fascination with underdogs and his appreciation of the power of the underdog narrative. When Mikhail Gorbachev visited New York in 1988, Rosey bought Gorby a bag of Nathan's hot dogs and tried to deliver the dogs personally. He lost the battle (to give Gorby the dogs) but won the war (for Nathan's publicity). As underdogs go, you'd be hard-pressed to find a greater political longshot than Henry B. Krajewski, the pig-farming candidate for president of the United States—and of course Krajewski was a Max Rosey client. In 1962, in the David-and-Goliath fight over building the World Trade Center, Rosey took the side of David: The Downtown West Businessmen's Association, a group of men who owned rickety electronics stores on the proposed site of the trade center. According to the book *City in the Sky*, Rosey and his sometime partner, Mortimer Matz, staged a mock funeral procession on behalf of the DWBA, carrying its leader in an open casket stamped with a placard that said: HERE LIES MR. SMALL BUSINESSMAN DON'T LET THE P.A. BURY HIM. Rosey used to call his journalist friend at Scripps Howard, asking: *Who is this guy they keep talking about, Irving Renewal?*

Rosey may have been able to afford the luxury of his little-guy clients by falling back on his work as the "King of Queens." He ran beauty pageants, dozens of them: Annual Donut Queen, Miss College Queen, and especially the Miss America pageant, which Rosey helped blow up into a cultural totem. But the pageants, to hear Jerry Cammarata tell it, were never Rosey's favorite stunts. He preferred a different sort of beefcake, loaded with nitrates, wrapped in a natural casing. He preferred his hot-dog contests: "Those were his babies."

The rationale for a Nathan's hot-dog contest was an obvious one. Even in the late sixties and early seventies, as Coney Island slid into decrepitude and Nathan's Famous, having gone public as an over-the-counter stock, started tussling with its new stockholders, thousands of New Yorkers still crowded Coney's beaches during the spring and summer. TV cameras fished the beaches for "brite" shots for the local news. It would be a simple thing to lure the TV cameras from the beach to the hot-dog stand. With the right bait. With a hot-dog stunt.

So Max Rosey and Mortimer Matz—longtime publicists for the Coney Island Chamber of Commerce and Nathan's Famous both—talked it over with Nathan Handwerker, the company's immigrant founder. Nathan had his hand in the pickle barrel at the time, because Nathan was cheap. He was so cheap that he used to feel the pickles in the bottom of the barrel to make sure his supplier wasn't gypping him with mushy pickles.

Nathan said:

"What is that? A hot-dog eating contest?"

Matz said, "Whoever eats the most hot dogs is the hot-dog champ."

"They pay for the hot dogs?"

"No! This is for publicity, Nathan."

"How long would that be?"

"Half an hour."

"No.

"Twenty minutes."

"No."

"Fifteen minutes."

"No. Twelve minutes! No more! No more! And I hope they had a big breakfast!"

That's the story, anyway. Its veracity is probably unverifiable in any robust journalistic sense, partly because Nathan is long dead, and partly because the story's exact date is disputed (more on that in a second), and partly because Murray Handwerker, Nathan's son and the former chairman and president of the company, remembers that "I was the one who initiated it"—i.e., the contest—since Murray's father was "a very, very practical man" who wasn't too keen on marketing stunts. All I can say, with the eyes of History upon me, is that, recently, at a deli in Manhattan, I got the preceding story straight from the mouth of Morty Matz.

Matz is alive and still working in PR. He asked me to call him Morty. Morty wore a light blazer, large glasses, and white sneakers. He wouldn't give me his exact age. Morty used to do publicity for lawyers in high-profile criminal cases; Jimmy Breslin once wrote a column about how Morty would advise criminal defendants to bring a raincoat on the day of their indictment, whether it was raining or not, so that they could drape the raincoat atop their handcuffs. Like George Shea, Morty graduated from an exceptional school—Amherst—and studied literature. (He used to drive Robert Frost around campus.) There in the deli, Morty ordered a salmon-and-cream-cheese sandwich on thin toasted rye bread. "Thin," he said. "It's got to be thin." I asked him whether his early hot-dog contests were well-covered. He looked at me funny. "It was popular from Day One," he said.

Day One. When exactly was Day One? Shea says that Rosey and Morty took over the contest in 1972. Morty says, "I think we started in 1973," but he adds, "We only knew from oldtimers that the contest was held before World War Two." In the files of the Brooklyn Public Library, a few books and articles mention informal eating stunts—a 1941 book called *Sodom by the Sea* says that Babe Ruth would sometimes eat two dozen franks in a single sitting, and according to a 1952 article in *Park East* magazine, "one of the stand's 'regulars' ate twenty-eight franks in a row" as part of a bet—but the earliest proof of a *formal* contest, at least as far as I can tell, may be an article published much later, in 1974, by the *New York Times*. Headlined CONEY I. AWAKENS FOR A 145TH TIME, and dated Monday, April 8—not July 5, interestingly—the story recaps Coney Island's opening weekend and ends by noting that "Nathan's Famous had a hot-dog-eating contest for a half dozen passers-by. Max Rosey ... oversaw the confusion, blowing occasionally on a silver whistle and shouting advice like 'Come, eat the hot-dogs, don't look at the camera' and 'Lady, lady, lady, what are you doing, stealing hot-dogs?'"

After 1974, the contest history starts to cloud up. By the 1978 contest—which was held on Memorial Day for about fifty spectators, and whose adult* champion, Kevin Sinclair of Sheepshead Bay, told a *New York Daily News* reporter that he "was looking for a rest room when he stumbled across the contest"—Rosey was claiming, to that same reporter, that he had "presided over the annual Memorial Day weenie eat for more years than he

---

* Until the mid-eighties, the contest was split into separate adult and child divisions; the kids ate for 6 minutes instead of 12.

can remember." Rosey also elaborated on the contest's backstory, explaining that "the first contest was held in 1917 and pitted Mae West's father, Jack, against entertainer Eddie Cantor."

No mention of Jim Mullen.

But it wasn't Rosey's job to handle the newspapermen, anyway. That job fell to Morty. Every year, on the day of the contest, Morty set up a little ad-hoc press operation inside the hot-dog stand. He was the back-end guy, the guy working the phone. Morty wasn't the showman. "Max was the showman." Max was the one who could fill Schweikert's Alley, that little jog behind the Nathan's stand, with a few hundred spectators packed tighter than a dozen shrink-wrapped franks. Max was the one who, with his straw boater and his bullhorn, could create tension with whatever contestants turned up, whether it was a Queens internist whose name was actually Dr. James *Weiner*, or a hirsute dude wearing an OFFICIAL BIKINI INSPECTOR T-shirt, or, in the 1984 contest, a "17-year-old, pretty, sandy-haired fraulein" from West Germany named Birgit Felden, who, according to the *Brooklyn Courier*, was "a member of the West German national Judo Team," and who took the title with a mere nine and a half hot dogs and buns. Expenses were minimal. Press was huge but local. With Rosey at the helm, the contest cruised through the eighties, even as Nathan's corporate continued to struggle with increased competition and, ultimately, a short-lived buyout.

Murray Handwerker retired in 1987. Three years later, Rosey passed away at the age of 79. Rosey, the Zelig of press agents; Rosey, the King of Queens—and he died leaving almost nothing to history. There is no Max Rosey Archive in any university library, prestigious or otherwise. He often talked of writing an autobiography called *Office in My Hat* but never got around to it. Jerry Cammarata worked with Rosey for thirty years but he doesn't have a single photograph of the man. There's barely even a trace of Max Rosey in newspaper databases or microfilm. "He never, *never* overshadowed his clients," says the Amazing Kreskin. "You rarely, rarely ever saw his name in print. He almost considered that a cardinal sin."

Thankfully, for the sake of hot-dog historians everywhere, Rosey's successor wasn't quite as modest.

·   ·   ·

George C. and Richard P. Shea grew up in Bangor, Maine, a place very cold and very far away from the rest of America. The Sheas' father, Maurice P. Shea III, was a prominent banker in Bangor, but he sent George, Rich, and his three other children to public schools, where they excelled. In a 2004 profile from the *Bangor Daily News*, their high-school swimming coach called them "wonderful young men," said that the entire Shea family (there were five children altogether) was "persistent" and "loyal," and added that George was especially confident: "There wasn't much he didn't think he could do." George went on to study English lit at New York's Columbia University, hoping to be a "great novelist," according to the school paper. Instead, Shea graduated in 1986, freelanced, waited tables (at which he "failed miserably"), and finally landed a job with the PR firm of Morty Matz. Around 1988, Matz set him to work on the Nathan's Famous account. By the time Max Rosey passed away a few years later, George was Rosey's natural successor—and an author of sorts, just not the kind he originally intended.

It took him a few years to develop into the George Shea we know today, the George Shea who channels P. T. Barnum for the benefit of ESPN's young male viewers. When Shea pops up in news clips from the early nineties, he's a spokesperson for his more staid clients; on behalf of an Upper West Side tenement owner, for instance, he's commenting to the *New York Times* on the likelihood of rent breaks. In 1997, when Shea went off to start his own firm—Shea Communications, together with his brother Rich—the skills he advertised were those of a fully modern PR firm, albeit with his Matz/Rosey heritage grafted on. A 1997 version of the Shea Communications webpage lists competencies in "Real Estate," "Election Campaigns," "Union Matters," "Legal Matters and Court Cases," "Crisis Management," "Publicity Stunts" ("Shea Communications is one of the few firms that still practices the light-hearted publicity stunt"), and "Stealth Media" ("Shea Communications generates media coverage that weakens the credibility of an adversary . . . with no link to the client").

George Shea has said that the contests were initially "a fun distraction from the more corporate PR." In the same way that black kids learn to "cold-switch" between two styles of talking—hip-hop slang and the King's English—the Sheas could cold-switch between business and ballyhoo. One minute, a Shea brother could be feeding square-footage rates to *Real Estate Weekly*, and the next minute he'd be on the phone with an ESPN reporter, feigning offense at ESPN's imputation that this eating stuff is all some kind of joke, right? *No, no. Imagine two Neanderthals in a cave. A rabbit hops into the cave. Whoever eats first, survives. This is the only sport there is.* "It was definitely the most exciting job that you could have," says Tom Maher, a former intern for the Sheas, "aside from maybe being a Navy SEAL."

Exciting, because there was nothing to lose. As late as spring 2001, four years after its founding, the IFOCE website listed three contests. Three. Matzo Balls, Pancakes, and Nathan's hot dogs. The IFOCE was imagination and bravado. Blank canvas. The Sheas could joke around as if no one was paying attention. They could joke that hot-dog eaters "are in peak physical condition—some peaking at 300 pounds." They could describe the Nathan's contest as a "grotesque display of gustatory prowess," *grotesque* being a word you won't find anywhere on the circa-2006 IFOCE website. And, paradoxically, it was this very atmosphere of loose, half-assed wisecracking that scored the Sheas one of their early business breaks, which was to entice a good reporter at a major New York paper to care about competitive eating.

That reporter, of course, is Gersh Kuntzman. I met Gersh for breakfast at Dizzy's, his favorite diner, in the Park Slope section of Brooklyn. Gersh has the angular, birdlike look of a guy who spends a lot of time in passionate conversations: glasses, neat beard, clavicle poking from the top of his shirt. He's prolific, both as a talker and a writer. He once wrote a 70,000-word book about baldness cures in two months. No disrespect to his book, *Hair!*, but Gersh's true legacy to American reportage may turn out to be his pioneering series of dispatches from the Nathan's contest. "I like to think of myself as the Homer of hot dogs," Gersh told me. Then he ordered a piece of apple pie with chocolate ice cream "to celebrate myself." He spilled some ice cream on his khakis and wiped them furiously, setting the stain.

As the sport's first true beat reporter, Gersh is the guy most responsible, after the Sheas and Takeru Kobayashi, for what eating has become. Before Gersh started covering the beat in the early nineties, the Nathan's contest only warranted a few lines in the *Post*'s Fourth of July wrap-ups. "You could easily just say, 'Ah, it's just a PR stunt,'" Gersh says. "Maybe it's not. Maybe there's actually people who are interested in this. And I covered it as if it was a real sport." Which is important—that Gersh approached eating with ambition, meaning preview stories, gossip items on Page Six, post-contest wraps, the works—but aside from giving the Sheas a powerful megaphone, Gersh did something more. He set the tone for future stories in the most specific sense of the cliché. And that's crucial, because deciding on the tone of an eating-contest story is hard. (Trust me.) Do you report it straight? If so, how do you make it *funny?* Do you just make a bunch of puns? If so, how do you convey that the eaters are serious dudes?

Gersh chose to approach it with puns—he was fond of calling pro eating a "man-eat-dog world"—but also with an epic mock-grandiosity. He gave the eaters nicknames that linked them to sporting heroes past: Steve Keiner was Steve "Ralph" Keiner, Ed Krachie was "The Maspeth Monster." He called the Mustard Yellow International Belt "the universal symbol of hot dog supremacy." Because Gersh's comic sensibility dovetailed with that of George Shea, his early stories read like collaborations. Gersh would report that "Krazy" Kevin Lipsitz, an avid spelunker, had grown too heavy to fit into the mouths of certain caves; Shea would respond, "That's an indication that the sport of competitive eating requires single-minded devotion." Gersh would bemoan the dominance of Japanese eaters; Shea would concur that without proper hot-dog role models, American kids "will switch to tennis, basketball, or curling." And this style of joking was a major break from Max Rosey's shilling in years past, because while George Shea shared with Max Rosey a love of the brazen sell, the verbosity of a wink-wink snow job—and while Shea was smart enough to realize that a twenty-first-century audience, numbed from decades of having been carefully and politely manipulated via ever more sophisticated branding and focus-grouping and demographic slicing, might get a nostalgic kick out of an old-school chain-yanking (*"Here are the teeth of Jim Mullen!"*)—Shea was a more literary soul than his predecessor, as well as more creatively ambitious. Instead of popping off one joke at a time, he built, by spinning out thread to his collaborator at the *Post*, a joke *framework*. A multilevel satire. The satire's primary target was American mainstream sport: the NFL, NHL, MLB, and their pompous, spoiled athletes. The satire's secondary target was the sports journalist who venerated those pompous, spoiled athletes. The satire's tertiary target was the fan, the fan who consumed sports media and imagined he had some connection to it all. "It was very *Onion*esque," says Gersh Kuntzman, referring to the popular satiric newspaper. The goal was to "create this thing that doesn't really exist, and give people some sense that they have owner-ship of it, which they never had."

This thing that doesn't really exist. The obvious truth about eating, plainly stated by one of its creators—a creator who's baffled by the fact that more and more eaters started showing up at contests without knowing the ground rules. They didn't know they were never supposed to believe in the teeth of Jim Mullen. So they did. And changed everything.

3

THE TWO-THIRDS RULE

TIM, IN NORMAL LIFE, is not a big eater but a broad one. He will eat anything once, including, he says, endangered species, fellow primates, or even aliens, if he were to meet them. Last year he ordered two hunks of lion meat from the Web and gave it as a Christmas gift to his father. They ate the steaks together and drank beer and laughed, trying to ignore the meat's toughness—it changed shape in their mouths but didn't break apart (lion's revenge), so they swallowed the bites whole.

When Tim was growing up in Connecticut, his Lithuanian grandmother used to make ethnic delicacies from caviar, and Tim became a caviar monster, loving the taste of it even as a little kid, astonishing his parents and delighting Grandma. He once read a biography of the pro football lineman Dexter Manley that mentioned Manley's love of chitlins, a Southern dish consisting of fried or boiled bits of a pig's small intestine. Janus had never eaten chitlins. Later, in college, on a road trip to an Arkansas blues festival, Janus spotted a hole-in-the-wall shack that advertised chitlins. He dragged his friends inside, sat down at the bar, ordered a chitlin sandwich on Wonder Bread, and bit in. "They were terrible," he says, but it was worth it. "It was, like, such a good feeling to *finally* know what they tasted like," says Janus. "And it was cool to eat them in a place where it's like—this is the real deal. This isn't some lame chitlin."

You might call him a gastronomic multilateralist. This makes him a different breed from Coondog, a picky eater who cares only about the shtick, and El Wingador, who disdains the show and cares only about chicken. Tim is a new kind of eater. He doesn't recoil from contest food. He's curious about it. And his curiosity has helped him rise through the ranks, because though it's a truism that the foods you eat well are the foods you like to eat, there aren't enough contests to make specialization feasible. To be successful—that is, to win contests and money and respect—you have to embrace the whole bell curve of whatever America's kitchens dish out. On the low end of the curve you get the occasional vile food. Spam. A slab of ennui, an existential pinkness. Rich and Carlene LeFevre ate six pounds of Spam, ran back to their hotel room, fumbled with the keys, fought for access to the toilet. "It . . . bounced," says Carlene LeFevre. "I don't know how to say that nicely." A nine-pound hamburger at the Plaza Hotel in Las Vegas was drier than Sheetrock, crumbly, a death march of a contest—even Sonya was revolted, and she eats Burger King 365 days a year. At the high end of the curve are the odd delicious surprises, food that's better than it needs to be: pastrami sandwiches at New York's Second Avenue Deli, cheesecake in Brooklyn.

But, most of the time, eaters are thinking not about taste but about how to conquer the food in the thick middle part of the bell curve, the vast American caloric middlebrow. This is what you do if you're an eater on the circuit. You go to middlebrow venues—food courts, shopping malls, casinos on Indian reservations—and eat middlebrow food. The middlebrow is culinary flyover country. This is the food that no one writes about but everybody eats. There are 1,671 Applebee's Neighborhood Grill & Bars in this country; 528 TGI Friday's restaurants; 300 Country Kitchens; 110 Cheesecake Factories; 360 Old Country Buffets, Country Buffets, and Hometown Buffets; 533 Cracker Barrels; 775 Outback Steakhouses; 1,470 Waffle Houses. On its corporate website, Waffle House—sponsor of the IFOCE's World Waffle Eating Championship—helpfully itemizes its historical contributions to the American stomach: 495,264,367 waffles, 957,041,599 cups of coffee, 1,173,838,328 hash-brown orders, 370,545,935 sausage patties, 786,449,152 bacon strips, 14,899,594 slices of ham, 1,527,602,959 eggs, 22,217,455 slices of pie, 123,587,123 T-bone steaks, and so on. By any measure, Waffle House is a hideously undercovered company. This is not the movable feast but the invisible feast. The feast you're not proud of. What you order late at night when you're drunk but have a little cash and you don't want to eat at McDonald's. It is comfort food metastasized, swollen and scary, removed from its ethnic context—the root of all comfort food is in the specific tastes of the bayou, the barrio, the old neighborhood—and cranked up to the point of toxicity with layers of whatever makes it decadent, bacon on hamburgers and eight cheeses on pizzas, raindrops on roses, buckets of fried chicken. Food to be eaten alone. This is a passage from Don DeLillo's *White Noise* that will probably make you hungry:

> No one wanted to cook that night. We all got in the car and went out to the commercial strip in the no-man's-land beyond the town boundary. The never-ending neon. I pulled in at a place that specialized in chicken parts and brownies. We decided to eat in the car. The car was sufficient for our needs. . . . There was a mood of intense concentration, minds converging on a single compelling idea. I was surprised to find I was enormously hungry. I chewed and ate, looking only inches past my hands. This is how hunger shrinks the world. This is the edge of the observable universe of food. . . . We sent Denise to get more food, waiting for her in silence. Then we started in again, half stunned by the dimensions of our pleasure.

Eating contests—in their shrunken focus, their involuted intensity—are like this DeLillo scene except for one key difference: the dimensions of a competitive eater's pleasure are much more circumscribed. Eating contests very quickly move past the initial pleasure, if any, and into discomfort. Comfort food becomes uncomfortable. Because eaters go into a contest assuming they won't enjoy the food, the conversation around the food is not about taste, but about physical properties like texture and weight. *How are the fries? Are they pretty moist?* If there's time to probe the food before the contest, the first action is never to taste. It's to feel. To peel off the outer layer and describe its texture: Wet? Flaky? Slimy? Crusty? How much resistance will it offer? How similar will it be to eating a Nathan's hot dog, the standard unit of measure in competitive eating? Is the consistency uniform, or is there a separate, denser core, as in a matzo ball? Is it springy, like a Nerf football, or solid, like an apple? ("Humble" Bob Shoudt, describing a plate of cheese fries: "They're very lubricated, but they're, like, *gluey*.") The eaters try to imagine how the food will disintegrate in the mouth or in a tub of water or iced tea or lemonade. The food is palmed, rolled around in the hand, to get a feel for density and weight. Sometimes it's actually weighed, if the eaters have access to a scale. Only then do they taste, a small bite—or, in the case of Eric Booker, smell: a single finger casually wiped across the food, picking up a hint of essence and lifted to his nose.

And then there are contests where the eaters are not allowed to see the food beforehand, so they wander around and guess. In March, a month after Wing Bowl, I followed Tim Janus to the Federation's "Title Rally" event at Verducci's Italian Market in New Jersey, where he speculated with his possible opponent Allen "The Shredder" Goldstein:

"They haven't told us what we'll be eating," says Tim.

"We just know what's available," says Goldstein.

"I like sweets," says Tim. "Sweets are my game."

"Ooh," says Goldstein, grimacing. "Sweets."

The Title Rally was a series of five head-to-head contests with five different foods: tomatoes and fresh mozzarella, escarole, penne pasta, sausage and peppers, and tiramisu. The contest is being filmed by a giant HDTV camera for airing on the nascent, content-starved INHD network, which has signed a deal with the IFOCE to produce a series of eating contests called the "Tour de Gorge." The eaters wait their turns in a staging area behind the contest table and are called up by George and Rich Shea when it's time. "Beautiful" Brian Seiken loses the escarole battle to his longtime nemesis, "Krazy" Kevin Lipsitz, and mutters, "You see that shit they gave me? That was like eating fuckin' seaweed." Allen Goldstein draws pasta against "Humble" Bob Shoudt and loses. Humble Bob says, "You wouldn't believe how slippery those suckers were." After the next round's sausage-and-pepper battle, the smell of the table is sharp and sweet, the smell of a dishwashing station at a banquet hall—the rot of admixture—or a picnic table on a hot day after the flies have had their fill. Now it's Tim's turn.

Wearing green, white, and red face paint in honor of the Italian venue, he stands in front of a tiramisu. He knows nothing about the tiramisu aside from its weight, four pounds. It is a black box. Tim intuits that the main mass is in the center of the cake, the soft goopy stuff, and not in the ladyfinger cookies on the outside. In the event that the contest is close, the cakes' remains will be weighed, so Tim needs to eat the most mass as quick as he can. His opponent is Brian "Yellowcake" Subich. They start. Subich slams down his fist on the tiramisu to get a feel for its consistency. It spatters, leaves his hand yellow: dramatic but ineffective. Tim is more methodical. He pretends the cake is a drink, drinking the soft center, then moving on to the ladyfingers until time is called. The scale is procured. Subich has neglected to eat his cookies; the cookies sink him. Tim wins the first title of his young career. He mugs for the HD cameras. Eric Booker grabs Tim's hand and raises it in victory; Charles Hardy pats his back. Beautiful Brian congratulates him: "Let's do a linguini now."

And if you're Tim Janus you move on. New malls, new casinos, same food. Toasted ravioli turns out to be chewy, like eating a whole pack of Now and Laters. Shoofly pie is the crystal meth of sweets and just as bad for your teeth; the hands and face and neckline of your shirt turn into sand, you kick up sandstorms of powdery crust with each motion, you look like a little kid at the beach building a sand castle. Matzo balls sponge up water and turn your gut into a cement mixer. A giant birthday cake disappoints—it's not luxe like a tiramisu, but banal like a cake your company gives the secretary on her fiftieth; it gloms onto your hand. Your hand is a glove of cake. You appear to be melting from the extremities.*

And it is exactly these foods, the ones that are difficult to merely ingest, that you complain about if you're Tim Janus. Not because they're untasty but because they are, in eating verbiage, "slow," which means they don't go down the gullet fast enough to make you feel pain—the very pain you have been training so gruelingly, throughout the spring and summer of 2005, to prolong and mentally overcome.

There are two ways to stretch the stomach: water and food. Water-training is drinking water very fast. The advantage of water-training, vis-à-vis food training, is that it's zero-calorie. The disadvantage is that water starts to empty from the stomach almost immediately. For an eater, the Holy Grail is a low-calorie, high-volume food that stretches the stomach to the max while keeping weight gain low.

---

* There is food at contests that isn't contest food—table spreads for the wives and girlfriends and kids but for the eaters, too, because if you happen to lose a short contest you're still hungry.

Tim searched for that food. At first he tried tabbouleh salad, but it made him feel "gross." (If he and his roommate Jen had been sharing a bathroom, Tim may have run into a common training obstacle in competitive eating—the roommate/fiancée/wife veto—but "we have different bathrooms," Jen told me, "which has made this work out just fine.") Next he tried scrambled eggs, but eventually abandoned them because of the prep work involved. Jell-O was next because it was easy; Tim could put away a gallon of Jell-O in twenty minutes. But then he started to feel as though the Jell-O was liquefying too quickly in his stomach. If Jell-O was going to liquefy, he might as well use the real thing, water, which he did—until he started to suspect that water's stretching mojo could be enhanced if combined with a periodic Big Meal of some sort. Two or three times a week, Tim ate eleven pounds of low-cal food like yogurt or cottage cheese, topping off the tank with a few pounds of water. Meanwhile he kept searching for the perfect training food.

In the whole time I followed Tim's progress, he only took one break from training, in early November of 2004, when he e-mailed, "The constant practice was making competitive eating seem more like work than like the fun it's supposed to be." By the spring of 2005 he was too far along even to think about letting up. "Every time I take a day or two off," he wrote, "I feel lazy." Tim was equally intense when it came to the contests. He never looked at the audience or cracked a smile. Afterward he rigorously analyzed his performance. He tried to account for every variable: swallowing speed, capacity, water consumption. He collected stats on other eaters that were too obscure even for the obsessively detailed gossip sites. They existed only in his own head. He kept, for instance, a mental database of the stomach capacities of every eater. R. LeFevre, twelve pounds. S. Thomas, eighteen pounds. E. Jarvis, thirteen pounds. C. LeFevre, ten pounds. He polled other eaters on their water consumption, finding that the top eaters like Sonya seemed to need less water during a contest to force down the food.

Synthesizing his analyses over a period of months, Tim came to believe that he had two inherent disadvantages as a competitive eater. One: He was a slow swallower. Two: His excessive water usage meant that he was "filling up on worthless stuff." In other words, he could consume a higher total volume of food and water than his opponents and still end up losing the contest, because water doesn't count.

So, while continuing to work on his capacity, Tim also sought advantages in odder, overlooked corners of the discipline. He had long schlepped Lipton Brisk Iced Teas to contests, preferring the taste to bare water. Now he broadened his beverage experimentation. He started carrying a Tupperware container to contests. He called it a "dunk tank." Before the contest he'd fill it with tea, and at the bell he'd toss the food in the dunk tank to soften it. He discovered that lemonade cut the saltiness of salty foods as well as iced tea cut the sweetness of sugary ones. Club soda was a brilliant softener that essentially pre-chewed anything carby he poured it on. By the summer of 2005, the flavored-beverage meme had infected the entire gurgitator corps, and every eater was bringing iced tea, lemonade, or club soda to contests.

In March, all of Tim's hard work came together at a mall in Auburn Hills, Michigan, just outside of Detroit. He'd flown here for the Gameworks Tex-Mex Roll Championship of the World, enticed by the unglamorous location, which meant that it was unlikely the field would be very strong. He wanted to win a contest. (Tiramisu was unprestigious, having been a one-on-one battle against a second-tier opponent.) I stood in a commons area as Tim clambered onstage as the mysterious "Eater X," seeming more confident than ever; for the first time he held up his arms and crossed them in front of his face, forming an X. (This would eventually become his signature move.) He poured club soda on the Tex-Mex rolls and washed them down with iced tea. Thanks to his enlarged capacity, he didn't flag in the final minutes as he'd done at Krystal burgers and cheesecake. Right before the results were announced, he grinned and flashed me two fingers: second place. Though he lost to Rich LeFevre, he beat Booker for the first time, ever.

"I just hope it bodes well for hot dogs," he said.

The Nathan's hot dog is a little more than six inches long. The bun is made of processed white flour. The dog is all beef, no pork, wrapped in a natural casing that snaps when you bite through it. According to *The Nathan's Famous Hot Dog Cookbook** by Murray Handwerker (1968), "Salt, spices, and sodium nitrate are added to the basic meat and then the mixture is chopped in a

---

* Recipes include Hot Dog Ragout, Hot Dog Salad Dressing, and Dixie Dog Casserole.

bowl-shaped machine. The blades revolve around so fast that crushed ice must be added to keep the meat from overheating." The basic process hasn't changed much, except for fancier machines and the addition of a few chemicals: sodium lactate and sodium diacetate to prevent the growth of bacteria, and sodium erythorbate to stabilize the food's color, according to Specialty Foods, which processes hot dogs for Nathan's. (Sodium erythorbate is also known to prevent the potentially carcinogenic effects of the dog's sodium nitrates.) The distinguishing characteristic of the Nathan's frank has always been the garlic-spiced mixture that Ida Handwerker, Nathan's wife, originally squooshed into every dog. It is this garlicky kick that creates the disconnect between food critics, who adore the Nathan's dog, and competitive eaters, who revile it. The spiciness that is bracing at five bites is smothering at fifty. The eaters, the ones who create millions of dollars' worth of free media for Nathan's every year, are the people who possibly hate Nathan's hot dogs the most.

But there is no avoiding the frank. If you want to be a competitive eater, you have to be in the Nathan's finals on July 4 at Coney Island, even though Koby is going to crush you by twenty-five dogs, guaranteed. Nathan's is the biggest media event in competitive eating, so a berth at the final table validates an eater's stature as no other contest can. When you tell people you're a competitive eater, says Tim, "they ask you, 'Oh, do you do hot dogs?' That's all they ask about. People don't really know about the other foods. So it sort of sucks to say, 'Yeah, I do hot dogs, but I never made it to Coney Island.'"

To make it to Coney Island, you have to win a regional qualifier. There are around a dozen every year across the country. In 2004, back when Tim was just starting out, he had entered a Nathan's qualifier in Hartford, Connecticut, near his hometown of Simsbury. It was his second contest ever. "I bit into that first dog and I was disgusted," he says. He'd been eating so healthily for so long, "I couldn't believe how greasy and salty it was." He managed to force down thirteen and a half hot dogs, good enough for fourth place. His second try, at Belmont Racing Park, was a sixteen-dog day (third place). Both times he was "experimenting with stupid strategies," as he says now. "I was [eating] all the meat first, because I thought the meat was the nastiest part." Tim was messing with an immutable law of hot-dog eating—

you cannot improve upon dog, bun, dog, bun—but he didn't catch on in time for his third qualifier in Long Island. Tim ate twenty franks in a row, and then started on the rolls. He'd eaten thirteen when he heard the emcee count down from one minute. He started cursing and throwing buns on the floor. Later that fall he tried a fourth time at Saratoga Park, posting his best total so far: sixteen and a half hot dogs and buns (second place). "I dehydrated myself, thinking that all the water soaked up by the buns would then be soaked up by my body," he says. "But that was pretty stupid, I think."

Tim had never quite overcome his initial disgust. The sense memory proved durable, his own private Proustian hell. For the rest of that year, a casual whiff of a Nathan's dog made him want to vomit. Now, a full year later, the sense memory had faded, but he was still terrified of resurrecting it. He had to find a way to step gingerly while still increasing his totals, because sixteen hot dogs and buns—sometimes abbreviated as HDBs— wouldn't cut it. He needed at least twenty HDBs. Twenty is the baseline for a serious Nathan's competitor, but twenty-five is even better. Twenty-five wins almost any qualifier. If he could eat twenty-five, he would make the A-list of hot-dog eaters: Sonya Thomas, Ed Jarvis, Charles Hardy. The B-list was more crowded: a dozen or so guys who could eat in the vicinity of twenty HDBs. If you were on the B-list, you had to beat the other B-listers while avoiding the A-listers at all costs. If you were known to be an A-lister, your road was easier, because guys avoided *you*. This was Tim's goal: to be avoided.

So he structured his training according to his ambition (twenty-five HDBs) and his fear (of the sense memory), deciding to practice eating HDBs in small, controlled bursts. He conducted short time-trials of five or six HDBs each. The trials went really well except for the few times he almost choked. ("You get scared, you know?") He found that he could eat five in a minute and thirty-four seconds, and six in a minute thirty-seven. If he could eat seven in under two minutes, he'd reach twenty HDBs, easy. Thanks to the small trials, he managed to stave off the negative sense memory, and was so successful that by mid-May he told me that "these last few runs it's been like eating a bouquet of flowers. I've gotten to the point where I like the taste of it." He stopped time-trialling and plugged away at his stomach capacity instead, until he could stomach thirteen pounds of food and water. This was impressive, because when I first met him, he couldn't eat eight pounds without feeling sick. Tim was pushing himself as hard as, or harder than, anyone on the circuit. When Sonya Thomas talked about her competition, she always mentioned Tim first, calling him "an American Kobayashi." Tim, cocky, guaranteed 25 HDBs on game day and supported his guarantee with some calculations incorporating his mental database of eaters' capabilities and historical hot-dog totals. The math was straightforward but the premises weren't. The premises were derived from Tim's nuanced and hard-won understanding of stomach capacity, which (Tim argued) is actually best described by splitting it apart into two separate kinds of stomach capacity. There's what Tim called "maximum capacity," which is the eater's absolute hard limit, the point at which the eater's "on the verge of throwing up," and then there's "functional capacity," which is slightly less. Okay—and the magic number, the number that determines how many HDBs an eater can eat in a twelve-minute contest, according to Tim, is *two-thirds of the functional capacity*. He used Koby as an example: "Kobayashi's capacity is twenty-four pounds. Two-thirds of that is sixteen pounds. That's 256 ounces. Divide that by five"—five, because an HDB, soaked in water, weighs five ounces—"[and] that's about fifty-one hot dogs."

Tim called this the "Two-Thirds Rule." He said, "I really swear this works . . . I hope it works for me. I hope I'm not the exception." He internalized the Two-Thirds Rule, stumped for it in his nightly phone calls with Crazy Legs and Humble Bob and Brian Subich, added it to the ad-hoc navigational beacons he steered by, full speed ahead. Tim was the picture of focused commitment. His brain was all nitrates now. When he lifted weights, he motivated himself by imagining that every weightlifting rep equaled one hot dog that he would eat at Coney Island. In May he told me that he had dreamed about hot dogs twice in one week. The dreams were interesting. In dream one, Tim has just competed in a Nathan's qualifier, and the results have been posted on the wall. Tim sees that Bob Shoudt has eaten nineteen, Brian Subich has eaten eighteen, and he himself has only eaten seventeen. In dream two, Tim approaches the Shea brothers to inquire about wild-card berths in the hot-dog contest. The Sheas assure him that "everybody's going to qualify," after which Tim feels an overwhelming sense of relief. A few days later Tim had a third dream, in which he got "completely hammered" before the hot-dog contest and was beaten by a newcomer named Santana. In the dream, Tim felt disappointment but also satisfaction, "because I'd put up a really great wild-card number and because I'd eaten twenty-three hot dogs while blacked-out drunk."

I polled other eaters to see if they had similar dreams. They all said no, except for Carlene LeFevre, who described a vague dream in which the sky was full of free-floating hot dogs. Tim's dreams were frequent and specific, and they weren't really about food at all. They were anxiety dreams. His sub-conscious was spinning out contest vignettes to deal with the pressure he'd put on himself to perform. Why the urgency? Tim believed that if he didn't get into Nathan's this year, he might never get in, because eating was perched on the edge of an era of bubble growth—like the stock market in the late nineties. "Eventually," he said, "there's going to be saturation in tal-ent, at which point I *will* get phased out. There are so many good guys, and it's a huge country."

The history of competitive eating is like the development of life itself. For long stretches of time, jack shit happened and things were pretty stable. Then, relatively recently, interesting and chaotic stuff started happening. Disequilibrium. The entropy curve shot skyward around 1999, which is when a barrel-chested man from New Jersey named Steve Keiner took his ball, stepped out of the sandbox, and went home.

More on that in a second.

There have always been two sets of people who make an eating contest work: promoters and eaters. The promoters want to make money for them-selves and a client. The eaters want fame, a trophy, money, and neighbor-hood bragging rights, in that order. The interests of eaters and promoters have always diverged. What was different in the pre-Keiner era—all those flat, stable years prior to 1999—was that this divergence didn't matter, because nothing was at stake. There was no money and the fame was local-ized, fleeting.

This changed when the Shea brothers took over in the early nineties and nurtured the contest into a media cherry, attracting national reporters, dan-gling the promise of actual fame. The neighborhood guys weren't prepared. They let the press get to them. It was a big deal to do talk shows and get mentioned on Howard Stern. Frank Dellarosa decided that if he were this big a deal, he ought to be making some money, so he changed his nickname to "Hollywood" and declared that he was now an actor. The next year he refused to defend his title. Ed Krachie was more magnanimous but equally perplexed. There is a documentary called *Red White & Yellow* that follows Krachie on his quest in 1997 to take back the hot-dog title from Hirofumi Nakajima, who'd beaten him in December 1996. Though the documentary is meant to be lighthearted, it's actually unintentionally harrowing, like a security camera that captures a murder. Ed Krachie, Hamlet-like in his vacillation, struggles to carry the burden of an absurd, jokey narrative (RECLAIM THE MUSTARD YELLOW BELT FOR AMERICA!) that everybody seems to care about way too much, including, unavoidably, Ed himself. And when these scenes are intercut with studio shots of George Shea and Gersh Kuntzman, deadpanning away, the whole thing starts to seem pathologically cruel.

Now for the Steve Keiner story.

Steve Keiner comes along in 1999. He's an electrical code inspector from Egg Harbor, New Jersey. He's the new Great American Hope. He's going to beat Hirofumi Nakajima and vanquish Ed Krachie's loss and blah blah blah. Well: Keiner won. He ate twenty and a quarter hot dogs* and did it. Except . . . according to videotape shot by a local news crew, Keiner "appeared to jump the gun, or jump the whistle," as George Shea told National Public Radio at the time, "and actually had a half of a hot dog in his mouth before the word 'go' was shouted . . ."

For Shea it was a chance to riff satirically on the phenomenon of the Instant Replay. He flogged the story to reporters. But construction workers from New Jersey have a tendency to take questions of honor pretty seriously, and Keiner fought back. He put up a website that reflected his ambivalence: both his desire to be seen as an honest competitor and his bafflement at the ridiculousness of the Shea-era Nathan's contest:

> I won fair, and square, and even if I had an inadvertent nano-second advantage I won by one and one quarter hot-dogs. . . . What has historically been a fun, and good natured contest has been blown

---

* Keiner insisted that he actually ate one hot dog more, for a total of twenty-one and a quarter.

up out of proportion. After all, we are talking about an international honor bestowed on me for eating the most hot-dogs in a set amount of time and not, of course, a cure for cancer. [*sic*]

"He was a real jerk," says Gersh Kuntzman. "He didn't get the joke."

The neighborhood guys, a stubborn group with little tolerance for bullshit, bowed out. Krachie moved to Florida. Keiner disappeared into eastern New Jersey and wouldn't return my calls or anyone else's. Dellarosa scored an agent and a bit part in the movie *Kiss Me Guido*, then, when the acting jobs dried up, got a job at a liquor distributor and had a heart attack three weeks before I sat down with him over breakfast in Queens, the day before the 2005 Coney Island finals. Dellarosa ordered wheat toast with a slice of tomato and asked me who held the American hot-dog record. Sonya Thomas, I said. His eyes bugged out: "A *woman* holds the record?"

The neighborhood guys were replaced by two new classes of eater: the jokers and the eccentrics. The jokers were guys like Kid Cary DeGrosa, a property manager in Las Vegas, or Crazy Legs Conti, who, in real life, manages a Penthouse gentlemen's club. The eccentrics were guys like "Krazy" Kevin Lipsitz, who wears a dingy ballcap with a stuffed polar bear glued above the brim and was the first Internet spammer to be sued successfully under a consumer-fraud statute (says Tom Maher, ex-intern at the IFOCE, "We didn't play that up in the marketing"), and Don "Moses" Lerman, who claims to have invented the modern sport of competitive eating by being the first to "cross over" from matzo balls—his original discipline—to hot dogs. They were the first eaters to need the IFOCE more than the IFOCE needed them. "They took themselves very seriously," says Tom Maher. "They got T-shirts made up. Jackets. Whole entourages. They talked to the media on their own. The message. This is to George and Rich's—a compliment to them. They didn't try to control the message. So they weren't trying to control the brand. They knew they had something special." Maher says that since the eaters "didn't feel they were being monetized," the Federation was "able to use the eaters' own vocalness and garrulousness to promote the event." The eaters would call up and say, "I really want to start a website and sell my own T-shirts," according to Tom Maher. "And George and Rich were like, 'Go ahead.'"

This is what Gersh Kuntzman so vastly underestimated. Gersh's satire wasn't strong enough to withstand the need—the need that was out there, powerfully, among the Americans that men like George Shea and Gersh Kuntzman took so much pride in manipulating—to be a part of something that felt like it mattered, even when it explicitly didn't.

And he underestimated, too, Shea's ambition to use eating as more than a way to differentiate his PR firm from all the rest—to use eating to make money. Tom Maher says, "When I showed up, it was corporate, meaning it wasn't just something off the cuff anymore, on the side. They knew it was going to blow up by 1998. That really was what a business major would call an inflection point." By 2000, the IFOCE was officially incorporated. By late 2001, Shea had signed the eccentrics and jokers to management contracts. Now, with a contracted corps of eaters, he could expand the contest circuit and develop TV shows. The Travel Channel, the Discovery Channel, and the Food Network green-lit *Gutbusters, Battle of the Buffets, Big Eats*, and *Gutbusters in Alaska*. They were zero-budget productions, so low-rent as to be laughable. Kid Cary, in an interview with a Vegas paper, poked fun at *Battle of the Buffets*, on which he was a contestant. "TV has dropped to a new low," Kid Cary told the paper.

"Well, that was not funny," says Kid Cary. "I got calls from the Travel Channel wanting to know why I said bad things about the show. I said, 'I was just joking! This isn't *War and Peace*, you know . . .'"

He also got a call from George Shea. "Comedy is not easy," Shea told him.

Kid Cary had never been a joker like Gersh Kuntzman was a joker; their humor was completely different, the difference between shtick and satire. But now both modes of humor had been squeezed out by a new seriousness. Now that eating was tied up with real money, self-deprecation was either dangerous or beside the point. "Don't misunderstand," Gersh told me. "I still love the sport. I think it's a lot of fun and George brings so much to it. But it's not parody anymore, it's just humor. It's not satire anymore, it's just comedy, which is fine, it's still fun . . ."

Fun, but bland. The joke has ossified into banality. Comedy equals tragedy plus time, and maybe tragedy equals comedy plus time. When the joke curdles but doesn't die. When the punchline sticks around after the union grips and cameramen have left for the day—stripped of context, feeding off its own tissues. The punchline extruded into a new dark shape. The punchline slouching forward into the dumb horizon. It needed to be put out of its misery for the good of everybody involved. And Tim Janus, though he didn't know it yet, was the perfect guy for the job.

It wasn't that Tim didn't get the joke. He did. It's just that he didn't *care* about the joke. To him the joke was peripheral. I would tease him via e-mail using Coondog O'Karma's scornful formulations—*Dude, what kind of sport promotes itself with a Virgin Mary Grilled Cheese Sandwich?*—and Tim would write back, calmly, imperturbably, that "IFOCE events are officiated better now than they've ever been before," and that something like the grilled-cheese Virgin was "just a backdrop" that "never overshadowed the event" and "never undermined the integrity of it."

Integrity. It was this aw-shucks earnestness that amazed everyone: the way, for instance, he refused to order, as so many other eaters had ordered, a navy-blue IFOCE T-shirt from the website to wear at contests, because he felt that it would be cheating. He wanted the Sheas to *hand* him a T-shirt one day, like varsity letters, after he'd earned it. As if being a competitive eater were some kind of privilege. As if the Shea brothers were doing *him* a favor and not vice versa. Once, after a contest, I saw Rich Shea look at Tim, smile, and say, in a pleasantly bewildered voice, "He's really sincere about it. It's all for real." Tim was humble to the point of self-abnegation. Maybe it wasn't surprising that an upper-middle-class kid would go out of his way to create obstacles where none needed to exist; to tough it out when he didn't have to; to stay in hostels and sleep in cars and airports; to "do the struggle," as he called it that day in Mississippi when he ate pounds of slimy blue Krystal burgers in a losing effort and then reclined in his bed at the Red Roof Inn and drank beers I'd brought from the convenience store next door. "It's almost like competitive eating's kind of like the frontier," Tim would tell me. "We're kind of doing it the hard way." He was struggling for future generations. He wanted to set a good example and live up to the standard set by his gurgitator elders like Eric Booker and Charles Hardy, whom he treated like *sensei*s. Early on, he wrote me an e-mail explaining why he stepped so softly. "One of the things I've really enjoyed about competitive eating is that I'm learning how to be a good sport," Tim wrote. "For the first time in my life I'm beginning to understand competitive camaraderie . . . and I'm proud of that personal growth. It's something I'm trying to nurture." Tim was like the coolest kid in high school who was also nice to the nerds. Jake Ryan in *Sixteen Candles*. He reduced the cantankerous gossipmonger Beautiful Brian to a fawning puddle. Even the renegade eaters liked him. Says Arnie "Chowhound" Chapman, "You see so many weirdos, and then you run into a normal person like Tim Janus, and it's like, wow, what a breath of fresh air." There was a sense that Janus was different, that he was, in a powerful way that benefited everyone by association, *good for eating*—he made it look stylish and athletic and sexy, he wasn't standoffish, he was a nice guy. Everybody cleared the decks for Tim because there was more at stake than just Tim's personal success. On his shoulders, the fad of competitive eating would be carried into a new promised land where everybody, promoters and eaters alike, could make some real money: the world of legitimate sport.

4

THE GURGITATOR ISLANDS

I USED TO WONDER if competitive eating was a sign of the apocalypse. What if? What if eaters really *were* "horsemen of the esophagus," in the words of George Shea—canaries in the coal mine, telling us how we were losing touch with our bodies and our rapidly toxifying environment? Eating seemed like a highly entertaining but empty vice, its very emptiness made terrifying by its intensity, and its intensity made terrifying by its emptiness. A dark phenomenon with dark consequences. Scary. But over the course of my year on the competitive eating circuit, as I humped around America in Southwest 737s from one gorgefest to another, I began to suspect that eating wasn't so easily pinned down. It didn't seem as discrete and monolithic as other cultural products with built-in KICK ME signs. Performance art. *Jackass*. Grand Theft Auto. Eating was broader, more slippery. There were a lot of variables, and a slight shift in audience, food, or venue could transform a contest's flavor—could make it go down easy or make it stick, like a chicken bone, in the spiritual craw. I started to see that eating was more like a political rally or a church sermon, or any institution that involved a call and response, a crowd and a performer and, most important, a place. Eating could bring out the best in the American character or the worst, or it could merely bring out two diametrically opposed tendencies and marry them for a brief berserk moment, as happened at the shoofly-pie championship in Lancaster, Pennsylvania, in summer 2005, which was attended by equal contingents of Philadelphia Eagles cheerleaders and Amish teenage boys (shoofly pie is an Amish delicacy), and after which my fiancée saw one Amish boy, maybe fourteen years old, in black trousers and suspenders, clutching a photo of a blonde cheerleader in a white bra. The photo's inscription read, "To Samuel,

Cheers & go Eagles, Caroline." Whether an eating contest felt life-affirming or soul-destroying, or just bizarre, all depended on the context.

It was in March 2005 when I saw, for the first time, an eating contest that felt perfectly calibrated to its context. The venue was the Acme Oyster House in Metairie, Louisiana, where I'd flown for the Acme World Oyster Eating Championship. The morning of the contest, I got up early and walked a mile from my hotel on Lake Ponchartrain to the Acme on Veterans Boulevard, about twenty blocks west of downtown New Orleans, across a grassy median from a Borders bookstore. I poked my head in the back door at 7:30 a.m. because I wanted to see the oyster-shucking operation. On most days, Acme employed three or four shuckers at its oyster bar on the restaurant floor, but this morning the restaurant had called in extra shuckers to prep the 1,908 oysters that would eventually be consumed by the eaters in that afternoon's main event. Five junior shuckers, all African-American but one, worked an assembly line in the kitchen, wearing rubber gloves to protect themselves from the sharp shells and prying open the oysters with squat, pointed knives. It smelled damp. To one side, off the assembly line, was Michael "Hollywood" Broadway, age forty-six, a gaunt man with wiry arms who tapped me with his fist and said, "I am the senior bad mothershucker in the house." Hollywood is the dean of all shuckers in New Orleans, having shucked for twenty-nine years, and he is also something of a media star. He said, "I've been on *Blind Date*, A&E, Travel Channel, Food Network, E!, *Gourmet* magazine," so he was used to doing what he did with me now, which was to pull live oysters from a big tub to his left (reef oysters, he said, mud-grown, from the brackish waters of the Gulf of Mexico) and narrate his technique to the soundtrack of his knife as he shucked: Smother the oyster. Press down hard with your hand. The more you press, the less work the knife has to do. Force against force. Go in perpendicular, knife point down. Pry. Don't push. Pop it open through the small side, the oyster's head. If that doesn't work, tap the wide side—the hinge—to make a flat area and crack through. Slide the knife to the wide side to sever the muscle and free the oyster for slurping.

"Hey, Hollywood," one of the shuckers teased, "you been talking since last night! What's up?"

"I'm doing an interview, son. Have your people call my people." Hollywood picked up a new oyster, shucked it, and pointed out the color in the shell. Color means it's a male. Males are sweeter. Always wipe the knife, so you don't get shell shavings in the juice. "If it ain't clean, it ain't worth eating. That's what I tell my customers. If they ask you how you like your oysters, don't say big or small, say clean and cold. Clean and cold, the Hollywood way." Hollywood was proud he could give the eaters the best, cleanest oysters. He picked up a shucked oyster and slurped it down. "Oh, they good and salty, good and salty," he said. "They'll love 'em." Hollywood said he wasn't rooting for any particular eater, but he had been amazed by last year's winner, Sonya Thomas, who'd eaten thirty-six dozen oysters in ten minutes. Out front at the oyster bar, faint-mustachioed and diamond-earringed Travis Pflueger, twenty-four, said he was trying to shuck the oysters extra-clean so that his friend Crazy Legs Conti would have a shot to beat Sonya. "They say she's a buck-oh-five and she throw it down like that," Travis said. "That's serious, man." He would periodically disappear out back to retrieve more oysters from the truck of Acme's supplier, P&J Oysters, founded by Croatians whose successors had been fishing oysters from the Gulf for 130 years, and then come back carrying orange mesh sacks of a dozen dozen. Travis started pulling oysters from one sack and said, "They shouldn't have a problem eating these today. They're small." An oyster is only water anyway, he said. To demonstrate, he squeezed an oyster dry with his towel, leaving a vague stain. "It's the original Viagra, man," said Laurie Brunet, Acme's manager and house mom, who was sitting at the bar with me. "Louisiana Viagra."

I drank coffee with Laurie and watched Travis shuck oysters and waited a couple of hours for the fog to burn off and the parking lot to fill up outside with eaters and contest-goers. Then I walked outside and saw that Acme had set up a state fair in its parking lot, complete with food tents (crawfish, corn) and a ticketing system (three tickets for a beer, four for a frozen daiquiri). A girl in a white wedding dress roamed the lot, handing out beads. A man's T-shirt read IT'S A GREAT TIME TO BE A REPUBLICAN. I saw Badlands Booker and Crazy Legs Conti taking pictures with fans. Bad rock music blasted through a PA system. Walking by four Louisiana Wildlife Fisheries officers in identical gray shirts, I heard one of them laugh, "I ain't gonna let the dynamic dago duo collect my money," and assumed he had a side bet with his buddies (of Italian descent) on the upcoming "heroes" competition, a one-minute contest to honor local state workers and firefighters and cops. Also on today's itinerary was a "neat-eating" contest for kids (in which they would try to construct the perfect ice-cream float), an oyster-shucking competition, and a "dignitaries" competition for local politicians and chefs. Chefs were considered dignitaries in New Orleans. Laurie spotted me and asked if I'd ever had a crawfish before. I said no, a small and harmless lie; I had eaten them once before and found them baffling, and I figured Laurie would have fun initiating a tourist into the society of crawfish-lovers, and I was right. She walked me to a crawfish booth, scored me a Styrofoam clamshell full of the buggers—I tried to pay, but my protestation of reportorial ethics was useless before Louisiana hospitality—and led me to a table of girls in black halter tops selling car calendars. *Hey, girls, this boy's never eaten a crawfish before, can ya show him?* I blushed as a heavily made-up brunette ripped the head off a crawfish and told me that the way to eat it is to, eh, suck it . . . and then Laurie ushered me to a picnic bench with two nice middle-aged women and their kids, making sure I wouldn't have to eat alone, and the women smiled and patted the open seat on the picnic bench, and we ate the spice-hot crawfish, all of us howling for water. Behind us, long tractor-trailers rolled by as part of Metairie's Italian and Irish parade, decorated in bright primary colors and showering not candy but food, actual groceries, from the windows, a throwback to some Tammany Hall boss's food-for-votes picnic.

It was starting. Rich Shea, George's little brother, presided over the "undercards," the one-minute contests for the heroes and dignitaries, after which I grabbed state senator Ken Hollis, Republican, of Metairie, and teased him about his poor total of twenty-four oysters. "I'm a gourmet oyster eater," he said. "I don't eat for speed. I like to enjoy 'em in a little sauce." We talked for a while about the bad old days of the Louisiana Senate, when it was thirty-eight Democrats and Ken Hollis, and how nowadays it was a red tide of Republicans. But today's contest was hardly political, unless it was a fund-raiser sponsored by the firm of Tabasco, Lea & Perrins. Hollis guessed that on his best day he could eat thirty-one oysters in a minute. "How many did you eat, Judge?"

"Forty-one," said the judge, a spry man with white hair.

"It's experience," said the senator deferentially. The judge had a great old

French name: Duplantier. Adrian Duplantier, U.S. District Court, Eastern District of Louisiana. He was seventy-eight years old. "I'm what they call a senior judge, but I'm still on the court," he said. "If they gave me two minutes, I think I could eat my age. You know how golfers say they could shoot their age?" He was holding a plaque commemorating his forty-one-oyster performance. "I have to bring my plaque to the courthouse," the judge laughed. "All my colleagues will think I'm crazy."

We fell silent out of respect for Miss Louisiana, a product of St. Charles Parish, who was now onstage. She said, "I can't do this alone, so please join in our National Anthem," and we did. Then Rich Shea spoke in somber tones about a recently departed fellow named "Crawfish" Nick Stipelcovich, a longtime denizen of the oyster contest and a beloved local chef. "Somewhere in the heavens, I venture to think the Southern part, is the very kind, big-hearted gentleman looking down with a resigning smile," said Shea—

"Craw*FISH!*"

"A giant!"

—and after a moment of silence the spirit of Crawfish Nick ceded the stage to a tiny Korean-American woman in a white IFOCE armband and white track pants that ended at her ankles, billowing around her skinny legs to provide the freedom of movement she'd need to put on her show. Sonya stood hunched over her circular oyster plates, a dozen per, and, with her cute little oyster fork, stabbed two or three at a time in a flash of toothpick wrists, no wasted motion, downing a dozen every fifteen seconds, four dozen in under a minute . . . "Sonya *THOMAS*, ladies and gentlemen, eighteen dozen! Lousiana! Oysters! In three! And a half! Minutes!" The crowd was stunned, agape. A man screamed, "She's doin' fawty dozen, *fawty dozen!*"

By now I'd seen Sonya eat four times at four contests, but I'd never seen her so . . . sensual. Unfreakish. It wasn't that she herself appeared any less severe eating those oysters, just that the contest's happy atmosphere had bled into my viewfinder, softening Sonya's hard edges. I got the sense that the contest would have been the same without her. To the locals here she was a great kick, but also just one in a long line of big eaters who'd walk into New Orleans oyster bars from time to time boasting they could eat so many dozen—big boys, "nasty boys" as Travis Pflueger calls them, guys like Boyd

"The Hammer" Bulot (he of the current house record at Acme, fifty dozen, the record it looked like Sonya was about to break), guys like U.B. Chase, aka "The Unknown Knight," who once ate, back in 1922, five pails of crawfish, then saved "the remainder of his supply for his supper," according to a contemporaneous *New York Times* clip; guys like Andrew Thevenet, former crawfish world record holder (thirty-three pounds in two hours), who once claimed, to a source of noted food writer Calvin Trillin, "There have been kings who didn't eat as well as I did." The New Orleans tradition of overeating was robust enough to absorb Sonya and frame her alongside all the old gluttons, who weren't really gluttons at all, as Trillin observed back in 1972 at the Crawfish Festival in Breaux Bridge, Louisiana. Back then, Trillin wrote, "in all of the discussion about excesses—about beer cans being thrown and immoral acts being committed in the churchyard and people walking half naked in the street—nobody had said a word about gluttony."

They didn't consider it gluttony because gluttony is a dire, consequential word and this sort of indulgence feels casual; it's been *made* to feel casual, which is the amazing thing about it, what separates the oyster contest and the New Orleans style of gorging from other communal eating spectacles like Wing Bowl. Wing Bowl is not casual. Wing Bowl is social, but only in the way that a race riot is social. People will die at Wing Bowl someday. No one will die in New Orleans at an oyster contest unless a neurotoxin is involved. If they suffer, it won't be from the binge but from what the binge covers up, the deeper problem that even that day in the Acme parking lot was visible in the obvious racial stratification of the chefs and the shuckers, the all-black shuckers being the ones who were emptying the circular plates of oyster shells into large trashcans and dragging them to the Dumpster. Yes, New Orleans was living a precarious existence then, and not in the Dennis Hastert sense—Hastert, prairie congressman and Speaker of the U.S. House of Representatives, who, after Hurricane Katrina flooded the city, said that "it looks like a lot of that place could be bulldozed." He didn't see the true precariousness, the more fundamental socioeconomic imbalance that couldn't be indefinitely overcome by minor eruptions of civic unity like the oyster contest. Still, what gorgeous fragility . . .

"EAT 'EM!!!! EAT 'EM *FAY-ASTER*, BABY!!!!!!"

A woman with short blonde hair and a scandalously sloping top had leaned over the railing in front of the stage and cupped her hands to yell at a man on the stage's far right, presumably her boyfriend. The boyfriend was losing to Sonya. Everyone was losing to Sonya. The man tried to communicate the futility of his enterprise by looking up from his oysters, staring solemnly at his girlfriend, and mouthing the words: "SHUT! UP! SHUT! THE FUCK! UP!" Sonya's eighteen dozen became twenty-six dozen, then thirty-six, which broke the record—and she kept going. "Oh my God," said Shea, "SonnnnYAAA!!!! SonnnnYAAAAA!!!! Forty-six dozen oysters in ten minutes! HISTORY HAS BEEN MADE!" And still she kept eating—not for the contest title, but to break Acme's house record, which only took her a few minutes extra.

The music started up again, a funk beat, as Sonya gave interviews to local press. After a few minutes, Sonya and the local TV cameras made way for a cover band in military fatigues and hats that said TOP GUN. The band launched into "Sweet Child o' Mine." The woman who'd screamed "EAT FASTER, BABY!" started dancing. She saw that a man was trying to take her picture, so she grabbed a few of her girlfriends and they all leaned into each other and leered and stuck out their tongues as every man within twenty yards craned his neck to catch a peek—*she's got eyes of the bluest skies as if they thought of ray-yay-yain!*—while behind them Judge Duplantier and Senator Hollis were kicking back with their people, and Michael "Hollywood" Broadway was autographing the T-shirts of IFOCE eaters with the slogan *Slow but good, Hollywood,* and even Rich Shea had cracked a beer—and I saw that the oyster contest was the best kind of eating contest because it wasn't about the food at all. Devotion to the food, to the oysters, was real enough, but it was only a means to an end. The food was an excuse for a federal judge and a state senator and Miss Louisiana and a New York carny barker and a voracious, toothpick-wristed woman in track pants and the world's most mediagenic oyster shucker and the disembodied spirits of Crawfish Nick and Axl Rose to gather together, in a parking lot next to an oyster house, and share a moment of American joy.

But food doesn't *have* to work that way. It doesn't have to be used as a way to get you outside of yourself, to connect to other people. It doesn't have to be social at all. It can be sealed off from the larger world. You and your stomach as a closed loop. DeLillo: *This is the edge of the observable universe of food.* The vast majority of eating contests follow the dictates of DeLillo and not Duplantier. The oyster contest is a party, but most contests are spectacles, and a spectacle requires separation between eater and fan. The eaters exist in a sealed-off universe of food as the audience stands there, gaping. The *New York Post*'s Gersh Kuntzman once argued to me that this hermetic quality was a good thing because "by making these guys spectacles . . . we can watch from the safety of the sidelines and therefore not have to *do* what these men do, nor *want* to do what they do, yet still be entertained." The eaters, in other words, are cautionary tales. Anti-examples. They are eating for our sins.

Actually, the gap between eater and spectator isn't quite so yawning. Some of the spectators relate to the eaters and perhaps even admire them as quasi-athletes. You wouldn't be wrong to call such spectators "fans." In Franz Kafka's story "The Hunger Artist," about a man who attracts crowds by fasting inside a cage, there are "constant observers" who make sure the hunger artist doesn't cheat by sneaking food, and Kafka writes that "strangely enough they were usually butchers." Fans of competitive eating tend to be skinny. I met a fan in New Orleans, Dave Hunley, who wore a Federation T-shirt to the Acme oyster contest and referred to his baby daughter, whom he was bouncing in his arms, as one of his "young gurgitators." I met a fan in Venice Beach, a deejay named Doron Oronstein, who said that he had lost ninety pounds in the last year, and was "living vicariously" by watching the contest, and if the Staples Center hosted eating events, he'd buy season tickets. (He also said, upon catching an Ed Jarvis T-shirt tossed from the stage, "Man, I am going to get so much pussy with this.") I even met a little boy, twelve-year-old Alex Marino, who told me he wants to be a competitive eater when he grows up. Alex's father had brought him to a Philly sports bar to watch the Federation's stars qualify for Wing Bowl 13. "It's just, like, unbelievable," said Alex, who had seen the eaters on TV. "Eating things is only a percentage of it. There's so many other things you have to keep in mind." He added that he'd rather be an eater than a linebacker, say, because he found most sports "kind of repetitive," including football and baseball: "Three ups and you're out. Three ups and you're out."

Alex is the exception. Most spectators obviously don't aspire to be eaters.

It's the other way around. The eaters aspire to be as healthy as the spectators. This aspiration is complex because it shifts during the course of a contest day. Right before a contest, when the music's pumping and George Shea is warming up the crowd, eaters are happy to puff themselves into the fearsome, gargantuan behemoths they are being hyped as. They're like any other species of athlete before a competition. Nervously excited. Tittering. Even the 400-pound eaters gain a certain buoyancy. They glide across food courts with the sullen grace of deep-sea beasts. At the bell, they fill their stomachs as best they can, and become heavy again. Buoyancy is replaced with a palpable sadness radiating from the gut. The eaters are now repositories of useless calories they immediately resent. Furiously, they set about erasing the visible evidence. Lips, cheeks, beards, noses wiped clean. Stained T-shirts changed or covered up. Tablecloths folded and stored. Floors vacuumed. The eaters congregate and trade gripes about the judging and the food. They discuss their elliptical machines, their diets, their prospects for the next contest. Modern eaters are devoted health nuts. Jim "Buffalo" Reeves and "Jalapeño" Jed Donahue actually lost weight after joining the circuit,* and the eaters who didn't lose weight, which was most of them, claimed to be trying. It used to be that old-time eaters would revel in the unhealthfulness of eating—Don Lerman once said, "I'll stretch my stomach until it causes internal bleeding"—but all the newer quotes stressed the athleticism and normalcy of eating, as if the eaters had been given a set of talking points. All the newer TV shows winnowed down the actual eating portions of the coverage to the bare minimum and focused instead on soulful interviews with the eaters and clips of the more attractive ones running and lifting weights. (Jason Bernstein, senior manager in programming and acquisitions for ESPN, says that if his network could air a 100-percent-clean eating show "without spilling, and without making a mess, I would still watch . . . throwing up, or spewing or whatever it is, that's not the case as to why we're doing it.") When I asked Don about his "internal bleeding" quote, he said, "I'd like to retract that comment," and went off the record. Even Eric Booker—420-pound Booker—spoke of his workouts. On *Battle of the Buffets,*

---

* I always hesitate to write "joining the circuit" because it sounds like "joining the circus," but perhaps these outcomes are not unalike.

a Travel Channel special filmed in Las Vegas, Booker claims in an interview, "I do a little cardio, I try to stay in shape—I mean, stay in eating shape, I should say." The interview clip is followed immediately by a shot of Booker at an "indoor skydiving" facility in Vegas. To skydive indoors, you put on a billowy suit and lie down on top of a big propeller pointed straight up, like a vertical wind tunnel. The suit fills with air, making you float. But Booker won't float. Two men from the facility grab Booker's suit at strategic points and give him a lift, but he's so heavy that one of the men stumbles from the strain. Booker's mass is overpowering the wind tunnel *plus two dudes*. The men regroup and try again, but the best they can do is bounce him up and down like a basketball.

An eater can only fight the contest calories so hard. There is no controlled study of the health of competitive eaters vis-à-vis the general population, but eating, at least the way Sonya Thomas and Tim Janus do it, is *prima facie* unhealthy. Most eaters don't go at it as hard as Sonya or Tim, and even both of them seem truly fit and undamaged by all that stomach-stretching. Still, the population of eaters is a grab-bag of foody maladies. There's the occasional serious health event—in 1991, Mort Hurst, a moon-pie eater from North Carolina, had a stroke after eating 38 eggs in less than a half-minute—in addition to acid reflux and diabetes. Diabetes would seem to be a career-ending injury for an eater, like an ACL tear for a slalom skier, but it almost never is. After diabetes played a part in claiming the right leg of Dave "Moe Ribs" Molesky, he continued to compete wearing a prosthetic limb. Even the victims of serious health events didn't necessarily retire. Wing Bowl eater "Tollman" Joe Paul bragged to my fact-checker, in early 2006, that he could "still beat anyone in mussels," having recently eaten 219 mussels in 10 minutes at a tavern in Bridgeport, Pennsylvania. "And that was after the stroke," said Tollman. He laughed.

For some guys, Moleskian/Tollmanian obstinacy manifests itself as a failure or inability to lose weight. Ed Jarvis at 420. Charles Hardy at 330. Booker sometimes at nearly a quarter-ton. Booker was the main one. I once talked to a Federation official who said that efforts had been made to persuade Booker to take his weight seriously. ("You can lead a horse to water," Hardy once told me, "but you can't make him drink.") These interventions always stopped short of actually preventing Booker from competing in contests.

"He's got an eating problem," the Federation official said, and argued that Booker would be a big guy even if he wasn't a competitive eater.

Which was probably true. Sometimes it's hard to tell whether the eaters are odd to start with or whether the eating makes them odd. Certainly, obsessive people self-select for this hobby. Documentary filmmaker Errol Morris says that "if you scratch the surface of any person you will find a world of the insane very close to that surface," and it seemed as though competitive eating had already done the scratching for me. To find the world of the insane, I needed only to show up at an eater's home and talk about food.

I could open the Long Island refrigerator of Don Lerman, for instance, and see that Don keeps nothing in his fridge—except for spring water and an O'Doul's—because Don is on a "TV dinner diet," which means that every morning he drives to Wal-Mart, buys three TV dinners, and eats them with a Slim-Fast shake. "I can't keep food in the fridge," Don says, "because I'd eat it all." Or I could sit in the living room of Carlene and Rich LeFevre, in their overwhelmingly pink home atop a mesa outside Las Vegas, and note the bowl of M&Ms on their coffee table, next to books like *Dr. Phil's Ultimate Weight Solution* and *The New Cabbage Soup Diet*, while Carlene keeps pulling delicious low-fat desserts from her fridge and feeding me: a parfait, a pretzel pie. She speaks of food as if every calorie must exact a cost in exercise: "I'll do anything to be able to eat." She favors a brutal cross-training circuit of jumping jacks, aerobics-style leglifts, and speed-walking that involves her own bedroom floor, *Oprah*, and clever use of the classroom facilities at the elementary schools where she substitute-teaches. "When the kids are working," she says, "I'm not sitting at my desk because I'm not burning any calories. So I tell the kids, 'Okay, children, I'm walking around and around the room, raise your hand if you need me!'"

Carlene and Don are flirting with the DSM definitions of disordered eating. They may have an old eating disorder or a completely new one. (*Vorolimia:* the tendency to gorge in public.) The difference between Carlene and Don is hard to pin down, but I'd say that Carlene is able to make her disordered eating work. She's manic, she's a little crazy, but she's not sad. She's a sweet woman with a sweet husband. They travel all over the country together in search of eating trophies and adrenaline rushes. They skydive, they bungee jump. Carlene isn't down the donut hole. She's kneeling above it, waving down at certain of her compatriots—waving, certainly, to Don Lerman, because when Don and I move beyond his kitchen into the rest of his Long Island house, I see that Don's obsession with eating is a nursery that launches other obsessions like a failed Middle Eastern state launches terrorists. In Don's living room, a neon sign hangs on the wall behind an eight-foot-long oak bar. It says, DON LERMAN'S BAR AND GRILL. This is Don's ultimate dream, to own and operate an actual Don Lerman's Bar and Grill. Don is retired now; he used to own a couple day-old-bread stores. Absent his own bar, he wouldn't mind doing *appearances* at bars—or, as he solicits on his website, "Grand Openings, Bar Mitvah's [*sic*], Bachelor/Bachelorette Parties . . . etc." I ask Don what services he could provide at a bachelorette party. "That's a good question," he says. "I see sports figures like Keith Hernandez, they go to bar mitzvahs, they sign autographs. And I guess I could do that, too, ya know? . . . But I haven't got no calls yet. I'm waitin' for my movie with A&E to come out. *Airlines.* They came to my house, they interviewed me, they took me to a buffet—I don't wanna give it all away . . ."

Don takes me downstairs. "I saved the best for last," he says, and pushes through the door to his trophy room, a smallish shrine with maroon carpeting where he stores his life-sized cardboard cutout of himself, his 50-plus Don Lerman hats, his sixty-one framed grip-and-grin photographs with reporters and the mayors Bloomberg and Giuliani (Bloomberg, lacking the showman's gene, appears bewildered, while Giuliani is all verve and teeth), his trophies of course, his thirty to forty custom-embroidered jackets, his oil paintings of himself as Charlton Heston (as Moses) and the King of Prussia . . . all of the things he says he wishes his late father, a candy salesman and a shoe-factory worker, were still alive to see. "I wish he could come back to Earth for *one* day," Don says, holding up his pointer finger, "to see what I've accomplished."

Don is stuck. He is at the end of the line. He has created his own cargo cult—a cargo cult of Don Lerman—and now he is waiting for his plane. Fame. *My movie. Airlines. I don't wanna give it all away . . .*

This happens all the time. Guys get stuck. It happens to guys with more going for them than Don Lerman, too—guys with wives, kids, families. It happened to Mike "The Scholar" Devito, who took five years to retire. It happened to Charles Hardy and Ed Jarvis, who have been threatening retirement since 2001 and 2004, respectively. I even watched it happen to Coondog O'Karma. Just when I thought he'd gotten out, like he said he had—just when I thought he'd quit eating for good—I'd check Arnie's AICE website and see:

> 6/27/05 Day two of the Spicefest featured The World Corn on the Cob Eating Championship where spectators were treated to a World Record performance by the charismatic and electrifying Dave "Coondog" O'Karma who ate an amazing 31 cobs of corn in 10 minutes . . .

> 6/23/05 Coondog toasts then coasts to victory at the second Quick Chek qualifier with 4.5 italian subs . . .

> 6/19/05 It was a big weekend for Coondog O'Karma, as he won the Byesville Coal Miner Festival Pizza eating contest . . .

Even Tim Janus was starting to get stuck. On the face of it, there was nothing to worry about when it came to Tim Janus. He had yet to incur any physical costs. He was young and clever, and thus far eating had made his life tangibly better: it had given him friends, a community, cash, a chance to travel and be on TV. And yet, as he e-mailed me in late June, his actual career plans were starting to become affected by his eating. "If you look at where the bulk of my income comes from, you'll see that it comes from my blue-collar pizza job," he wrote. "I think if only people knew that about me, they'd be a little bit less interested in me. But I don't say a word about it, and I'm kind of reluctant to give up the trading entirely because I know that as long as I'm still trading, some reporters will always be interested in my story."

One time in Manhattan I had beers with Tim and his mother, Lucinda. She was a thoughtful and funny woman. She wore earrings shaped like the moon and the sun. She's a psychologist by profession. It was enlightening, because I could hear Lucinda try to justify, in real time, the value of what her son was doing. "It still seems to me like such a strange hobby," she said. "Um, I wonder what brings all these different people together to do this thing that seems so, for lack of a better word, weird to me. You know? I mean I guess there are lots of weird things in the world but this one seems—"

Tim interrupted, "There's one thing about the weirdness, though." He said that eating wasn't weird, it was special. It was more special even than golf or tennis, because you can play golf or tennis any day of the week. With eating, he said, "You can't do it when you want to. You have to wait for this opportunity. So it makes it more special because it's rationed, you know?" He continued, "So you have to like the essence of it. You really have to like the essence of it a *lot*, and then you care about it."

But it was hard to make this argument stick. Eating seemed so strange, so weird, there was no convincing people—so at this point, all an eater could do was play his trump card, call in his rhetorical *deus ex machina*:

ESPN.

ESPN started covering the contest in 2002 after a young business reporter named Darren Rovell discovered that stories about competitive eating were always among the most e-mailed stories on ESPN's website, Page Two, along with stories with headlines like DEER FORCES MAN TO FLEE OFFICE. Rovell says, "Why shouldn't we be at an event where people are interested and there are very few reporters on it? So let's blow it out. Let's blow out the coverage." Rovell and ESPN started by running stories on the Page Two website; the next year, in 2003, they ran a *SportsCenter* piece on Koby; and in 2004, they made the leap to a live broadcast that garnered 765,000 households. "What *was* offbeat ten years ago is no longer offbeat now," says Jason Bernstein, who is ESPN's tennis guru and helped develop its eating programs. "Look at the X Games. The X Games are a major worldwide competition that, again, could have been classified as offbeat ten years ago." Bernstein continued, "That said, I don't expect—I don't want to compare competitive eating to the X Games"—he laughed nervously—"or the Great Outdoor Games." (He also made it clear that ESPN was not promoting obesity: "I'm not sure that this would be, that this event would constitute a statement from the network about obesity in the United States. Again, we certainly are not looking to rock the boat in that regard and we are very sensitive to all those issues.") Bernstein told me that "competitive eating, I think, is a—well, it's fascinating if nothing else," and he saw ESPN's role as "connecting the grassroots effort to the mainstream television effort." ESPN hasn't bet big on eating—"Let's be honest," says Bernstein, pointing out that in 2005 the network would devote just four hours of original programming to competitive eating—but ESPN still has twenty-four hours of programming to fill, so why not take a chance? "Before it's big," says Bernstein, "let's *help* it become something big."

And now that ESPN broadcasts the Nathan's contest, there's a feeling that the sport has really made it. At the very least, eating was at least as legitimate as any other weird sports on ESPN, as Tim argued, like the World's Strongest Man, or arm-wrestling, or the lumberjack competitions. Tim used to hear Don Lerman talking about eating being an Olympic sport, and thought he was crazy. But why? Why is Don crazy? Food is more important to us than running and jumping, the roots of track and field. Yes, eating contests are wasteful, but so are Olympic equestrian events, and so are mainstream non-Olympic sports like NASCAR (which burns enough gas to keep the Saudis happy) and golf (which squanders precious water keeping all those landscapes so green). Is eating too visually ridiculous for the Olympics? One word: biathlon. Two words: rhythmic gymnastics. Too corporate? Please. Look how hard snowboarding sold out after the 2002 Winter Olympics. Ross Powers might as well have been a NASCAR driver. In fact, competitive eating is the *perfect* twenty-first-century sport because it's sold out so hard already. It's pre–sold out. Its athletes go beyond slapping a brand name on their shirtsleeve, they actively *consume* the product, they're shitting out the product. The logic has an undeniable pull, especially when talking with someone like Tim Janus—who is not an eccentric like Don Lerman, who is a young, smart, functional, self-aware guy—and you listen to him describe, calmly, his latest training revelation. You find yourself nodding your head. Tofu bricks, he'll say. High volume, low fat. (Nod.) Don't even cook 'em—it's faster that way. (Nod.) Top it off with a splash of salsa for the electrolytes. (Nod.)

Makes sense, sure.

I have to say that I kept nodding for a long, long time. I nodded during cheesecake, pumpkin pie, oysters, tiramisu, and shoofly pie. I nodded through Tex-Mex rolls and four Krystal qualifiers, through grilled cheese and Wing Bowl.

And then, one day in May, at an event that had nothing to do with Tim Janus, I stopped.

I'm staring at a tarp. The tarp is blue, the color of the ocean on maps. Yellow Nathan's Famous logos dot the tarp. The tarp is in Las Vegas and covers a long table, the competition table, which is covered with hot-dog detritus from the contest that has just now taken place: the very first Nathan's Famous hot-dog qualifier of the 2005 season. Rich LeFevre is the winner with twenty-seven hot dogs. He has beaten his wife, Carlene, and his main challenger, Ron "Hizzoner" Koch, a staff photographer for the MGM Grand casino just across the street. We are in front of the New York New York casino in the shadow of the fake Brooklyn Bridge. And I'm staring at the tarp—specifically, at the mess Rich LeFevre has left in front of his little patch of blue ocean—trying to figure out why the contest sucked.

Maybe I've seen too many of them. Maybe I've heard George Shea's shtick so many times I can predict his next set piece, or maybe the inherent artifice of Vegas, combined with the hot-dog contest, is like a Hershey bar dipped in a pixie stick. Maybe I'm upset about Kid Cary. Kid Cary was not here today. Every year in the late nineties, Kid Cary would hire a couple of Bunnettes to wear flag-patterned vests and show some leg in honor of the Vegas hot-dog champ. The Kid is no longer the champ, but I was hoping he'd crash the party anyway. Last night I called him to say hi. "I didn't hire any Bunnettes this year," he said, sounding very tired. "I sent my DVD* to George and the head of Nathan's, but I never heard back. I guess nobody gives a shit."

No Kid Cary, no Bunnettes, no shtick or cheesy prurience. *In Vegas.*

So now the contest is over. Three or four reporters, holding tape recorders, have approached the competition table, asking Carlene and Rich the same questions I myself asked fifteen contests ago. I tune out the questions and answers and focus on the blue tarp. The other reporters are trying

---

* . . . *With Relish: Kid Cary's Greatest Hits.*

not to look—I don't blame them, it's gross—but me, I'm transfixed. Rich has deposited an array of rejected bun parts and chunks of franks. To be clear: not vomit, but crumbs. Vomit would be better; vomit is a car crash, bloody, thrilling. This is just sad. This is just a coy assemblage that, against the map-blue backdrop of the tarp, resembles a little island archipelago. The Gurgitator Islands.

I stare at the Gurgitator Islands because I have nothing better to do.

I stare and stare.

A mental wall crumbles.

Something's missing.

I realize that for the first time since my initial forays into the Krystal hamburger circuit eight months ago, when competitive eating was new to me and I was juiced to cover any contest, I'm covering a contest without the eaters I know and like the best. Tim Janus isn't here. Neither is Coondog or El Wingador. Without Tim's stream of training anecdotes and earnest logic, or Coondog's shtick, or Wingador's feral tropism toward anything that smells like a barbecue grill, I'm lost. I'm alone with the dry bones of the spectacle itself. For the first time, my view isn't obstructed by my own newbie's enthusiasm or the enthusiasms of my favorite eaters. I've got a clear shot at what I'm actually dealing with. And what do I see? I see . . . a marketing pitch. An unhealthy food product. A person wearing a hot-dog costume. Canned music. A few scribes and TV cameras. One shill in a suit. Additional shills in T-shirts. It's so obvious to me now: Janus and Coondog and El Wingador have been propping up the spectacle. They've made it funnier, fairer, denser, more delicate, more poignant—in every way better, to a startling degree.

Has eating returned the favor?

That's been my question all along, the one that's made me a serial flip-flopper: *They're idiots, they're heroes, eating's crushing them, they're getting the better of it, it's a moral victory, it's a deathwish*, ad infinitum. I've had a year to decide if a person can extract meaning from a professional eating circuit—whether that person is a competitive eater or just a guy who follows them and sticks a tape recorder in their faces—and the whole thing remains a mess to me. I still change my mind a few times a week. It makes writing a book kind of hard. Look: if the eaters have taught me anything, it's that to run straight at trash culture, to engage it and live inside, is a complex and contradictory act. One, it's self-destructive in the extreme. It's fucked up! Because however alienated you already are, you're risking even greater alienation by becoming a competitive eater. It's like leaving a homeless shelter on a cold night to sleep in a dark alley. There's a mordant humor in the attempt, a febrile willingness to make things worse before they get better, like the self-abnegation of certain holy people, only in complete reverse. If twenty-first-century America is telling us, in a hundred ways, that what we are is a mouth connected to a bag, a wet sack of cells and orifices, and our highest patriotic purpose is to inflate this bag to bursting and soak this wet sack to saturation with cheap food and cheap TV, then maybe this running toward trash culture is a new kind of subconscious bodily revenge committed* for the same reason men smoke unfiltered cigarettes and teenage girls cut their wrists: to feel something, even if it's bad. *Reductio ad absurdum.* Okay, here I am, a mouth, a gut, a set of ears and eyeballs, a big bag of shit, howya like me now? But then trash culture is *so* toxic that it's impossible *not* to build a nest there, and its very awfulness ends up actually sharpening the intensity of the yearning to smooth it out, to make it comfortable and livable. Trash culture becomes more enveloping than it has a right to be: broader and bigger, more alluring, a thing startlingly maximalist, containing multitudes.

I was hoping, all along, that Janus and Coondog and El Wingador might be able to reckon with trash culture directly, to extract what they could on their own terms and then get the hell out, to safer ground. And, amazingly, they had, except for the part about getting the hell out. Competitive eating had made their lives tangibly better. Wingador had earned respect, a marketable local brand, some personal pride, cars, a Superbowl-style ring; Coondog had gotten a temporary reprieve from middle age; Tim had found a group of friends and a fun hobby/sport that got him recognized by random people in St. Louis Indian casinos and Wisconsin airports. The three of them weren't suckers, they were rational actors, and their achievements proved they weren't crazy to have become eaters. But hadn't they also given something up? Hadn't they lent this dumb spectacle, *which doesn't deserve them,* their best

---

* Damon Runyon once wrote that his fictional character Nicely-Nicely Jones "dearly loved to commit eating."

traits and hopes and qualities, their energy, their health—and who got the better part of that deal? Look at trash culture. Really look at what forty dollars buys you in the electronics section of Wal-Mart or what forty minutes teaches you on basic cable; read any forty wire stories on competitive eating; *WITNESS IT, WIT! NESS! IT!*—this deep phenomenon, raw, greedy, blurry-edged, excandescent from all the outsized fiery hope people like Janus and Coondog and Wingador have been slopping into it—could a person really play chicken with something like that? Gurgitation was not flirtation. It was a commitment. *Gurgitation,* from the Latin *gurges,* meaning "whirlpool" or, more loosely, "abyss"; *regurgitation,* derived from the Latin *gurgitare,* meaning "to engulf, flood": literally, "to flood oneself again." As a gurgitator, you clear a space. You make the vacuum you. You invite the flood. And once you let trash culture in, once you hold it like a fluid in your cells and shudder with the coursing weight of it, once it absorbs all your good and hopeful traits, it spouts back out of you to rejoin the bigger flow. You're only a way station. I keep thinking of the toxic sludge of Lake Ponchartrain, post-Katrina: confusing, dense, sick in the aggregate but spotted with uneven beauty. The lake crashing through all those neighborhoods, buckling walls, taking what it wanted, taking oil and baby books, combs, DVDs, heirloom jewelry, motorcycles, guns, the lake carrying along the priceless and holy effects of decent people—but drink a spoonful and you're done for.

Competitive eating wasn't apocalyptic, meaningful, vapid, funny, cornpone, clever, it wasn't a sign of societal decay or the next great American sport, it wasn't a lark or a fatal indulgence, it wasn't any of those things alone or even all of those things fused together. There was only one broad flood— and every joke, every victory, every risk, every media hit, every moment of joy was a piece of flotsam on the water, which explained why the subjective experience of competitive eating shifted wildly depending on time and place. It was an illusion caused by the flood itself, by the fact that extremely different pieces of flotsam happened to float by at different times—when really, but really, it was all happening at the same time, in the same place. How could the eaters answer my questions about America when they were deluged and I was, too? When we were all treading water in something vaster than anything any of us could see to the edge of, could comprehend, could begin to fight?

5

CONEY ISLAND

AND THE CIRCUIT ROLLED on, oblivious of my crisis of conscience. Gurgitation paused for no man. This was hot-dog season, son, crazy season, when the thoughts of every eater turned to Nathan's and Nathan's alone. After Vegas there were eleven American qualifiers left, eleven chances to make the big stage. The calculus was tricky. Tim wasn't sure which qualifier to choose. There were thousands of permutations. He spent his free time on e-mail and IM, peddling gossip with other B-listers about whether Sonya would show up in Philly, Virginia, New York, or Hartford. He briefly considered the qualifier at the Molly Pitcher Travel Plaza on the New Jersey Turnpike, but Molly Pitcher was late in the season and he wanted to get it out of the way early. He also considered flying to Atlanta, traditionally the domain of one Dale "Mouth of the South" Boone, a flamboyant loudmouth and a seventeen-hot-dog guy on his best day. Tim even thought seriously about the qualifier in Manchester, England. But George Shea said no, so it was out.

Eventually, Tim settled on Hartford, near his hometown. On May 21, trailing me and his MTV documentarian—I kept having to duck in front of the camera so as not to spoil the shots—Tim arrived at an outdoor stage in the middle of a shopping-mall parking lot. His gym-rat buddy Susan and his father's law partner had shown up to cheer him, but he didn't need it. He coasted to a twenty-two-and-a-half-dog total, easily beating Allen Goldstein and Beautiful Brian. He made his split times and only flagged near the end. According to the Two-Thirds Theory, he should have eaten twenty-five hot dogs and buns; Janus blamed the discrepancy on his own tentativeness, his fear of the unknown. "I'd never gone that far out into open water," he said. "Now that I know there's nothing to fear, I'll go balls to the wall on the Fourth." He was positive he could eat twenty-five in the finals. "Twenty-five I can guarantee," he said. "I know what I can do."

It was an audacious promise, but not the most audacious promise I heard in the early summer of 2005. That prize belonged to Coondog O'Karma, who in June left a cryptic message on my voice mail to the effect that he was "planning something cool." When I called him back, Coondog said that after the Coney Island finals, he would persuade Takeru Kobayashi—the hottest thing in the world on July 4—to leave his nice room at the W Hotel in Manhattan, the free meals, the fan adulation, the scrum of national and international reporters . . . and fly to Cleveland so he could eat against Coondog in a pizza contest on a local TV show hosted by an old man and a dwarf.

Coondog was planning to kidnap the hot-dog champ. And he wanted me to help.

The eaters arrived in New York a few days early, and why not, since their hotel rooms were paid for. Festivities officially began on July 1, at the traditional press conference at City Hall, attended this year by the city's sports commission. Kenji Oguni, the second Japanese contestant, showed up with his arm in a sling from a motorcycle accident, and Koby showed up with blonde hair, veiny arms, and chest muscles variously described as a "six-pack," an "eight-pack" (Brian Subich), and "a six-pack with two Bud tall-boys" (Gersh Kuntzman). Even as muscular as he was, his face was thinner, more kidlike than just six months prior. That afternoon, most of the eaters popped over to the final qualifier in front of Shea Stadium, where Carlene LeFevre, who had vanquished Dale Boone in Atlanta, discussed the finer points of flaxseed with Ron Koch, who had beaten her in Tempe. Sonya Thomas snacked on free hot dogs, her purse overflowing with a hoard of free Cheez Doodles some Nathan's flack had been handing out. I spotted Nathan's CEO Wayne Norbitz in the crowd. I asked him what was going through his mind as he watched the contest. He smiled and said, "I look to make sure the logos are straight and the cameras are rolling." Afterward, the eaters walked inside to watch the Mets game. The Sheas handed them gift bags that included various Nathan's-branded merchandise—a pen, a pencil, two keychains, a noisemaker—as well as a pair of sunglasses and an envelope with $100 in cash. The next day, the eaters rested. Tim packed a duffel bag to take to the W Hotel, where he would be sleeping that night with the A/C blasting on high; he had come to believe that body temperature was an important factor in contest preparation. Into his bag he placed seven bananas, high-fiber English muffins, a pack of Swedish Fish, crumb cake, Rice Krispies treats, and glazed donuts. That night he stretched his stomach with the bananas, the muffins, and a gallon of water, and in the morning he woke up and ate the sweet stuff to get his blood sugar up. And then he waited with the other eaters for the Bus of Champions to take them to Coney Island.

Coney Island, as Gersh Kuntzman says, is a dump. He means it as a compliment. Its grittiness is reassuring. While Tim is pounding sugar and waiting for the bus, I'm on the F train to Coney, and when I get there I see what Gersh means. The stage has been set up in front of a giant Nathan's billboard that runs along Stillwell Avenue on the side wall of the hot-dog stand. The left side of the wall is home to what the Sheas call the "two-dimensional Mount Rushmore of competitive eating": a giant photo montage of past contest winners, incorporating a digital clock that counts down the days, hours, and minutes until the next contest. It reads three hours, zero days. Off to the side is a small green tent with a dingy paper sign that says EATERS ONLY. Inside are coolers stocked with Coke Zero and Lemonlime Powerade, and a tub of red and white carnations reserved for the grand entrance of Takeru Kobayashi. In front of the stage is your standard set of media bleachers. Coney Island is still surprisingly dirty, for all the talk of revitalization. Right across the street from Nathan's is a line of frumpy stores spilling trash into the sidewalk gutters. I'm just blocks from Max Rosey's Astroland (*Who is this guy they keep talking about, Irving Renewal?*) and the brand-new Cyclones minor-league ballpark.

For me, Coney is anticlimax—not the show itself but the curtain call. Every constituency from eating's past and future is here. There are recent fans like Ian Gellman, fifteen, who, thanks to the Discovery Channel, possesses a keen understanding of the Belt of Fat Theory, alongside old fans like Harold Kay, seventy-four, from nearby Luna Park, and his friend Greg

Packer, forty-one, both of whom saw Kobayashi shatter the hot-dog record back in 2001.

"I figure fifty at least he's gonna do," says Kay. "And that's good."

"Well, maybe sixty," says Packer.

"Well, I don't know, sixty."

There are even Japanese fans who speak no English. "Toro umiyamada," the *oogui* blogger I met in Tokyo, is here. She says a giggly hello. There is a guy dressed as Uncle Sam on stilts. There is a girl in a sari dancing with Amos Wengler, the longtime troubador of the hot-dog contest, in the fenced-off area where the Bus of Champions will soon pull in. The crowd is starting to fill in. In the crowd are button-wearers ("It's about integrity / ARNIE KRISS for Brooklyn DA") and sign-holders. KENJI OGUNI 2005. SWALLOW SONYA SWALLOW. YOU GIVE ME LEFEVRE! Tim's sign says simply EATER X. It's tiny and made of poor-quality cardboard. The crowd starts getting so thick it's difficult to move. Noisemakers are passed out. Cops proliferate, directing traffic. "You see how we are?" says an old shirtless man with wraparound sunglasses. "Americans? We're happy. We love life. This is what they hate." By "they" he means the terrorists. "They've done nothing since the thirteenth century. No patents, nothing." He starts talking about the neutron bomb.

The media are here, too, starting with Gersh, who is trying to help Amos Wengler write a new song that reflects the realities of the 2005 circuit. Gersh sings:

> *Ko-bay-ossh-ee, Sonya Thomas.*
> *Biggest eaters in the world*
> *And Judgment Day's upon us.*
> *Forty pounds of grilled hot dogs*
> *And then it's . . .*

He trails off, searching for a rhyme. "On us . . . Honest . . . Then go home to Mamas . . ." Gersh squints in a gesture of futility. "I don't know," Gersh says. "It's not bad. It's the best I can do. Believe it or not, if you actually need it I have a rhyming dictionary in my bag."

"Ehhhh," says Amos Wengler.

Lined up across the media bleachers are thirty or so video cameras. TV reporters jostle for space to do standups. CNN. TV Asahi. I run into a Eurotrash-looking guy in dark glasses and Gola shoes and ask where he's from. He says he's French, working on a documentary about American fatness. "There is no such thing anywhere else in the world," he says. "I don't judge—people do exactly what they want to do."

The Fuji Blimp is here, flying overhead.

I write in my notebook, "FUJI FUCKING BLIMP."

And then, finally, the eaters are here, too, stepping off the Bus of Champions: Hardy, Booker, Don Lerman, Ron Koch, Crazy Legs, both LeFevres, Kenji Oguni, Florida banquet chef "Jammin'" Joe LaRue, U.K. porkpie champ Rob Burns, a young newcomer from California named Joey Chestnut, an old newcomer from Moonachie named Pat From Moonachie, Sonya, Koby, Ed Jarvis with his fanny-pack annex, Tim Janus. I ask Tim how he feels. "Not as hungry and intense as I'd like," he says, "but this crowd is amazing!" The ESPN feed goes live. George Shea proclaims the presence of Koby, who is carried onto the stage in a hot-dog chariot, Pharaoh-style, as he bats away the flying carnations and takes his place at the table with the mere mortals, to the left of Sonya Thomas and the right of Eric Booker, who wears an enormous white airbrushed shirt that says *Badlands* and, below it, *Hungry &* *Focused* in cursive script. Koby wears a yellow Nathan's headband and a white tank top to show off his biceps. On the ESPN broadcast, the editor cues a fuzzy shot of some kind of Zen temple with Asian string music in the background. A sports analyst named Paul Page, who along with Rich Shea is providing color commentary, introduces Koby as being "from the empire of Japan."

Five, four, three, two, one, GO . . .

It's on.

Okay—now is when the made-for-TV nature of the modern Nathan's contest becomes painfully apparent. I'm squished in among a few hundred people on the left side of the stage, with no prospects for getting closer. The camera guys are the only ones with unobstructed views. It's like being at a U2 concert or a Super Bowl game—you get better angles watching at home. ESPN's viewers, for instance, have already been treated to studio-filmed set pieces of three eaters: Koby, filmed against a white background; Sonya, ghostlike in layers of white pancake makeup, wearing a black cape against a stark red backdrop and saying, creepily, "I am the Black Weedow . . . I beat all the men . . ."; and Tim Janus, applying his red, white, and blue makeup, with prominent Xs under his eyes. ESPN has already flashed a graphic listing the "heavy hitters" of gurgitation, along with some of their vital stats: Koby, Sonya, Booker, Jarvis, and Tim Janus. Janus is clearly being set up for lots of airtime, and not just because the Internet betting site, BetUs.com, has given him 5-to-1 odds to win: Tim has also agreed to wear a "helmet cam," a black ESPN ballcap fitted with a mirror and a camera that offers viewers a simultaneous view of Tim's plate and his mouth, and to which ESPN will often cut away in the next twelve minutes.

The first two or three minutes are uneventful. In a box on the upper left of the TV screen, ESPN keeps a running tab of hot-dog totals that, for the moment, remain predictable: with a little less than nine minutes to go, Koby has eighteen, Sonya fifteen, Jarvis eleven, Carlene eleven, Hardy eight. George Shea fills the dramatic vacuum with showmanship. His podium starts to rise, revealing itself to be a cleverly disguised portable scissor lift. As it rises, he lifts his arms skyward to the Fuji Fucking Blimp until he's level with the giant floating hot dog that is part of the Nathan's restaurant's façade, and the crowd roars and keeps roaring as, with seven minutes left to go, we get a new set of totals: Koby in the lead with twenty-five, Sonya trailing with twenty-two. The camera cuts to a shot from Tim's helmet cam. He appears to be struggling with the dogs. A graphic reads, "Day Trader by trade; Eater by disposition." Rich Shea jumps in and claims that Sonya is about to "break away" despite the fact that Koby is starting "to put distance between him and the other eaters . . . Cookie Jarvis is going to fall behind . . ."

And that's when it happens.

Shouting from the far side of the stage. Extreme stage-left. With 6:35 left to go, an IFOCE official, from what has to be considered no-man's-land— since all the top eaters, including Tim, are situated at the table's center— starts yelling the name of Joey Chestnut.

Chestnut, Joey Chestnut with twenty-one HDBs!

Chestnut, this twenty-one-year-old dude from out west, an unknown quantity to the whole New York crew—gooberous shaved head, prognathous jaw, unfortunate teeth, he'd only eaten twenty and a half HDBs at his qualifier—has twenty-one HDBs with more than half of the contest left to go!

His showing is so unexpected that, initially, ESPN doesn't catch on. At the moment ESPN is showing not Chestnut but a frontal shot of Tim Janus, who has yet to reach the fifteen-HDB mark. Janus hears the screaming, pauses, looks to his left, stares at Joey Chestnut for two or three long seconds, and returns to his hot dogs. A full minute goes by. "Eater X better catch a breath," says Rich Shea, and ESPN finally cuts to its first shot of Chestnut. Shea says, "Chestnut performing better than I thought he would . . . twenty-four I'm being told for Chestnut, that's a great, great competition, this kid's got a future . . ."

Under three minutes to go. Koby's at forty, Sonya's at thirty-three, a personal best and a new women's record. "The story here today for me, though, is this man right here, Joey Chestnut," says Rich Shea, "unbelievable, a rookie out of asparagus, who has shaken off even Rich LeFevre, it's just an unbelievable thing to see a young kid break out like this, pound for pound Chestnut might be the best rookie we've ever seen . . ."

"Ladies and gentlemen, witness it!" screams George Shea. "WITNESS IT!"

"You know," says Rich, as ESPN shows Janus struggling with less than a minute and a half left, "he's learning a lesson today, like all eaters, good eaters, bad eaters, Tim is gonna go through some growing pains, he's having a difficult time, I think, right now but it won't take him long to get out of that."

After some brief last-minute drama—a close shot of Koby shows his hand shaking badly, and Joey Chestnut spends a few terrible moments with his hand in front of his face, looking like he's about to launch ("Chestnut's in trouble, Chestnut must hold that down")—Koby pounds his forty-ninth dog at the buzzer, and Chestnut avoids launching on live TV, bending over the table in agony, his cheeks full, his fist defiantly raised. Rich says, "He's gonna leave a real man . . ."

Chestnut: 32 hot dogs and buns.
Tim Janus: 22½.
Sonya: 37.
Koby: 49.

"I am very sad," Koby tells ESPN's Darren Rovell, through his inter-preter Bobby Ikeda. "I came here to beat it, but maybe next year I will. . . . I will be back, I will be back." Sonya tells Rovell she's "a little bit disappointed. My goal was about forty." The press envelops the winners and doesn't let go for half an hour. The rest of the eaters mill around and wait for reporters to notice them. "My my my," says Rich LeFevre, "that was amazing. At least I wasn't fourth this year. It was a strange contest this year."

I find Tim off to the side, autographing the back of a girl's shirt. It's hard to believe that after all that stress and preparation, the stomach-stretching and trial eats, it's finally over.

"You'll be back?" the girl asks.

"I hope so," Tim says. He seems deflated, but the fan attention is perking him up:

"Warrior! Will you sign it?"

"How do you like New York?"

"How do you feel?"

"Does it hurt?"

This last inquisitor is wearing a bikini. She is a bubbly young chick with a serious Brooklyn accent. "Nah, it feels okay," says Tim. "But if you rub it," he adds, lifting his shirt to expose his belly, "it'll feel better."

Across the country, 660,000 households watched Tim Janus spray hot-dog debris. This represented a 16-percent drop in overall ratings from the 2004 broadcast. However, in the coveted eighteen-to-thirty-four-year-old male demographic, the rating jumped 19 percent to what ESPN programmer Jason Bernstein called "a serious number." Of all the shows on ESPN that day—including a baseball game, *Baseball Tonight*, even *SportsCenter*—the hot-dog contest attracted the most young males. Said Bernstein, "We're pretty pleased."

Tim Janus, however, was not pleased. The next day, July 5, I saw him in the lobby of the W Hotel, checking out. "I felt like a jerk because Chestnut crushed me," he said. "I knew something was wrong all week . . . it was really fucked up . . . in Hartford I had an excitement that allowed me to kind of not even taste the first ten or twelve hot dogs, you know? I almost felt like I was eating candy, you know? Here, I knew they were hot dogs from hot dog one. I had to muscle through those twenty ... use pure will ... I just felt huge disappointment today. To everybody. To myself, to ESPN, to the Sheas ..."

"I saw George pat your back," I said.

"And then I saw him just *beaming* when he talked to Chestnut. And you see that and you wish that were you, you know? You made somebody *so* happy about your eating, you know?"

Tim seemed terrified that he had been replaced. Later that night he wrote me a terse e-mail. "I lost my place in the hierarchy of eaters yesterday," he said. "Chestnut blew us away, and now he'll be the young guy everybody goes to." On top of this indignity, Tim had suffered a deeper one: the indignity of being betrayed by his own body. Tim had guaranteed twenty-five hot dogs. He had developed a theory, the Two-Thirds Rule, to explain why he must eat twenty-five hot dogs. Either he was the rule's sole exception or the rule was crap. He had not eaten twenty-five hot dogs, and he couldn't explain why except to cite a vague lack of excitement that was "really fucked up." It seemed possible that Tim had reached an upper limit. Chestnut was a swallower. His esophagus was more amenable than Tim's, and he needed less water to force down his food—two huge advantages in any contest, because it meant that Chestnut could eat faster *and* waste less of his stomach capacity on water. To keep up with Chestnut, Tim would need to make sure he didn't slow down, ever, which would require a monstrous stomach capacity on the level with Kobayashi's: twenty pounds or more. Tim had already discounted that possibility as "absurd."

This seemed like the end of the line.

I didn't talk to Tim again for a long time. I cocooned myself in my home office and wrote this book. I gave myself permission—I admit that this was more difficult than I'd anticipated—to stop checking ifoce.com and speedeat.com and beautifulbrian.com twice a day, every day. It wasn't until late August that I caught up with Tim again, on the phone. He asked me if I'd seen the IFOCE web page lately. I loaded it and saw: *Janus Sets New Record at GoldenPalace.com Event.* He was the top news story. At the Nebraska State Fair, flanked by the famous Virgin Mary Grilled Cheese Sandwich—February's inaugural Passion of the Toast had swelled into a fourteen-contest circuit—

Janus had eaten thirty-one grilled-cheese sandwiches in ten minutes. He'd beaten Sonya's record by six sandwiches. How had Tim gotten so good so quickly?

"I've been working on my capacity a lot," he said. "I thought the only way to give myself a future in this is to get my capacity [up]." At Coney Island, his capacity was 13 pounds. Now, he said, it was 14.5 pounds. He could now eat 6.5 pounds of food, sit back for five or six minutes, and then chug a gallon of water—8 pounds—in three minutes. He was training with a new kind of food he'd discovered at Whole Foods. The only problem with this new food was its expense—Whole Foods is not cheap—but Tim was willing to pay it. I asked Tim what the food was. He told me. Then he begged me not to print it. It was so effective that if other guys started using it he would lose his edge. All cordiality drained from his voice. It was an odd moment. We negotiated a truce: I could inform readers that Tim had discovered a certain type of *noodle*, but I would not divulge its ingredients or brand name. Satisfied with this, Tim lightened up again and told me that he believed there was no intrinsic limit to his stomach's expansion. He was not going to stop. He repeated this three, four times. *I'm just not gonna stop. I'm starting to believe I can push myself endlessly if I just don't stop.* "I've got nothing else to do. I enjoy doing this stuff, so why not give it a shot. I mean, if I had a career that was really demanding, or a family or something, I wouldn't be doing this. But I don't, and I enjoy this. So I'd be angry if I didn't try." Given another two months, he thought he could do 16 pounds, just two shy of Sonya Thomas. Eventually he could work all the way up to 20 pounds, in the ballpark of Kobayashi's capacity. "I wonder," he said. "Why *isn't* it possible? The stomach is just tissue and it can stretch, and it can tear a little bit and regenerate like muscles do, and why can't it keep going?" He knew that Sonya and Koby had big head starts. "But I'm saying—why can't you *outwork* somebody?"

This conversation creeped me out.

It was the first time that I'd ever felt a moral imperative to warn an eater about the risks of what he was doing. I saw in Tim the same focus and obsessive drive that had made Kobayashi so superabundantly capable, the same willingness to experiment, and since the Japan trip I'd learned more about Kobayashi that made me question the safety of high-level gurgitation. A few weeks after Coondog and I got back from Japan, Koby sent us an e-mail:

I am always thinking about how I can battle in a world beyond my appetite.... When I cannot eat any more is when it is physically impossible to fit anything else in my stomach. To ignore the limit means death. You cannot breathe. Another thing that will stop me from eating is sickness. In the past, I have attended three competitions with stomach ulcer, but they were painful competitions.

You cannot breathe. Koby was not speaking poetically. A few months later I stopped by the L.A. fashion warehouse of his translator, Bobby Ikeda. "He can eat way more than anybody's ever seen him eat on TV," Bobby said. "*Way* more." This is why Koby never appears to be laboring after a contest: he's not testing the upper limit of his capacity. The really insane volumes were being consumed in Koby's *practice sessions*, not in contests. Bobby said that in practice, Koby would eat until his stomach pressed against his diaphragm and messed with his breathing. "It's scary to see him breathing funny," Bobby told me. "He's, like, choking, almost. Not choking but fighting. It's fuckin' *spooky*, man." How does Koby overcome that? "Mind, body, soul, whatever," said Bobby. "I don't want to go dog-deep, but he's deep." Bobby smiled. "Either that or he's just fuckin' nuts."

What else was Koby—and now Tim Janus—risking? Ulcers. Gastric reflux disease. A specific kind of esophageal violence called a "Mallory-Weiss tear," an affliction common to anorexics and bulimics that makes them vomit blood. Gastric rupture. Gastric rupture was the really scary one, though I had never met an eater who claimed to worry about it, or had even heard of it. I would have been happy to tell Tim the story of Assunta Petroccia, say— a twenty-six-year-old Australian girl, whose case was representative of most gastric rupture victims. On December 17, 1999, Assunta went on a bulimic binge. She ate no more than 1.5 liters worth of chicken, chocolate, and chocolate milk. The next morning around 8:00 a.m., she reported to the hospital with abdominal pain. Doctors misdiagnosed her condition as constipation and gave her six doses of morphine, a laxative, and two enemas. Nothing worked. While doctors continued, over the next hours, to puzzle, Assunta's stomach burst, flooding her peritoneal cavity with acidic juice; early on December 19, sixteen to eighteen hours after first reporting, Assunta went into toxic shock. Her heart stopped. Later, at the coroner's inquest, a doctor testified that by eating her food so quickly, Assunta had effectively paralyzed her stomach, causing both valves to clamp off and the internal pressure to build and build. "It's a closed system," said the doctor, who added, "the blood supply in the wall is gradually cut off by this pressure and so the wall starts to die." The dead tissue is weak. It splits. The patient dies.

By 1968, only forty-nine cases of spontaneous gastric rupture (in all of modern medical history) had been reported in the medical literature, so it's definitely rare, but only eleven of those forty-nine survived. I had a stack of terse journal articles. Assunta's story wasn't even the saddest. There was the girl, age eighteen, who, prior to her death, *told the nurse her stomach had burst, and then she collapsed.* A twenty-three-year-old bulimic female fashion model who ate a nineteen-pound meal: dead. A forty-year-old white woman reported to Mount Sinai, *perspired profusely and had a sense of impending doom.* Most rupture patients were women. A sixty-one-year-old nun from Altoona, Pennsylvania, took sodium bicarbonate for her constipation and *collapsed on the floor in severe agony* from a 5-centimeter gastric rupture. A nun! *Death ensued before the closure was completed.* An eighteen-year-old bulimic girl reported to New Haven Hospital with a necrotic (dead) stomach that contained more than 15 liters, or 4 gallons, of undigested food in large chunks. She survived after *a stormy postoperative course.*

Except for this last woman, who ate 4 gallons (!) and lived to tell, the fatal volumes of food ranged from 1.5 to 3 liters, rarely cracking a gallon. Don Lerman can eat a gallon at an Indian buffet without even trying. The gurgitators have obviously adapted to volume eating, so they'll probably never bust a gut, but it's hard to feel comfortable with that conclusion because the gurgitators keep eating more and more every year. How do they know, especially the ones at the very top, like Tim and Koby? Now that they've worked so hard to short-circuit every feedback mechanism that would normally prevent them from eating to the point of death, how do they know, as Koby says he knows, "when it is physically impossible to fit anything else in my stomach"?

Here's my theory:

I don't think Koby *does* know.

I think he's just been lucky.

But he knows the risks, and Tim doesn't, or won't acknowledge them. He will not acknowledge that he is just guessing. *That even the gastroenterologists are guessing.* Tim had worked so hard to normalize competitive eating, to make it less weird. It's why he worked so hard at it. It's why he followed a schedule. It's why he wanted so badly to scrounge at the beginning, to sleep in hostels, sacrifice—because that's the American narrative of what you do if you want to succeed at something. You struggle. You sacrifice. Tim had slotted competitive eating into the larger American success narrative, and he had done it so gracefully that he'd lost touch with how strange his new environment really was. He never considered that his body might be as mysterious and random, in its own way, as the stock market. What's so American about competitive eating isn't the gluttony but the steroidal confidence in self-transformation it inspires. Tim had so masterfully constructed an American narrative around an American aberration that when the narrative bumped up against the boundaries of the aberration, it was the aberration, not the narrative, that had to give way:

Why can't you just outwork somebody?

I sent Tim an e-mail describing gastric rupture and recommending that he call a good gastro. "I'll be researching some stuff as a result of your e-mail," he wrote back. "Thanks for your concern." This statement was followed by 380 words of meticulous speculation on what he called the "Catch-22" of contest-specific water consumption.

Coondog's Coney Island wasn't an emotional wringer like Tim's. It was the opposite, a chance for reconciliation. Coondog spent most of the Fourth at the second annual Coney Island Hamburger Contest at Peggy O'Neill's, just a short walk up Surf Avenue from Surf and Stillwell. As he and Arnie set up the tables and prepped the event, they could hear George Shea's voice boom from the direction of Nathan's, and for Coondog it nearly killed him. "I can't help it," he said. "I want to be down there." After the Nathan's contest was over, Charles Hardy, Coondog's old friend, walked down to Peggy O'Neill's to say hello. For a long time the two of them hadn't even e-mailed each other, on account of the IFOCE-AICE rift, but lately they'd been talking on the phone again. Two weeks ago, Hardy had retired from his job as a New York corrections officer. He looked good. He was still a big guy, but he had lost enough weight to let him stop taking his diabetes medication, and in a few weeks he would fly on an airplane, for the first time in years without needing a seatbelt extender. He had a kickass pension, and a brownstone he could sell for big money. Hardy grabbed Coondog in a bear hug, and Coondog hugged back.

"Did you see Joey Chestnut?" Hardy said. "Man! He did his thing, man, did his fuckin' thing." Coondog pointed at me. "Tell him," he said, meaning me, "who's your nigga?"

"You my nigga, man," said Hardy, laughing. "I spotted you a fuckin' block away."

They chatted for a while as Arnie and his wife, Deb, set up the contest. Since the chili debacle in Vegas, Arnie had figured out how to run an eating league. He'd hired a professional emcee, for one—essentially benching himself as emcee, for the good of the team—and, just as important, he had dialed back the tone and frequency of his e-mail missives, focusing instead on trying to grow the business. Now Arnie's league was prospering. Despite his new professionalism, though, Arnie was a sucker for old-school aesthetics. The production values on display at Peggy O'Neill's were a throwback to Nathan's contests from the late eighties, when Matz and Rosey arranged picnic tables in skinny Schweikert's Alley. No scissor lift. No blimp. The only camera crew was from a local Spanish TV station. Arnie arranged wooden chairs behind a few long tables covered with a red checkered tablecloth that repeated the words EAT EAT EAT ad infinitum. Even the names of the competitors harkened back to the neighborhood ethnics of old. Thomas Martinez. Robert "The Italian Macho Man" Polimeni. Rafaez Marino. Jerry "The Mouse" Canna. Lenny "Lenman" Bartolone. Chris "The American" Schlesinger. Ian "The Caribbean Giant" Armel. James "The Crooner" Quigley. I volunteered to keep track of Coondog's burger count, which meant I had to spend the contest crouched on my knees, flipping the little notepad Arnie had anchored to the edge of the table. The woman flipping numbers next to me had a Tweety Bird tattoo on her thigh. Coondog finished second. Spanish TV stuck a camera in the face of the third-place finisher, Chris "The American" Schlesinger, asking, "And how does it feel like now?"

Coondog and I took the train back to Park Slope, where we rented *Cool Hand Luke* and crashed with a friend of mine who was on vacation. I went to bed. Coondog slept on the couch. And in the morning, we kidnapped Kobayashi.

Not really kidnapped. More like spirited away. We plucked the hot-dog champ from New York City, where his plate overflowed with interview requests and talk-show-appearance opportunities, and spirited him away to Cleveland. For a long time now, Koby had been wanting to see an American baseball game, and Coondog had told Koby he could make it happen. Coondog worked his connections with Cleveland's Fox 8 TV station—where he films the Pizza Pan Pizza Fight of the Century every week on *The Big Chuck and Lil' John Show*—to score Koby some tickets, on the condition that Koby give Fox 8 an exclusive interview. Coondog also hoped to get Koby on the Pizza Fight show.

So there we were—Koby, his girlfriend Nari, Coondog, and me—in LaGuardia Airport, the day after Coney Island. As we waited for our plane, Koby and Coondog drilled each other with Coondog's homemade Japanese-to-English flash cards. Once we got to Cleveland, we rented a car, checked into a downtown hotel, and met up with our interpreter for the weekend, Mina Sakamoto. Two hours later we were pulling up to the gated parking lot at Fox 8 TV. This, if it went off, would be the most memorable Pizza Fight in Coondog's long career. On the Pizza Fight more than thirty years ago, as a geeky teen, he'd eaten against the great Mushmouth Mariano. Since then, he'd eaten against a bear, a professional cage fighter, his best friend Phil "The Big Tomato" Angelo, and me. Now he was going to eat against the world's undisputed Number One.

"The champ is here!" says Coondog. "I got one behind me, too."

"Hey bay-bay!" coos the female security guard.

"There's my girl!"

"Yeah! Hey!"

"Gimme a kiss. This is my friend Kobayashi."

"Ooh! I saw you on TV!"

"She saw you on TV!" says Coondog to Koby.

"Yeah!" says the security guard woman.

"That's the Big Tomato!" says Coondog, recognizing Phil Angelo, his best friend, the one who banged out Jerry Lee Lewis chords on the piano back in May. Of course Coondog has invited all of his friends to the taping, and the friends have brought their wives and kids. Coondog makes sure Koby meets them all. *Big-Tow-May-Tow. Little-John-san*—he's *chisai*, small. Coondog explains the format of the contest to Koby. "You eat a pizza. Just one. One little teeny one." Coondog asks Koby if he'll wear a hat and T-shirt that say PIZZA PAN PIZZA. Koby balks. Coondog feels horrible. There is a short, tense negotiation; it looks like the whole thing might fall apart. Finally it's agreed that Koby won't wear the shirt or the hat, and everybody's cool with that. Fox 8 does a pre-contest interview with Coondog, who says, "He could probably eat it in one bite. Koby-san, two bites, two bites, right?" Coondog says he doesn't expect to win—it's all for fun—but admits that winning "would be the highlight of my life."

Lil' John steps to the mike.

"Testing testing one two three," he booms. "KOOO-BEEEE-AW-CHEE!" He says it with very hard syllables, especially the *ch* sound, making Koby sound like a Native American chief. The crowd is riled:

Ko-BEE! Ko-BEE! Ko-BEE!

USA! USA! USA! USA!

The camera guy's still fiddling. Lil' John is pissed. "I'm not paid by the hour," he cracks. Coondog takes advantage of the lull to show Koby a picture of Mushmouth, saying, "I beat him when I was fifteen years old. He was Cleveland's greatest . . ."

Now the camera guy's ready. Everybody quiet. Cue the theme from *Rocky*. Applause.

"It's the Pizza Fight of the Century! This is a non-title exhibition match! In this corner we have four-time defending champion, direct from Nagoya, Japan, it's the world champion hot-dog eater, Kobeochee!"

YEAH, KOBEEEE, YEAH!

"And our undefeated champion from Cuyahoga Falls, Ohio, in the most famous match in his illustrious career, King! Coondog! O'Karma!"

WOOOO!!!!!

"And our referee tonight is Biiiiiig Chuck!"

"Thank you Johnnny," says Chuck. "Mr. Kobeochee, it is an honor to have you here tonight." He pauses to let Mina translate; Mina translates; Koby nods. "We will abide by the Marquis of Queensberry rules . . . gentlemen, make a good clean fight, shake hands, when you hear the bell come out eating."

Ding . . .

Coondog's fast out of the gate. Big bites. Ten seconds. Koby is fast, too, but *Coondog is ahead*. Amazing. Twenty seconds and Coondog's halfway done. He is beating the greatest eater in the world. *Ganbare*, I shout, *ganbare*. Have courage. After twenty seconds it looks like he might win—but then, at twenty-nine seconds, Coondog looks up at Koby and takes a huge gulp of water. It's enough of a pause for Koby to down his last piece, open his mouth . . .

Ding!

Thirty-two seconds. Koby by a single bite.

Kobeochee! Wooooohoo!

KoBEE! KoBEE! KoBEE!

Koby wipes his face, smiles, and nods his thanks. Coondog claps for his little buddy. Lil' John hands Koby the Pizza Pan key to the city: a two-foot-long, gold-painted, key-shaped slab of wood created by Coondog's friends at the paint store. *Tune in next week for another Pizza Pan Pizza Fight of the Century!*

"Man," says Coondog to Koby, "you were great. I thought I almost got you."

As they always do, the crowd gathers around the TV monitors to watch the replay. They watch the first bell. The early Coondog lead. The final Coondog gulp of water. God, it was close, it was close . . . if only Coondog hadn't needed that final gulp . . .

Why did he take the gulp?

"I think Coondog choked," says Big Chuck, jokingly.

"If you watch the replay with him there, heeeeeeeee backed off a little bit," says Fred, the owner of Pizza Pan Pizza.

"Uh-uh," says the security guard woman, shaking her head. She's not buying it. She has seen Coondog eat too many times. Coondog *never* flags at the end like that.

That evening, after dinner with Mina, our translator, I get into the hotel elevator with Coondog to head up to my room for bed. Coondog leans back against the glass. He says he was glad that Koby won. It would have been awful for him if he hadn't won—to go through all those negotiations, all that stress, only to lose . . .

"Does that mean you let him win?"

"All I wanted to know is if I had him," Coondog says. "That's all I'm saying, Jason. That's all I'm saying. If I could take him. And I'm not saying yes or no but I'm *satisfied*."

The elevator dings. We've reached our floor. The doors open. Coondog starts walking to his room, then stops and turns around. He can't help himself.

"I did my last three pizzas in under thirty seconds," he says. "What do *you* think?"

One last thing to do in Cleveland.

On July 6, two days after Coney Island, we take Koby and Nari to a baseball game. We have finagled press passes for the Indians-Tigers game at Jacobs Field, hoping that Koby will be able to go early and meet the players and possibly even throw out the first pitch. As soon as we walk in the gate and see the players down on the field, Coondog starts yelling:

"Hey, do you want to meet the Coney Island hot-dog eating champion?"

"Is that him?"

"That's him!"

"No shit."

"Sugoi!" says Koby, happier than I've ever seen him.

One Indian whistles, beckoning other Indians. Outfielder Jody Gerut, pitcher David Riske. Two Indians become three, then four. They barrage Koby with questions: Do you ever get sick? No? How about afterward? Hot dogs the only thing you eat? What's the most you've eaten? You drink water with it? They all know about Koby. They must have watched the contest together in the locker room. Coondog asks each new Indian to introduce himself so Koby can remember. Matt Miller, relief pitcher. Ben Broussard, first base. Bob Wickman, relief pitcher. "Now, when *I* eat, look what happens," says Wickman, patting his paunch. "You're in good shape."

"Show 'em your stomach muscles," says Coondog.

Koby smiles and lifts up his shirt.

"Oh my GOD!"

"Man!"

"Unbelievable."

"I gotta start eating more hot dogs."

The Indians suddenly tap the fence and start jogging, one by one, toward the outfield in a slow trot that resolves into a team wind sprint. We make our way to the dugout, running into more players on the way. *Congratulations. Thank you veddy much.* Young slugger Grady Sizemore asks Koby to autograph a baseball for him. "Sweet," says Sizemore, grinning at his Koby ball. Koby pauses as he's about to step onto the field, and bows, gracefully; once he's on the field proper, the barrage of questions begins anew—this time from beat reporters and local TV crews. *What's the hot-dog guy doing here?* Mina translates as the press bores in: Tell us your technique. Your trade secret. Maybe it's a dumb question, but how exactly do you find out you can eat fifty-three and a half hot dogs? What did you weigh before and after? Do people recognize you when you go out? What kind of pitch do you plan on throwing tonight? (By now the Indians' press guy, seeing Koby get thronged—in fourteen years, he says, "I've never seen a celebrity-type person attract so much attention"—has told the front office to let Koby throw out the first pitch.)

"I'm just hoping that I won't fail," says Koby with typical *nihongo* modesty.

"He's a friend of mine," Coondog tells a reporter, who gives Coondog a look that says: *And you are?*

"This is David O'Karma," I jump in, "corn-eating champion of the world."

"CORN-eating?" says the reporter.

"COONDOG O'Karma," says Coondog, correcting me. "Yeah, corn on the cob."

I look into the dugout and notice that the figure next to the water cooler, sipping from a paper cup, is none other than centerfielder Coco Crisp. I am about to have one of those blessed reportorial moments when the heavens part to reveal a slice of the immutable sublime, such as a meeting between two men named Coco Crisp and Coondog O'Karma:

"Hey, Coco," says Coondog. "I'm a—I'm *the* world corn-eating champion."

"Is *that* right?"

"Yeah, I'm the Pizza Pan pizza-eating champion on Big Chuck and Lil' John."

"What's your name?"

"Coondog."

Coco sips his water. "Cooon-doggg," he says, languidly, and smiles. "You know," he says, "I think I can take him"—gesturing to Koby, who's still being interviewed—"if I'm eating Vienna sausages. The little ones. I think I might be able to. The little Vienna sausages. The little wienies? I think I might be able to eat sixty-three of those."

"Yeah," laughs Coondog. "I was one of the best, and he tripled what I did. He's just amazing."

"Peyton Manning," says Coco. "Nobody ever threw forty-nine touchdowns before. He almost did fifty. You know? Who could throw—who had the better season? Did Peyton Manning throw more touchdowns, or will he"—he points to Koby—"be able to eat more hot dogs? They were tied after this year. Forty-nine and forty-nine." Coco laughs. "But all-*time*-record, he has Peyton beat, fifty-three to forty-nine."

Koby finishes his interviews, and we have some time to kill before the first pitch, so we go upstairs to the press cafeteria and munch on beef and potatoes and a few hot dogs I've bought for Koby, at Nari's request. Three men at another table see Koby eating the hot dogs and walk over, one by one, each with his digital camera. Koby, unfailingly accommodating, poses for three pictures of escalating hamminess, so that by the last picture he is holding a hot dog to his open mouth and pretending to bite it, just like earlier today, when we took him to the Rock and Roll Hall of Fame, and he saw the giant hot dog suspended from the ceiling on wires—a stage prop once used by the jam-band Phish—and knelt down, mouth open wide, so Nari could take a picture. Now, a little after six, Koby gets antsy and says he wants to warm up, so we take him down to the field, where I scrounge a glove for him and Coondog and watch the two of them play catch on the dirt track near home plate.

It's like *Field of Dreams*.

I feel like I'm about to cry.

Is this why Coondog and I were dying to bring Koby to a ballgame—to produce this exact sort of pleasant droning between the ears, this warm wastedness? Subconsciously, is this what I wanted? To anchor a mania as strange as pro gluttony in a solid, venerated American tradition? To tame its scorching newness with sentiment? To bring it into the fold of something we already understand, like a hot dog, or a baseball game, or Peyton Manning's passing record, or a heroic narrative like the one I was now writing about Coondog O'Karma? Is this how we convince ourselves that we're creating something worthwhile, not just spinning our wheels—we reflexively structure our new stories like the old ones, with beginnings, middles, and ends, with transcendence? Cool Hand Luke, who got the better of the Boss and communed with God in that crappy little church! Rocky Balboa, who went twelve rounds with Apollo Creed! Coondog O'Karma, who swallowed pizzas like they were Doritos, who sneered and flexed his muscles and tossed large barbells at local television cameras! Coondog O'Karma, who was a question in Trivial Pursuit and a blurb in *GQ* magazine! Coondog O'Karma, who swallowed eighteen hot dogs in twelve minutes, thirty-one ears of sweet corn in ten minutes, forty-five hard-boiled eggs in eight minutes, twenty-five donuts in twelve minutes! Coondog O'Karma, who shrank his universe to the size of a skinny Japanese guy and exploded it for all of Cleveland to see!

It was lovely to think about . . .

"Ko-BEE!!"

He's on the mound now, in his Indians jersey and a borrowed cap. Three young boys, who won the rights to an Indians "first pitch" in a charity auction, have just thrown their pitches, one after the other, but Koby's pitch is the true ceremonial pitch, the true capper. He goes through a full windup; he releases the ball in a hard, graceful motion; the ball whips into home plate at something approaching pro speed, and the crowd *ooohs*. The Indians' team mascot, "Slider," who looks like a giant purple Elmo doll, shakes Koby's hand and pats him on the back, escorting him over to us, to me and Coondog, so we can take Koby into the stands. Before we even step off the field, Koby's mobbed. "Kobee-ochee! Over here. Look right here. Kobee-ochee! Look right here, buddy." It's a gauntlet of cell-phone cameras. Coondog tries to hurry him along, but is rebuffed. "Kobee-ochee, right here, babe." Koby stops, searches out the camera, smiles vaguely, and tries to reach the gate, but is stopped by a half-dozen more kids sticking out their ticket stubs for him to sign. "These are all gonna be on eBay," says Coondog. "He doesn't mind, do you think?"

"I don't think so."

"Kobayashi, I love you! I love you!"

A boy snaps a camera-phone pic. We somehow get Koby to our seats, right behind third base, and sit down.

"Kobayashi! Kobayashi!"

Six boys, screaming, thronging.

"Keep eating hot dogs!"

"Kobayashi!"

Six boys, eight, nine.

"Kobayashi!"

"Can you get to sixty?"

"He's gonna buy you hot dogs!"

"I'd buy him hot dogs, but I don't think I can afford it!"

"Guess who I'm sitting behind," says the man behind us. He is talking on his cell. He leans forward and says to Koby, "How many did you eat this year?"

"Forty-nine," we say.

"Danny," says the man, "it was forty-nine this year. Fifty-three last year. Can you say hi to my son? He doesn't believe me."

It turns out we're in the wrong seats. We should be on the first-base side, not the third-base side. An Indians press aide offers to escort us to our actual seats. We start walking. Heads swivel. Old men and little kids reach over and through the railings, waving, straining to touch him. A paunchy old stadium employee grabs Koby by the shoulders and shakes him, *Ha ha ha, you shoulda been here for hot-dog night*—Koby is polite but we can tell he's a little scared, they don't grab you like that in Nagoya. Coondog hurries him along, pleading with the mob for space. A dude comes running along the concrete shouting, *Kobayashi, Mr. Kobayashi*, holding a digital camera, Koby stops to let him take a picture but the dude's camera flashes an error message—we keep walking and so does the dude—I elbow him in the chest, hard, and he curses me out . . . now in our new seats, Koby's thronged again by kids begging for autographs: "He's so good at eating, it's awesome, it's fun." "He's like the best. Nobody can eat hot dogs like him." "Seeing him eat all those hot dogs on TV makes me want to eat more hot dogs." "He must train or something." "We watched it live in my house." "I'm going to take on the mission of eating fifty hot dogs." "Yeah, I'll challenge him in a couple years."

We settle into the game. In the bottom of the fifth and then again during the seventh-inning stretch, the Jumbotron cameraman films Koby eating a hot dog, blasting Koby's image to the whole stadium and summoning new waves of autograph seekers. It's palpable, this swarming need for people to watch Koby perform this magic trick with hot dogs—so palpable, really, that it becomes impossible not to wonder about its eventual withering, the entropic heat death of the fad. How long can competitive eating keep growing? "I know we've questioned that at ESPN," says the network's Darren Rovell. "It's kind of like if Kobayashi keeps winning and they don't get a ringer, how many times can you show a competitive eating contest?" Gersh Kuntzman, over a piece of apple pie at his favorite diner, Dizzy's, started talking about "saving the sport from itself." If you put eating on TV, he said, you make it just another "mass-produced," "plastic" product. "You lose the *purity* of things," he said. "If Dizzy's opens a Dizzy's in twelve cities, it's not Dizzy's anymore. What is it? A place where I'd get a bad piece of pie?" He sighed. "So I don't know, if you let the genie out of the bottle . . ."

If you let the genie out of the bottle, ESPN starts thinking about ways to fit a stomach cam in the digestive tract of Kobayashi. George Shea starts recruiting Fortune 500 sponsors like Verizon. The Clinton Station Diner in New Jersey introduces a fifty-pound "Mount Olympus" hamburger, and Arnie "Chowhound" Chapman gets to work organizing teams of firefighters and cops to tackle it. Joey Chestnut, Tim's Coney Island vanquisher, becomes Joey "Jaws" Chestnut, regularly besting Sonya Thomas in Federation events and pushing the rupture threshold of stomach capacity. Remove eating from its natural ecosystem—lighthearted stunts, steady coverage in smaller media, the occasional cheap cable special—and you remove any guarantees of sustainability. You release the phenomenon into the wilds of big American risk and reward.

I think this is why Americans love Koby, and why he loves them back: he let the genie out and he made it work. He pushed into the big unknown and came back with fame, money, a cute girlfriend, and commercials on ESPN. He's like those bacteria they pour on top of oil spills, which break toxins into their harmless component parts. He can do it, and we need to think that we *big, fat, infantile, stupid assholes* can do it, too—that we can shovel past the shit to find something better on the other side. Because if not, if we can't make it by throttling up, who's going to help us throttle back? *Real Simple* magazine? Ralph Nader? Wendell Berry? Wendell Berry is a crank. There's no mainstream constituency in American life for smaller and softer. The Hummers won't evaporate into metallic mists, and we don't have another hundred million years for Mother Nature to crush us some more crude oil. We're a nation stuck in a Coen Brothers plot, stakes ratcheting higher with each scene. We can't scale back. We have to scale everything else up. We have to find hope in our own core destructive impulses, because they're part of us, they're not going away. Hope in ambition, in acceleration, in size, in expanse.

That's what kept me going, what got me past the crises of conscience inherent in writing a book about something so ostensibly soulless. Whenever I'd despair, I would try to think about what the book's index would look like, if it had one. I'd list the names and places to myself and would take great pleasure in thinking that Don Lerman might collide with Don DeLillo, and Errol Morris with Eddie the Geek; that *Trillin, Calvin* would bump up against *Tomato, Big* and that if I could crush these people into a small space, even artificially, I might create a few of those moments when America really seems to work, when we can take all this hope and dread and shit and cram it together and find wonder in the odd harmonic convergences it's bound to create, in which everything seems to fuse and cancel out, the hope against the shit, the dread against the crazy newness, to provoke this feeling of null clarity like when you're buzzing on wine and the difference between Coondog O'Karma and Coco Crisp can melt, temporarily, into nothing.

It's the feeling that Koby, laden with autographed baseballs, will describe to us a little later, after we get back from the baseball game and take the elevator up to our rooms:

"I feel like I am under a spell. And when it is over, I will have to go back to reality."

So that's why Axl Rose is in this book. *Maxim* magazine and *The Picture of Dorian Gray*. Shaving Katie and Miss America. M. F. K. Fisher and "Beautiful" Brian Seiken. George Wallace, Charlton Heston, the Virgin Mary. The smell of New Orleans by the lake, the smell of rubber in Cuyahoga Falls. El Wingador and the silver-striking hammer of the Black Cloud Mine. *Sixteen Candles, Guys and Dolls, Stand by Me, Kiss Me Guido*. Turducken and Sumner Redstone. Spam, the food. The Amazing Kreskin is in this book, and Kurt

Vonnegut Jr., and the Gameworks Tex-Mex Roll. I made the book big and sprawling, I threw everything in, because it's the impulse encoded in me, deep in my American bones.

It was getting late. Coondog left us for a while to go thank the Fox people for arranging our passes. For an inning or two, Koby had to fend for himself against the fans still trickling down to pay their respects. He left to go to the bathroom, came back, and said that while facing the urinal, the man next to him had whipped out his cell phone, called a buddy, and told the buddy he was peeing next to the great Kobayashi. A few outs later, Coondog loped down the steps and sat down next to Koby. They didn't talk for a long time. They were both deeply tired. They had withdrawn into their joy. Tigers up 6–1. The Tigers were making it look easy against the Indians' beefy ace, C.C. Sabathia. As a Fox anchor would quip later on the ten-o'clock news, "The big fella lasted about as long as a hot dog in front of Ko-bee-auch-ee." The sun went down over third base, spraying the diamond with haze. The electric lights clicked on with no visible effect. The players blurred into ghosts. Koby and Coondog leaned into the left-field haze, watching the Indians get creamed.

EPILOGUE

THANK YOU,
BLUEBERRY FAIRIES

AN EATER'S STORY doesn't end unless he says so, and he never says so. There is no true retirement in competitive eating, and no one, not journalists, not family members, has the heart to finally shut off the lights and put the stools up on the table so that the eater gets the hint to leave—the eater, sucking the marrow from his chicken bones, muttering in the dark about the ninety-nine-pound woman.

In August, Dave O'Karma e-mailed with a classic good news/bad news situation. Good news: he had been assigned his first magazine article that wasn't about competitive eating. Bad news: the assignment entailed sparring a few rounds with heavyweight female boxer Vonda Ward. Although Vonda is six foot six and 195 pounds, Dave told me he wasn't worried. "It only takes one punch and I hit hard," he said.

Vonda Ward eventually declined to fight Dave, which was probably for the best.

Anyway, he didn't need the boxing story. While Dave had been training for his Vonda fight, his editor had asked him to write a second piece, this one about a Negro League baseball team from Cleveland. It was Dave's first non-gonzo assignment. "I don't have to do the stupid stuff," he told me. "I'm thinkin' maybe I don't have to get my brains bashed in or my stomach split open. Maybe I was meant to develop carpal tunnel syndrome."

In September, Dave e-mailed again. "Here's a snippet of my new play," he wrote:

> May I set the stage? I shall impersonate a man.
> Come, enter into my imagination and see him!

His name . . . David O'Karma . . . a simple house painter,
no longer young . . . bony, hollow-faced . . .
And he conceives the strangest project ever imagined . . .
to become a dilettante of the strange,
and sally forth into the world
to experience all things odd . . .

Dave's song was actually from *Man of La Mancha*, but at first I didn't catch that he was goofing with me. "Don Quixote is a fave book and play and a part I always wanted to play when I got old," he eventually e-mailed. "I thought the Dave O'Karma/Coondog was much like Alphonso Quijana's transformation into Don Quixote and . . . funny?"

El Wingador's post-eating career also involved a near-miss with boxing. After Wing Bowl 13, a promoter in Philly approached Bill about fighting a former hockey player named Frank Baya Lewis. "I said yeah, I'll fight him, because I'm a psycho like that," Wingador told me. "My agent says, 'Bill, what's wrong with you? We're trying to make you more businesslike. There's no reason to go out and be a goon.'"

Wingador, it turned out, was trying to reinvent himself as an entrepreneur. The summer after Wing Bowl, Bill and a few family members collaborated to buy an old 500-square-foot custard stand next to a batting cage in Westville, New Jersey: the future site of "El Wingador's Restaurant." The restaurant would serve pork shoulder, his aunt's recipe, and wings, of course, served with a special Wingador touch: a side of Spanish rice instead of the traditional bleu cheese. Bill's ambitious business plan—five franchised restaurants within the first year—left little time for competitive eating. "I am so done," he said. "I don't even miss that shit."

In June, Bill called and left a message on my voice mail, asking if I knew the time and place of a Salty Ball contest in Wildwood.

As for Wing Bowl itself, the foul beast was also going through a phase of reinvention and rebirth. The chaos of Wing Bowl 13 had its consequences. Arnie "Chowhound" Chapman filed an FCC complaint against 610 WIP for unfairly disqualifying him. The *Inquirer* picked up the story, writing that "this is believed to be the first FCC complaint surrounding Wing Bowl, which frequently pushes the taste envelope." The station decided to wipe the slate clean for Wing Bowl 14. On its website, WIP announced that, for the first time ever, Wing Bowl would be a ticketed event. Additionally, "NO previous Wing Bowl participants will be eligible to compete in this year's Wing Bowl. No 'El Wingador,' No 'Sonya,' No 'Cookie.'"

WIP was calling it "The Virgin Wing Bowl."

Tickets sold out immediately.

On February 3, 2006, Joey Chestnut set a new Wing Bowl record with 173 wings.

Around the same time, Bill Simmons signed a deal to make his eponymous sauce available at any ACME, Clemens, Superfresh, or Shop-Rite.

According to Bill's friends, he was already talking about returning for Wing Bowl 15.

A week after the twenty-two-and-a-half-dog fiasco of Tim "Eater X" Janus, he flew to Las Vegas for the inaugural Alka-Seltzer U.S. Open of Competitive Eating, scheduled to air on ESPN later that month. The Open was the largest gathering of gurgitators since Glutton Bowl three years prior. Thirty-two Federation eaters, including Tim, plus a handful of alternates, stayed in the off-strip Stratosphere hotel and were shuttled in waves to the ESPN Zone restaurant in the New York New York Casino, where the Open was being filmed over three days. The first day, Charles Hardy, who had officially retired to become the Federation's new commissioner, handed out the official contest shirt, which was blue and expensive-looking, covered with Alka-Seltzer logos, and made of stretchy fabric, like a Tour de France jersey. The eaters surrendered utterly to the shirt. Wandering the casino floor in packs, they looked like the world's slowest cycling team.

Because the Open was structured like the NCAAs—a series of one-on-one battles in a thirty-two-eater bracket—half the field was eliminated on the first day. The Open necessarily became less about the competition than about the camaraderie. Eaters took the opportunity to get to know each other, and to sample the local strip clubs, often at the same time. They also made a point of encouraging each other in competition ("Clear that mouth, Don, CLEAR THAT MOUTH!"), which resulted in an organized chant of "X! X! X!" whenever Tim stepped to the table. He cruised through the early rounds and surprised his comrades by beating third-ranked Rich LeFevre in the chopped-salad quarter finals. He reached the potato-skin semis, where he lost to Sonya. Tim was happy with his showing. "I really am glad I got a chance to redeem myself a little bit," he said. "Just a little bit." After the penultimate night of filming, Tim found himself at the center of a coterie of girls, who crowded around him and made the "X" sign with their forearms, posing for photos. A Krystal eater from Tennessee named Lynn Curley glanced over, shook his head, and said, "I think we have the first ever competitive-eating groupies."

"First viable groupies, anyway," said Rich Shea, sipping a beer.

Looking over at the scrum of snapping flashes, I saw another first. Tim wasn't the only gurgitator attracting the cuties. The cuties were also asking for pictures with two fresh-faced circuit newcomers from sunny states: California's Chris Coble, twenty-three, a trim triathlete, and Florida's Hall Hunt, twenty-four, a born-again Christian who resembled a young Dan Marino. Hall Hunt, in his own way, was just as earnest about eating as Tim. "Before every contest," he e-mailed me once, "I always bow my head and pray just like I do every time I sit down to a meal":

> My prayer goes a little something like this: "Thank you Lord for today. Thank you for this food that you have given me. I pray this food nourishes my body to be healthy and strong. I pray that in everything I do I can always follow your will and give you all the glory Lord."

> I feel that any talents God has given me I need to use them. Whether it is in the class room doing school work, working hard with my job, loving traveling and doing mission work in other countries, being a servant to others and doing whatever I can to make someone else's day a [little] better, lifting weights, running, competitive eating, or whatever else. Anything I do, I want to do it well.

In the months after the Alka-Seltzer Open, Hall Hunt and Chris Coble—along with nineteen-year-old Patrick Bertoletti and twenty-one-year-old Joey Chestnut—would cohere into a new class of young, white, middle-class, male, credibly athletic eaters, fulfilling Tim's long anxiety about his own obsolescence. The American gurgitator corps would start to look like the Japanese corps in its heyday: a bunch of fit, invincible collegiate guys with time to burn and nothing to lose. Tim would no longer be either the best-looking or the most dedicated eater on the circuit. Four months after the Alka-Seltzer Open, at the 2005 Krystal finals, Joey Chestnut would come within five burgers (sixty-two burgers total) of beating Kobayashi himself (sixty-seven); Tim, despite doubling his 2004 total with forty-one burgers, would finish back in sixth place. "It's a lot more competitive now," he would tell me. "Guys are really busting their humps. Guys are doing water two times a day . . . it's begun to accelerate. It's continuing to accelerate . . . the time is beginning to tick away, and I'll be out . . ."

Back in Vegas, on the morning of the Koby-Sonya finals, I decided to take off. I flew back to Philly on what I hoped would be my last Southwest flight for a long time. Two weeks later I watched the Alka-Seltzer Open on ESPN. Whereas Glutton Bowl was all eating, the Open was all cutaway: clips of George Shea deadpanning, Chris Coble running, Tim Janus lifting weights, Brian Subich coaching his football team, and Eric Booker rapping, all of it spliced together with clips from the eating battles. The eating clips were short, pared to the bare minimum, as if ESPN were embarrassed by its own programming. It was a sports show with no sport, and a reality show with no reality.

I couldn't tell if I was looking at the apotheosis of competitive eating, as per E. L. Doctorow. I didn't know if the Alka-Seltzer Open was weighing every ESPN viewer down. But it was weighing *me* down. Which is why, a few weeks after the Open, I had to drive to a remote little town in Maine.

In Machias, Maine, population 2,334, the economy runs on blueberries. Machias grows and harvests 85 percent of the world's supply of wild blueberries. In Machias you can buy a car at Blueberry Ford or stay the night at the Bluebird Motel, and during the annual Maine Wild Blueberry Festival, held in August, the town's one coffee shop, owned and operated by a native of Detroit, will sell you a blueberry chicken-salad sandwich, a bottle of blueberry cream soda, and a cup of blueberry coffee, although my advice is to skip the coffee and buy a second cream soda instead.

In the summer of 2005, I found myself wanting desperately to visit Machias, on Maine's Down East Coast, because of what I thought Machias represented. After a year of hanging out with people named Coondog and Cookie and Moses and Shredder, I had a jones for a simple, old-fashioned pie contest. Kids. Cherubic faces stained with pie. I wanted a palate-cleanser, a place untouched by the Sheas and the gullets of ringers. This is exactly what the website of the Machias Centre Street Congregational Church seemed to promise me: "a real old fashioned, country good time." The church, which runs the festival, advertised a Chicken BBQ, a Children's Parade, a Fish Fry, a Quilt Raffle, a Blueberry Musical, and a Pie Eating Contest, whose entrants were advised to "WEAR AN OLD SHIRT OR A LARGE NAPKIN!!" It was perfect. Machias is eleven hours from New York City and two and a half from the nearest airport, in Bangor—the hometown, incidentally, of George and Rich Shea. Unless the Sheas were home on vacation, I'd have Machias to myself.

So my fiancée and I booked a room and drove up Coastal Route 1 on a Friday, past little gas stations with no bathrooms, past a hundred "cottage for rent" signs, and parked our car in downtown Machias. We walked a block north on Centre Street to the Congregational Church, the site of Saturday's pie contest. The festival-goers were still trickling in. They skewed to the extremes, young and old. We saw the centaurlike elderly of Machias, old faces fused to young bodies, grannies with the calves of U. Penn rowers. Inside the church's cafeteria, the tables were piled with blueberry literature featuring a bar graph titled "The Power of Blue™, Nature's #1 Antioxidant Fruit™," hailing the wild blueberry as more cancer-peventing than oranges, spinach, garlic, kale, strawberries, and broccoli florets. Outside, surrounding the church, were craft tents, a food stall with Wicked Good Smoked Salmon Paté for six dollars, ten-buck lobster rolls for charity, fliers for a PTA auction (OLD TIME SCHOONER PAINTING, 18 HOLES OF GOLF, WAXMELTS, PROPANE HEATER, BUSH), tables full of handmade jewelry, and of course the giant stage at the top of the hill with the banner that read SPORTSCENTER . . .

SPORTSCENTER. As in, ESPN's SportsCenter.

It was too improbable to process, like seeing a man waterskiing on I-95. I needed some time. We walked into the church, where a cardiganed local-history expert was giving a talk on the swashbuckling life of the church's original preacher, James Lyon, who once captured a British sea vessel and threatened to invade Nova Scotia. I tried to focus on Preacher Lyon, failed, and instead flipped idly through the church bulletin, where I read:

> ESPN, the cable television sports channel is sending a crew to broadcast our pie eating contest and more as part of their "Fifty States in Fifty Days" special programming . . .

Yep.

Shea was here.

Even in Machias, I couldn't escape gurgitation.

I scribbled my fiancée a note ("SHEA IS HERE") and tried to suppress a laugh. We left the church to get a beer at A.J.'s, the local bar. I wanted to sulk. Walking in, we overheard a conversation about ESPN. It was like that the rest of the day, too: anywhere we went, we could tune in bits of ESPN-related conversation, fading in and out like radio stations on a long car ride. I felt better when I talked to the ESPN producers about the pie contest. "That's the church," a female producer said, waving her hand. "We don't promote that." She was apparently unaware of her own network's role in the Alka-Seltzer Open, which was great, because it meant that Shea wasn't here after all. This was just a fun local thing. And then I felt depressed all over again when I chatted with the Congregational Church ladies and they asked me if I knew Sonya Thomas:

"Have you been following that amazing ninety-eight-pound woman? Forty-four pounds of lobsters?"

"And how many brats did she eat?"

It took me a good night's sleep at my B&B to get over it. Saturday morning, I woke up and went downstairs for breakfast. The B&B's owner told me that his son was so excited about ESPN coming to his town that he was going to run in that morning's Children's Race, even though he had a medical condition that made his knee joints flop around like fish. "He literally can't race," the owner said, "but he's racing." He wanted to be on ESPN.

Okay—I was being kind of a dick.

Machias is a poor town. There aren't many jobs. The census trend is negative. Kids can't wait to leave. (There's a reason George and Rich Shea didn't stay in Bangor.) What's so awful about showing the kids of Machias that their town has something cool enough to make ESPN come to *them?*

As noon approached, the area around the church steps filled with 300 or 400 people. Bill Richardson, age eighty, a local, confirmed for me that the crowd was "distinctly biggah" than last year's. At noon, an old man wearing a green ten-gallon hat and a mustache took the microphone. This, I learned later, was Norman Nelson, the preeminent citizen of Machias: a veteran of the Normandy invasion, the "town vaudevillian," in Bill Richardson's words, and also a candidate for town selectman at age eighty-seven. Norman described the contest thusly: "It's a bit different from the lobstah-eating contests and the crab-eating contests. It's fun to see the expressions on their faces when they get up from the pie. It's really wonderful." The pies were then brought out, and the kids were loosed from their holding pen inside the church. They romped down the steps to the table, some smiling, some serious. The kids would not be allowed to use their hands; in anticipation of handless eating, the judges had Velcro'd the pies to the table. Someone blew an air horn and the kids were off, into the pies. All we could see of the kids was hair and a slice of forehead, except for the chubbier kids, whose faces spilled out over the pie pans' silver rims, an exodus of cheek fat . . .

"Thirty seconds!" shouted Norman. "You bettah get goin'! You don't want anyone to beat you by a mouthful!"

As each age group had its moment in the ESPN cameras, as the table was cleaned after each contest and more pies were procured for the next bracket, Norman insisted on reducing the contest time, from 120 seconds to 90 and finally to 60 for the adults. It was over quickly. ESPN interviewed several of the kids, and that afternoon, through the open window of my B&B room, I heard a child's cry rocket down Centre Street: "I WAS ON ESPN!"

Dana and I had one last thing to do in Machias. That night we cut our dinner short to try to get tickets for the Blueberry Musical. I ordered a slice of double-crust blueberry pie, fat as a dictionary, to go, in a foam clamshell that I carried to the church. The musical, we learned, was sold out. We gave the usher a sob story and she took pity, seating us up front, in the chorus section. For half an hour we listened to the Machias town band burning through jazz standards and also the theme songs of all four branches of the

U.S. military, during which the veterans of each branch were invited to stand and be recognized. When the band was finished, a man walked onto the stage whose face was a crystallization of the distinctive features of both Garrison Keillor and Newt Gingrich: Keillor's wide brow, Newt's silver hair. The man wore a navy T-shirt, khakis, sneakers, and a blue-and-green vest with vertical stripes. This was Doug Guy, author of the musical. Doug Guy said:

"Welcome to the United Church of Christ, where God speaks. God speaks to us every year when he tells us to hold a party and invite everybody." He added, "The one thing we want people to remember is that no matter who you are or where you are, you're welcome at this church . . ."

He turned abruptly to his side, where three men had joined him onstage wearing identical T-shirts and vests. They all gathered around a standing microphone and sang, barbershop-style, to the tune of "O Tannenbaum":

> *Oh blueberry, oh blueberry*
> *The fruit of our best wishes*
> *Oh blueberry, oh blueberry*
> *They sometimes stain the dishes*
> *Open your heart*
> *Give life a chance*
> *They're full of antioxidants!*
> *Oh blueberry, oh blueberry*
> *It goes so good with fishes*
> *. . . and lobstah!*

It got a big laugh, the first of many. The show, called "Miracle on Centre Street," was patterned loosely on *Miracle on 34th Street*, with the plot focusing on an "intern" from the Maine Wild Blueberry Commission in Augusta. The intern, along with her two young children, travels to Machias to help the locals punch up their festival. All three Augusta visitors wear bright red shirts, in contrast to the rest of the cast, dressed in blue. The prideful intern, a stand-in for the state government, is gradually indoctrinated with blueberry propaganda from the locals, who crack gentle jokes about Augusta and self-deprecating jokes about Machias. Along the way, the cast tries to convince the intern that the famous Machias "blueberry fairies"—played by a half-dozen little girls in blue tutus and fairy wings—are real. The show's conceit is broad enough to include an Elvis impersonation, a joke that relates erectile dysfunction to "upswings in the Washington County economy," a row of church ladies banging tambourines and kicking up their skirts to reveal multicolored Spandex underwear, and political humor, as expressed in Doug Guy's solo number, "I Heard Limbaugh Dissing Hillary," whose lyrics slaughtered Rush and poked mild fun at Al Franken before concluding in a dulcet choirboy flourish:

> *So now I never know what I should believe*
> *Say it enough times it must be true*
> *So now I doubt all that I can hear*
> *Except for that fact so dear*
> *That the best berries on earth are blue!*

After the finale, which involved the full cast—anchored by a cane-swinging Mr. Norman Nelson—singing the town's theme song, "Blueberry Blues," we all clapped and filed out of the church, across the frayed red carpeting and down the steps, where the cast formed a receiving line and smiled as we descended into the cold. Yellow school buses had been arranged to taxi elderly residents back to their homes. The buses idled, coughing exhaust. No one seemed in a hurry to leave; the townspeople and tourists, scarves whipping in the cold, formed football huddles at the bottom of the steps, retelling the best jokes and the best songs. I opened my Styrofoam clamshell and swallowed my double-crust blueberry pie in like four bites. I reran the whole show in a crude mental loop. I felt it unfurl into something gently profound. A philosophy, a catechism. Laugh at yourself, it was saying. Co-opt the crazy ones that threaten you. Throw your family and friends on top of the craziness like a blanket. Outlive the goobers in Augusta and the cowboy president. Believe in an unclenched Jesus and humble food, especially when it's high in antioxidants. And keep some laughter in check for the big finale, when the oilfields dry up and the ice caps melt, flooding the coast inland to Bangor, and the rising tide really does lift all boats together.

ACKNOWLEDGMENTS

AFTER ALL, how can you fuck up a hot-dog book?"

Those are the words of Jerry Cammarata, protégé of the great press agent Max Rosey. I hope Jerry is as wise as he seems. And if I did fuck up this hot-dog book, please don't blame any of the following people:

At *Philadelphia* magazine, thanks to editor Larry Platt for his support and encouragement; Tom McGrath, who suggested that I write a piece on Wing Bowl instead of the Mummers and thereby changed my life; and Vicki Glembocki, for giving me my first and third magazine jobs, and for generally being a great editor and friend.

Family. Thanks to my parents, Frank and Sharyn Fagone, to whom this book is dedicated, for their support, and for taping radio shows and TV talk shows whenever I asked, which was usually at the last minute; and thanks to my future in-laws, Rich and Lynn Bauer, for the use of their kitchen scale.

Media. The *New York Post*'s Gersh Kuntzman, keeper of eating's "vast oral history," unlocked that history for my benefit, with considerable wit. I'm grateful to the 610-WIP AM morning crew—Angelo Cataldi, Al Morganti, and Rhea Hughes—for their open-ended invitation to hang out in their studio. Same thing with the crew at Fox 8 Cleveland, especially "Big Chuck" Schodowski and "Lil' John" Rinaldi. Thanks to David Giffels of the *Akron Beacon-Journal*, that leading expert of Coondog lore, for his stories and his support. Eric "Badlands" Booker graciously allowed me to reprint his song lyrics, as did Doug Guy, author of the blueberry musical in Machias, Maine. Thanks to those who helped me track down obscure eating-contest effluvia: Dave Davies of the *Philadelphia Daily News*, David Helfrich of WIP, author Tony Perrotett, Mark "Big Rig" Vogeding, Mortimer Matz, Lou

Reda, and the Amazing Kreskin. Thanks also to the Wing Bowl Nerds—especially Brian Dwyer and Joshua Camerote, and also Josh Taylor and Andrew Watson—for giving me access to their vast library of Wing Bowl footage, and for being generally cool guys.

Experts. An early conversation with the sociologist Gary Alan Fine at Northwestern University clarified much for me, as did a fascinating lunch with the psychologist Paul Rozin of U. Penn. Thanks also to the several gastroenterologists who answered my questions, including Dr. George Triadafilopoulos at the Stanford School of Medicine, Dr. Edgar Achkar at the Cleveland Clinic, and Dr. Robert Coben at Thomas Jefferson University Hospital. Dr. Triadafilopoulos and Dr. Coben also reviewed certain science-heavy portions of Chapter 3 in part I. I'm certain that any remaining errors are in passages that have not been reviewed by the doctors; any such errors are mine alone.

Readers. Sasha Issenberg, Neel Master, and Kitty Morgan read and dissected the entire first-draft manuscript, talked me through numerous problems, and suggested so many great ideas that the writing process sometimes felt like a collaboration between me and my smartest friends and colleagues. It's no coincidence that Sasha, Neel, and Kitty are also wonderful friends who encouraged me, early on, to pursue the book. I owe them hugely. I also owe Robert Huber, Robert Morlino, and Chris McDougall for offering key comments on various other parts of the book. The best advice I could give to aspiring writers is to know people as sharp and generous as these six.

Researchers. I'm indebted to Dan Morrell for his careful work fact-checking portions of the book. I received invaluable research help from Victor Fiorillo and Daryl Lang (who was also kind enough to let me crash more than once on his sofa bed in Park Slope) especially, but also from April White, Emily Grosvenor, Robert Morlino, and, in Japan, the estimable "toro umiyamada."

Translators. Without the imperturbable Marina Kinno translating e-mails and making our interview subjects feel comfortable, Coondog and I would have been lost in Japan. Thanks also to Kaori Kaneko for additional translation work, and thanks to Marina's husband, Thomas Nixon, for putting up with us and for stepping up to the sushi table to fill a last-minute void for

Sushi Battle Club: The Speed. Here in the United States, Mina Sakamoto did stellar interpreting work in Cleveland, and Genevieve Weber translated manga and helped me make sense of the neon riot of *TV Champion* and *Food Battle Club.* Robert Ikeda, Koby's translator, was also helpful on several occasions in arranging time with Koby.

Eaters and eaters' family members. I'm grateful to Don Lerman, Rich and Carlene LeFevre, Mike Devito, Joelle Cachola, Deb Chapman, Debbie Simmons, and Lisa O'Karma for inviting me into their homes and, often, feeding me. Particular thanks to Eric Booker, Charles Hardy, Ed Jarvis, Sonya Thomas, Brian Subich, Frank Dellarosa, Joe Menchetti, Joseph and Loretta Cordero, Bob Shoudt, and Kate Stelnick, among others, for sharing their recollections. In Japan, the hospitality of Kenji Aoki was particularly humbling; I also appreciated the efforts made by Toshio Kimura, Kazutoyo Arai, Yuko, and Nobuyuki Shirota to make us feel at home. Extra thanks to Shirota for dubbing a good portion of his VHS library of Japanese eating tapes.

Arnie "Chowhound" Chapman and Bill "El Wingador" Simmons. Arnie and Bill were incredibly open from the get-go, and always made me feel welcome wherever we were traveling.

Tim "Eater X" Janus and David "Coondog" O'Karma. These two men are the heart of this book, and also the ones who had the most to risk, personal-credibility-wise, in sticking their necks out to help me get interviews. Tim and Dave trusted me to tell their stories fairly, and I hope I've repaid that trust.

Christopher Jackson at Crown, my original editor. It's kind of unfair that I get to pass off Chris's best ideas as my own, but such is the advantage of working with a brilliant guy. He was open and curious and engaged; he'd think about the book while walking or biking and then would call me with these great incisive riffs. Chris seemed able to hold the whole book inside his head, so that whenever I got brain-fried and lost in the little details, he could bring me back to the big picture. Chris was an early believer in the book's approach and a fierce advocate within Crown as the manuscript came together. It's a far better piece of writing for his having edited it. Additional thanks are due to Rachel Klayman, senior editor, for her tenacity, her energy, and her attention to detail, as well as the fastidious Genoveva Llosa, Chris's assistant, for keeping me on track, and also to Lucinda Bartley, Rachel's unflappable assistant, and to production editor Jim Walsh. Finally, Kristin Kiser's support and encouragement meant a lot to me.

Larry Weissman, my agent. Without Larry, this book never would have happened. He saw the idea's potential early on and had faith that I could pull it off even before I did. Larry became an agent because he wanted to do hands-on work with writers; my reams of e-mails and late-night phone calls must have tested his original resolve. But he proved to be more than a patient reader, idea springboard, and surrogate ego. He was a friend. And for that I want to thank him—and also his whip-smart wife and business partner, Sascha Alper. Larry and Sascha's passion, energy, and work ethic were all humbling, as was their graciousness in letting me crash at their place on multiple occasions, and also their decision not to press the issue re: that nasty food stain I left on their couch.

Finally: Dana Bauer, my fiancée. Eaters often say that their sport is a crucible for spouses: if the spouses stick around, the spouses must really love them. I feel the same is true for the spouse of a person who writes a book about competitive eating. Over the course of a year and a half, Dana gave tirelessly of her time, her critical eye, and her Jetta. At contests, she often noticed telling details I missed, and she improved endless drafts with her sharp, cut-through-the-BS suggestions—this despite enduring catcalls at a strip club, cell phone calls at 4 a.m. from Vegas, and more high-level gurgitation than anyone not writing a book about it should ever see. And she's still here. And still wants to marry me. I am lucky, lucky, lucky.

ABOUT THE AUTHOR

JASON FAGONE is a writer-at-large for *Philadelphia* magazine, and he was named one of the "Ten Young Writers on the Rise" by the *Columbia Journalism Review*. He's a graduate of Pennsylvania State University.